ENCYCLOPEDIA OF HORSES

Debby Sly

PaRragon

Bath · New York · Singapore · Hong Kong · Cologne · Delhi · Melbourne

First published by Parragon in 2008

Parragon
Queen Street House
4 Queen Street
Bath BA1 1HE, UK

Created and produced by

13 SOUTHGATE STREET WINCHESTER HAMPSHIRE SO23 9DZ

DESIGN Laura Watson, Sharon Rudd
EDITORIAL Jennifer Close, Jo Weeks

ISBN: 978-1-4075-2444-3

Printed in China

CONTENTS

ENCYCLOPEDIA OF
HORSES

ABOUT THIS BOOK

We are far removed from the era when humans relied on horses as much as we rely on modern transport today. For many of us, our only experience of horses and ponies is for leisure or competition riding, and whilst we may consider the horse essential to our enjoyment, he was once essential to our survival.

THE HORSE AND US

The first part of this book looks at how horses evolved before beginning their long relationship with us through domestication. We look at how horses behave in the wild, which reminds us of our duty to understand and appreciate their needs now that we have removed them from their natural existence to the artificial one that suits our needs.

Their care, in sickness and in health, is given as a guide, but the good handler will work out what suits each horse best, which doesn't always mean 'going by the book'! A round up of the many equestrian activities and sports is included, and it is sobering to compare how horses serve us today with how they served on the land, in industry, and in war in the past.

BREEDS

There are over 200 breeds of horses and ponies worldwide, and most of them are included here. It is fascinating to be reminded of the diversity that there is in the equine family. Whilst, sadly, many draught breeds are almost redundant beyond being bred for meat, it is also heartwarming to see the efforts being made by dedicated horse breeders and enthusiasts to protect and promote individual breeds.

SYMBOLS IN THIS BOOK

Symbols at the head of each breed description illustrate aspects of each breed.

Environment relates to the climate and landscape of the general area in which each breed originated. It is specific to the origins of the breed itself rather than the breed's ancestors or current distribution.

Horses may be hotblood (Arab, Barb, or Thoroughbred); coldblood (heavy breeds); or warmblood (crosses between the two).

Uses are self evident, other than that sports includes showing, and racing includes harness racing.

The size guide gives an indicator of the breeds' relative size and height. Breeds are categorized by size, the pony section being 14.2 hh and under, and the horses covering breeds that are over 14.2 hh.

Up to eight colour swatches show the most common coat variations for a breed.

ENVIRONMENT					
	DESERT AND SEMI DESERT	FOREST AND WOODLAND	MOUNTAIN AND HIGHLAND	OPEN HABITAT INCLUDING GRASSLAND MOOR AND HEATH	WETLANDS AND MARSHES
BLOOD	HOT	WARM	COLD		
USES	RIDING	SPORT	RACING		
	DRAUGHT	CARRIAGE	RANCH WORK	WILD AND SEMI FERAL	
SIZE GUIDE	PONY 14.2 hh	LIGHT 17 hh	HEAVY 19 hh		

1.80 m (6 ft)

COAT COLOURS

BLACK   BROWN   CHESTNUT   DUN   GREY   BAY   PALOMINO   COLOURED   ROAN

THE NATURE OF THE HORSE

Given thousands of years of evolutionary experience, which should have ensured that the horse developed an inherent fear of Man, the nature of the horse is such that he has submitted to the demands of humans since his first domestication. From being hunted as a source of food to then providing transportation with which we could hunt, explore, and invade, the horse has served us well. We owe him a great debt and, by understanding how he evolved, how he thinks and reacts, what his needs are, and using that knowledge sympathetically in his training and care, we can begin to repay him.

EQUINE EVOLUTION The horse we recognize today evolved from a small, fox-sized creature that inhabited the earth over 55 million years ago. The species has been developed and refined and is now represented by over 200 different breeds.

EVOLUTION OF THE HORSE

A full study of the evolution of the horse merits a book of its own but, based on fossil evidence, it is believed that the earliest known ancestor of the horse lived about 55 million years ago (during the early Eocene period). *Hyracotherium*, also known as 'Eohippus' or 'the Dawn Horse', was a fox-sized creature with four toes on his front feet and three toes on his back feet. This prototype horse scampered around in the forests of the American continent, which, at that stage, was joined to Europe.

FOSSIL EVIDENCE

A series of horse fossils show what would appear to be a line of evolution traced from the earliest *Hyracotherium* (55 million years old) through to *Equus* (the modern-day horse). The fossil series was originally believed to show gradual, straight-line evolution with the end result being

FAMILY The tapir (*below*) is a distant relative of the horse. *Hyracotherium* (*left*) would have looked more like this juvenile tapir than the modern horse.

the horse we recognize today. However, further fossil finds and increased investigation of this theory now show that horse evolution didn't follow a straight line – there were many branches that produced various species. It just so happens that the modern horse, *Equus*, was the only branch of the tree that has survived through to the modern day. Some of the other species co-existed alongside their ancestors, others rapidly became extinct.

FAMILY TREE

The evolutionary line that takes us through to *Equus* shows a number of consistent traits – a reduction in the number

of toes, an increase in overall size, an increase in size and number of grinding teeth, and a lengthening of the face.

NOTABLE ANCESTORS OF EQUUS

Co-existing with *Hyracotherium* was *Orohippus*. *Orohippus* was very similar in appearance but had altered teeth to give more of a grinding action, indicating that he was feeding on tougher plant material. By the middle Eocene, there was *Eppihippus*, still fox-sized but now with five grinding teeth.

In the late Eocene and Oligocene period, the climate of North America was becoming drier with forest giving way to grass. A larger, leggier animal evolved; *Mesohippus* had a straighter back and longer legs, neck, and head. He had six grinding teeth and three toes, front and back.

Miohippus co-existed in some areas with *Mesohippus*. He was larger and had a longer skull, and produced the first significant diversity in the family tree, having up to a dozen different descendants.

MERYCHIPPUS

By the Miocene period, *Merychippus* had appeared, 17–11 million years ago. The environment was still changing from forests and jungle to open plains. *Merychippus*'s legs and neck were longer and his eyes were positioned on the side of his head, giving greater speed and vision. He still had three toes but most of his weight was now carried on the middle toe. He was starting to look like the modern horse.

PRIMITIVE HORSE Przewalski's Horse (*above*) is the only remaining truly wild species of horse. The similarities between Przewalski's Horse and its distant ancestor *Pliohippus* (*right*) are easy to see.

PLIOHIPPUS

Pliohippus is considered to be the 'grandfather' of the modern horse. He existed about 6 million years ago (mid-Pliocene period) He was the first one-toed horse, was about 12.2 hh (1.2 m), and gave rise to another burst of species diversification that included *Dinohippus*, the closest known relative to *Equus*. During the late Pliocene (2.6 million years ago), the first major glaciations allowed some species of *Equus* to move to the Old World. In Africa they diversified into the modern zebra. Asia, the Middle East, and North Africa saw the development of desert onagers and asses. In Europe, Asia, and the Middle East, the true horse, *Equus caballus*, thrived. Up to a million years ago there were enormous herds of *Equus* species in America, Africa, Asia, and Europe. But, about 10,000 years ago, mass extinctions wiped out all the horses in the Americas. From then on there were no horses in America until they were reintroduced by Spanish *conquistadores* who conquered the New World in the 16th century.

THE HORSE FAMILY

There are eight extant species of the horse family Equidae, of which *Equus caballus* is by far the most numerous. The Asiatic Wild Horse, *Equus ferus*, was originally discovered by the Russian explorer Nicolai Przewalski in 1879, although the nomads of the Gobi desert had been familiar with him for years. They claimed to have crossed the breed with their racehorses to improve their stamina. The horses were officially declared a new species in 1881 and were named in honour of the man who introduced them to the rest of the world. Fortunately, as it turned out, there was great interest in them and many were captured to be shown around the world in zoos. This proved to be opportune as by the 1970s the horses were extinct in the wild. In recent years, however, herds have been taken from the zoos and re-established in their natural habitat to once again run wild. The Asiatic Wild Horse, also known as Przewalski's Horse, is a short (about 13 hh/1.32 m), stocky, and powerfully built animal with a heavy head and wide chest. Its coat is a sandy dun colour with black lower legs, with some striping on them, and a black mane and tail. The mane stands erect but there is no forelock and the muzzle is a mealy colour.

ZEBRAS AND ASSES

The other members of the *Equus* family that are truly wild are zebras and asses, which still roam their native habitats in large herds. As well as having a different appearance to the horse, they have other characteristics which differentiate them. For example, horses have chestnuts (horny calluses) on all four legs whereas zebras and asses have them on the forelegs only. Zebras and asses have five lumbar vertebrae (as opposed to the horse's six), their ears are relatively long, and their manes relatively short and upright.

Instantly recognizable by their 'tiger stripes', herds of truly wild zebra still survive in parts of Africa. Three different species survive today; the most numerous is

EQUUS CABALLUS The modern horse is the result of over 55 million years of evolution. He was upheld for many years as a textbook case of 'straight-line' evolution, but further fossil finds proved that there were many branches of the horse family tree.

EQUUS FERUS The Mongolians call the Asiatic Wild Horse *Takhi*, which means spirit. Up until the mid-20th century, the Asiatic Wild Horse could still be found in the wild. It was hunted to extinction but survived in zoos. It has recently been reintroduced to the wild.

EQUUS AFRICANUS The Somali Wild Ass pictured is a sub-species of *Equus Africanus* (the African Wild Ass). Found in Ethiopia, Somalia, and Sudan, they stand at a height of between 1.25 and 1.45 m (4¼–4¾ ft). The species faces extinction as there are thought to be fewer than 1,000 left in the wild.

EQUUS ZEBRA Facing a high risk of extinction – there are thought to be up to approximately 33,000 still living in the wild – the Mountain Zebra is distinguishable from Burchell's Zebra by the different stripe pattern on their heads and bodies.

Burchell's Zebra, *Equus burchelli*. Less common is the Mountain Zebra, *Equus zebra*. The rarest of all is Grevy's Zebra, *Equus grevyi*.

WILD ASSES

Most of us are familiar with the domestic ass, or donkey, but this name only came into use in the late 18th century. His truly wild ancestor is the African Wild Ass, which, in its native habitat of Ethiopia, Somali, and Sudan, is facing extinction – fewer then 1,000 remain.

Hermiones and onagers are different names for the wild asses of Asia. They are more 'horse-like' than the African Wild Ass, having much longer legs and a high crouped body. The Asian Wild Ass is found in India, Iran, Turkmenistan and Mongolia. There are believed to be up to 30,000 of them living in the wild. Another sub-species is the Kiang. These are far more common, with a population of approximately 70,000, and are found in Iran, Turkmenistan, India, Mongolia, and China.

Meet the ancestors

All members of the horse family are classed as Perissodactyles – the order of hoofed animals that bear their weight on the middle (third) toe. There are three families within the order Perissodactyles: Equidae (asses, horses, and zebras); Tapiridae (tapirs); and Rhinocerotidae (rhinoceroses). DNA evidence suggests the horse and rhino families diverged 50 million years ago.

EQUUS GREVYI Grevy's Zebra is the largest of the Zebra species and the most closely related to the primitive horse. They are found in North Kenya and South Ethiopia but are currently in great danger of extinction. There are only about 3,000 of them left.

EQUUS HERMIONUS The Asian Wild Ass is more horse-like than his African counterpart, having a longer thinner face, and is generally taller at 1.5 m (5 ft). They are also endangered as their numbers have dropped to around 20,000. They can be found in India, Iran, Turkmenistan, Mongolia, and China.

EQUUS BURCHELLI This is the zebra with which we are most familiar. Also known as the Plains Zebra, Burchell's Zebras appear quite short and dumpy and thrive in the grasslands and savannah of East Africa. There are well over 600,000 of them in existence.

EQUUS KIANG The Kiang stands at up to 1.42 m (4½ ft) and they appear to be about halfway between an African Wild Ass and an Asian Wild Ass. Their ability to thrive in their inhospitable habitat in Tibet and Nepal means that their survival gives the least cause for concern among the Equidae family.

WILD HORSES

The only truly wild horse in existence today, apart from the species of zebra and wild ass, is the Asiatic Wild Horse (Przewalski's Horse). There are many herds, worldwide, of feral horses, i.e. horses that were once domesticated but escaped to live in the wild, but Przewalski's Horse is unique in that he carries a different chromosome count to his feral cousins. He is a genuine wild horse.

FERAL HORSES

Domesticated horses that have escaped to form 'wild herds' are known as feral horses and ponies. Probably the most famous examples are the Mustangs and Brumbies of America and Australia. But a surprising number of countries have their own feral herds of equines of various shapes and sizes. Even among the feral herds there are those, such as the Mustangs and Brumbies, that live a relatively wild and isolated existence and others that are left to roam free but have regular contact with humans.

The British Isles are home to various herds of famous mountain and moorland pony breeds such as the Shetland, Welsh Mountain, Exmoor, and New Forest Ponies. But these, along with the Chincoteague Ponies from an island off Virginia, are herded up annually to be sorted and branded.

CAMARGUE HORSES The famous 'white horses' of the Camargue live on the salt marshes of the Rhône delta in southern France. They enjoy a semi-wild existence but are actually kept to be ridden by the herdsmen who manage the fighting bulls bred in the area.

HERDS AROUND THE WORLD

Herds of free-roaming feral horses are found in a number of countries. Canada has several herds, including the Sable Island Ponies off Nova Scotia, as well as herds of feral horses in British Columbia. Known as the 'Wild Horses of Alberta', it is believed that about 300 of these tough little horses remain. Their environment is extremely harsh and they have developed a unique physique to cope with it – large hooves to paw away the snow in search of food, and short, strong legs to handle the rough terrain. They have Roman noses, which denotes their Spanish origins, and many carry the primitive dorsal stripe.

Namibia is home to the Namib Desert Horse. They are quality horses with good conformation and movement, possibly descended from the Shagya Arab. Their numbers have been drastically reduced by the harsh drought conditions that are regularly experienced, but small numbers are now being relocated into protected areas.

ISLAND HORSES

Abaco Island, in the Bahamas, 240 km (150 miles) off Florida's Gold Coast, is home to the few surviving Abaco Barbs. Officially recognized as a breed by the Horse of the Americas registry, this once thriving herd of over 200

WILD PONY This pony is wading through the saltwater tidal flats off Assateague Island in the United States. The wild herds found on this island are Chincoteague Ponies, named after the smaller neighbouring island. Each year they swim across from Assateague to Chincoteague where they are sorted and checked over.

horses has dwindled to a band of eight. It is believed they swam to the island after being shipwrecked when Spanish explorers first arrived in America during the 16th century.

Greece is home to the 'Wild Horses of Cephalonia'. A small herd of several dozen still exists and they are now being aided in their survival by a local charity. It's the same story the world over – where farmers have livestock they want to graze, they resent the presence of horses sharing their livestock's forage.

AUSTRALIA

Australia is home to the legendary Brumby. Cherished by romantics but despised by many farmers as a pest, they can still be found in their thousands. Most live in the Northern Territory and North Queensland, along with a small number on the east coast. New Zealand's Kaimanawa Horses – a mixture of Exmoor, Comet, and local breeds – have roamed free since 1814.

FERAL HORSES The wild horses of Namibia show plenty of quality and would not look out of place in many competitive disciplines. They have endured terrible hardship in the past when drought conditions have devastated their numbers but find some refuge in National Parks.

Feral donkeys

Domestic donkeys are found worldwide. They are popular pets in wealthier countries and in poorer countries they are still relied upon as a tough, and relatively cheap, workforce. The male is called a Jack and the female is a Jennet or Jenny. Mules and Hinnies are hybrids produced by crossing an ass with a horse. Crossing a Jack ass with a mare produces a Mule, and a stallion crossed with a Jenny produces a Hinny. Following the introduction of motorized transport in the early 1900s, many donkeys were abandoned and large feral herds became established, notably in parts of Australia and the United States.

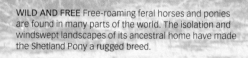

WILD AND FREE Free-roaming feral horses and ponies are found in many parts of the world. The isolation and windswept landscapes of its ancestral home have made the Shetland Pony a rugged breed.

LIFECYCLE OF THE HORSE

Many domesticated brood mares enjoy a very cosseted life. Turned out on good grazing, with plenty of food and shelter, they are monitored and assessed throughout their pregnancy. Compare this to the feral or wild in-foal mare who has to keep up with the herd in search of food and water. For the same reason, a new-born foal knows instinctively that he must get up and be ready to run as soon as possible.

PREGNANCY AND FOALING

Mares reach puberty by the time they are two, but they are not normally bred from until they are three. The mare starts to come into season (on heat) from early spring at intervals of approximately three weeks. Once a successful mating has occurred, the gestation period is just over eleven months. Two months into pregnancy, the embryo is only about 10 cm (4 in) long, but by eleven months, the foal will weigh between 38 and 48 kg (83–106 lb) and will have increased in length to about 110 cm (43 in).

Signs that the mare is close to foaling are that her belly drops noticeably, the udder enlarges as it fills with milk,

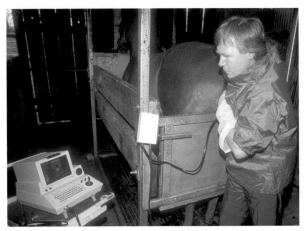

MONITORED An internal examination, six weeks after mating, enables the vet to determine whether or not the mare is in foal. If she is in foal, as the embryo develops it can be monitored using an ultra-sound scanner. This allows the vet to check that the embryo is developing normally.

and wax appears on the teats. When foaling is imminent, the mare will become restless, often lying down and getting up repeatedly as she feels the foal moving inside her. Involuntary uterine contractions move the foal into the correct position so that his nose and forefeet are stretched forwards towards the pelvic arch. The cervix dilates.

Voluntary contractions allow the mare to push the foal out through the pelvis and cervix. The forefeet appear first, followed by the head. The largest part of the foal to push out are the shoulders; once these are free, the rest follows very quickly. The foal is encased in a protective membrane that breaks as he is born, allowing him to start to breathe.

As soon as the foal is standing, he will begin to drink from the mare's teats. This nutritious first milk is called colostrum and contains many antibodies that help to build immunity against the bugs and bacteria in the foal's environment.

FAST DEVELOPER As the new-born foal moves around, or when the mare gets up, the umbilical cord will break. The mare will start to lick the foal, which warms him and dries him out. Within about 15 minutes of being born, he will begin trying to get to his feet.

Who's who?

Male and female horses are known by different names, depending on their age. These names apply to ponies as well as horses.
Mare – a female horse over four years of age
Filly – a female horse under four years of age
Stallion – a male horse (entire) over four years of age
Colt – a male horse under four years of age
Gelding – a castrated male horse

GROWTH AND DEVELOPMENT

Within hours of birth, a foal can gallop and flee with the herd from any danger. By six weeks old, he will have doubled his birth weight. At one year old, he will have achieved half his total adult size and weight. At four to six months old, the foal will be weaned. From his early days, he will have nibbled at grass, hard feed, and forage. Over the months, he becomes less reliant on his mother's milk.

Most horses reach their adult height by the time they are four or five. Handling and educating a foal can begin at just a few days old to teach him to accept human contact. At a few weeks old, he can be expected to be led around, handled all over his body, and to begin to pick up feet when asked, all in preparation for his working life.

GETTING TO WORK

Horses benefit physically and mentally from being worked carefully through their formative years. Despite this evidence, many horses are left virtually unhandled until they are four, when suddenly they are expected to accept human contact and demands. Most, with careful handling, are still perfectly willing to be backed (have a rider on their back) and to begin their ridden education. But the conditioning benefits of toning and strengthening their bodies, and allowing their tendons, ligaments, and joints to be prepared for an athletic future will have been lost.

REACHING A PEAK

Apart from horses bred to race on the flat, who run competitively at two years of age, most horses start their serious competitive careers at four or five years old. At this stage the horse is still maturing physically and mentally and most riders would consider a horse to be at its peak, competitively, from the age of about seven through to twelve years old. Advances in understanding the physiology of the horse, and in nutrition and veterinary care, mean that many horses compete to a much greater age than this.

STICKING WITH MUM By the time he is six weeks old a foal will have doubled his birth weight but won't stray far from mum. At four to six months old, he will be weaned from his mother.

Guide to age

In human terms, as a very approximate guide, the following age comparisons can be made:

Age of human	Age of horse
20 yrs old	5 yrs old
40	10
50	15
60	20
70	25
80	30
90	35

Ponies tend to live longer than horses, but a fair life expectancy for a horse is between 20 and 25 years.

BEHAVIOUR AND COMMUNICATION

Horses are, first and foremost, herd animals. Domestication and careful and correct training has produced an animal that will work happily as an individual for us, but he will never completely lose his herd instincts.

HERD BEHAVIOUR

In their natural state, horses live in herds made up of mares, young stock, and one dominant stallion. They graze in a relatively tight bunch, with the older mares on the outside of the herd acting as lookouts. There is usually a lead mare who tops the pecking order – she will lead the herd to fresh grazing and water whilst the stallion brings up the rear. The dominant mares keep younger horses in order, telling them with a swift nip or kick what is unacceptable behaviour. As the young males mature, they are driven out of the herd by the stallion. They can choose to leave quietly or fight for the right to remain and 'own' the herd. Stallions occasionally fight to the death but more often one backs down and leaves before any serious damage is inflicted.

HERD INSTINCT Horses naturally group together to find safety in numbers. In the wild, the herd is mainly preoccupied with finding sufficient food and water to keep themselves alive.

MUTUAL GROOMING In the wild, grooming is an important process that helps individual horses to bond. Similarly, grooming helps handlers to bond with their horses as well as keeping the coat in good condition.

HUMANS AND THE HERD

The domesticated horse is brought up in a very different environment to his wild ancestors, but the good handler will consider the horse's ancestral needs. Once a horse has learned to accept a rider, he must be taught to curb his natural flight instinct. By a slow introduction to new sights

and situations, a horse can be taught to turn to his rider for instruction rather than run away from situations that scare him. In a herd the young horses take a lead from the older horses, and a good trainer will use an experienced horse to give a lead to a youngster in new situations.

BODY LANGUAGE

Horses use body language to communicate with each other, and we can learn to understand their body language too. The horse's ears tell us a great deal about his state of mind. When relaxed, the ears will point forwards and outwards, ready to pick up any sound in front or to the side. To check for any noise behind him, he will flick one or both ears back. When resting, the ears flop outwards as the muscles controlling them relax. If the horse is angry, aggressive, or in pain, he will flatten his ears back against his skull.

When a sound attracts his attention, he will prick his ears forwards, and turn his head and neck – and sometimes his whole body – towards the sound. This position allows his ears and eyes to focus directly on the source of interest.

Rapid flicking of the ears backwards and forwards indicates that the horse is unsettled and nervous about surroundings. But a relaxed movement of the ears forwards and backwards is a good sign. When ridden, the horse will often point one ear back to listen to his rider.

VOICE

The horse produces various sounds to communicate with others. Snorting, by expelling air forcefully through his nostrils, makes enough noise to alert his herd mates to some distant danger, without giving away his position.

Fight or flight

Horses are not naturally aggressive – their first instinct is to put as much space as possible between themselves and the thing they fear. Acute hearing and sense of smell, and virtually all-round vision, help them detect danger. Their speed helps them to escape it. If cornered, they will turn and fight – with teeth and hooves. And the reason horses buck is to dislodge an attacker from their backs. Predators such as wolves would leap onto the horse's back and the horse's last defence was to buck and writhe to throw the beast off. For this reason, it is essential that young horses are introduced to a rider slowly and sympathetically. A horse rarely bears his rider any malice but if he feels a weight on his back, his primeval instincts tell him to get rid of it.

Horses squeal to show excitement or to warn another horse to keep its distance. When two horses meet, they will often sniff noses and then one or both of them will squeal. The nicker is a soft, low gutteral sound, which is a sign of welcome to other horses and also to humans. A whinny or neigh is a long, loud gutteral sound, which is the horse's way of calling out to his friends to let them know he's around. An angry or fearful horse may emit a roar to intimidate and scare the object of his fear or anger. When a horse is surprised by something, or just showing his wellbeing, he will emit a loud blowing noise.

FIGHTING BACK

The horse can also use his limbs and neck to communicate his mood or intentions. The neck can be used aggressively in a snake-like, lunging manner to position the horse to deliver a bite. Lifting a hind leg, or turning the hindquarters towards someone is a prelude to a kick. Pawing the ground with the front feet is the horse's way of investigating something or showing that he is anxious to be on the move. Horses will also strike out with their front legs in a defensive or attacking move; when seriously threatened, the horse may rear up and strike out with his front feet.

EYES

The horse's eyes should be bright and alert in normal circumstances. If the horse is in pain or exhausted, the eyes will be almost closed. If he is alarmed by something, the eyes will widen. To show anger or resentment, the horse will roll his eyes back to show the whites of the eyes.

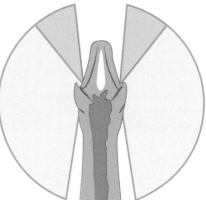

FIELD OF VISION The position of the eyes at the side of horses' heads allows them almost 360 degrees of vision. Monocular vision allows them to see on either side (light shaded area), while they have a comparatively narrow binocular field (dark shaded area). Horses have two 'blind spots' – one directly in front of the face and one directly behind the body – a very good reason for never approaching a horse from either of these two positions.

SIGHT The horse's sight does not pick up as much detail as the human eye, but they are far quicker to spot movement. Horses can also see better in the dark than we can. Horses do see degrees of colour – yellow, greens, and blues are more obvious to them than reds, for example.

FLEHMEN To savour a particularly interesting smell, horses use the action known as flehmen. Having breathed in a scent, the horse curls his upper lip over his nostrils. This action traps the scent inside the nasal cavities.

IF ONLY THEY COULD TALK Touch and ear positioning is an important part of communication between horses, and can give crucial clues as to mood.

SMELL, TOUCH, AND TASTE

Horses rely on their highly developed senses to explore and deal with their environment. The horse's large nostrils and nasal cavities enhance his sense of smell. In the wild, horses used their sense of smell to detect predators, to recognize fellow herd members, and to detect sources of water. Smell is important to the stallion in particular to detect mares that are in season.

Horses use touch to communicate with each other and will nudge or nuzzle a companion with their nose or head. Their whiskers help them to sense and explore objects that interest them. We use touch to communicate our own wishes to the horse – the touch of our legs on his sides allows us to direct and control him when ridden, as does the hand on the rein via the bit.

Like us, horses can distinguish between bitter, sweet, salt, and sour tastes, but they can tolerate far more bitter-tasting substances than we can. We often assume that horses have a sweet tooth, hence the habit of feeding them sugar lumps and mints as treats. But it could simply be that the horse associates kindness and a particularly close degree of attention from humans with the action of feeding him a treat, rather than the taste itself having a particular appeal.

HORSES IN MOTION

In advanced dressage, the horse is taught to perform all kinds of movements, but they all find a basis in the horse's four natural paces: walk, trot, canter, and gallop. As riders, we learn to understand and feel the sequence in which the horse moves his legs and uses his body in each pace in order to stay in balance with him and, in more advanced riding, to be able to train him in a way that will improve his paces and his jumping technique.

WALK AND TROT

The walk is a four-beat gait as the horse moves each leg individually. If you listen to his footfalls, you will hear four separate hoof beats.

The trot is a two-beat gait. The horse springs from one pair of diagonal legs to the other. If you listen to the footfalls, you will only hear two hoof beats within each complete stride. There is a brief period of suspension as the horse springs from one diagonal pair of legs to the other. A good rider will seek to make use of this moment of suspension to give the trot a really good spring and lift to it, which will enhance the performance of the horse, particularly in dressage.

CANTER

The canter is a three-beat gait, so you will hear three hoof beats within each stride. There is a brief period of suspension when all four feet are off the ground, before the stride

FLYING HORSE Racehorses are bred and shaped to produce a good gallop. This shows the moment of suspension when all four feet are off the ground.

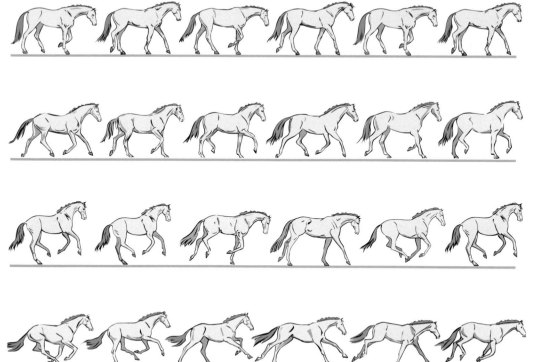

WALK The sequence of footfalls in this four-beat gait is as follows: outside (right) hind, outside fore, inside (left) hind, and inside fore.

TROT The sequence of footfalls in this two-beat gait is outside hind and inside fore together, then inside hind, outside fore together.

CANTER In this three-beat gait, the outside hind goes forward, inside hind and outside fore move forwards together, followed by the inside fore.

GALLOP The sequence of footfalls in the gallop is near hind, off hind, near fore, off fore, followed by all four feet being off the ground before the pattern restarts.

Jumping action

To take off, the horse lifts his shoulders, places both his hind feet together, and uses the power and flexion of his hocks to propel himself off the ground. In mid air, he keeps his front legs tightly folded and tucks his hind legs up underneath himself. On landing, he extends his front legs forwards and down to meet the ground. He raises his neck slightly to help keep his balance.

pattern is repeated. To keep properly balanced, the horse is said to 'lead' with one or other front leg as he goes round a corner. If he is circling to the right, he will appear to be leading the stride with his right foreleg. In fact, once you understand the sequence of footfalls, you will appreciate that the right foreleg is actually the last leg in the sequence to move! But it should appear that the right foreleg leads on a right circle, and the left foreleg leads on a left circle.

GALLOP

The gallop is a four-beat gait in which the horse extends his whole body, from the tip of his nose to his tail. The sequence of footfalls is near hind, off hind, near fore, off fore. Because the walk is also a four-beat gait, it is often said that if a horse has a good walk, he will also have a good gallop.

JUMPING

All horses can jump to some degree or other, but to be top-class, competitive jumpers, riders spend many hours improving their horses' athleticism and technique. A horse with a good jumping technique will bring his forearms up high and bend his lower leg tightly against his forearm to give him as much clearance over the fence as possible.

NECK AND NECK These point-to-pointers (amateur racehorses) show the speed and exhilaration of horses galloping and jumping together. The speed, strength, and courage of the horses make for an exciting spectacle.

MODERN BREEDING

The way breeds are defined today is governed by breed societies, registers, and stud books. Before the advent of such things, a breed would have simply meant a group of animals living in a particular area. Without interference from humans, and shaped by their environment, the animals in the group would, over time, share similar traits in terms of overall size, conformation, and temperament.

STUD BOOKS Stud books record the ancestry (pedigree) of each horse or pony that is accepted as a registered breed. The oldest stud books are those of the Arab and Thoroughbred breeds. Some are operated as closed stud books and others as open stud books.

REGISTERED BREEDS

In modern-day breeding, for a breed to be recognized, or for new offspring to be registered as a particular breed, certain criteria have to be met. Different countries, stud books, and breed societies apply varying levels of criteria as to what defines a 'breed' and therefore which horses and ponies can or cannot be registered as a breed. In America, for example, breed status is given to many types of horse and pony that in Europe would be considered a 'type' or crossbreed. Today, there are just over 200 recognized breeds of horse and pony worldwide.

CLOSED STUD BOOKS

A closed stud book, such as that of the Trakehner and Thoroughbred, will no longer accept any outside or 'fresh' blood. Any new horses entered in the stud book must be the progeny of horses that are already registered in the stud book. The registered animals form the foundation of the breed, and the breeding of all subsequent entrants can be traced back to these foundation animals. A closed stud book has the advantage of maintaining purity of type within a breed but it obviously limits the gene pool, which can lead to undesirable traits becoming accentuated. Occasionally a closed stud book may be reopened temporarily to allow additional approved fresh blood to be added.

WARMBLOOD In an effort to produce the ultimate competition horse, the traits of the Thoroughbred have been enhanced by the toughness, calmness, and more extravagant movement of some of the cold-blooded breeds.

HOTBLOOD The Arab shows a purity of blood and type over thousands of years and is regarded as the father of all breeds.

OPEN STUD BOOKS

Some stud books have appendix or part-breed registers, allowing a greater number of horses to be kept under the umbrella of one breed. All racehorses in the United Kingdom must be entered in the Weatherbys Thoroughbred register, but there is also a Non-Thoroughbred register, which allows part-Thoroughbred horses to be registered and, if they prove good enough, raced. Similarly, the American Quarter Horse Association has a stud book in which the offspring of registered Quarter Horses can be entered, but they also have an Appendix for offspring of Quarter Horse/Thoroughbred crosses. These horses are entered temporarily in the Appendix and can 'earn' a place in the stud book by fulfilling performance criteria.

An open stud book, as operates in many parts of Europe, allows much more flexibility. Many breeding records were lost during the two World Wars. This left many countries with little choice but to start again from scratch. An open stud book allows the progeny of approved pedigree horses to be registered even if the parents are of different breeds. Most warmblood breeds were produced by crossing the heavier draught or carriage horses of a particular country with the more finely bred Thoroughbred. Further crosses or outcrosses produced the warmblood breeds. So the open stud book allows breeders to experiment with different mixes of blood to produce a horse showing the type, conformation, temperament, and performance ability required of a particular 'breed'.

HOT, WARM, AND COLD BLOOD

All horses and ponies are defined as being one of three blood types: hot, warm, or cold. This has nothing to do with their blood temperatures but relates to their origins. The most well-known hotblood breeds are the Arab and the Thoroughbred. The Thoroughbred is the Arab's direct descendant and has a recorded pedigree going back several hundred years. Hotbloods are considered more high-spirited than other breeds but training and environment heavily influences how a horse's temperament develops. Hot refers to the original environment of the Arab Horse – the deserts of the Middle East and North Africa.

Heavy horses are coldbloods. These heavier, slower-reacting, and more placid horses descended from the northern forest type of horse. Their stocky build suited the colder northern climates in which they originated.

Warmbloods include ponies and crossbreeds produced by crossing hotbloods with coldbloods, in varying degrees. They combine the quality and athleticism of the hotbloods with the steadier character of the coldbloods.

TYPES

A type refers to a certain stamp of horse that has been produced to do a particular job, rather than an actual breed. A hunter, for example, is judged by the accepted attributes required for the job of a hunt horse; soundness, strength, and manners. But any number of breeds, or crossbreeds, could meet these requirements.

COLDBLOOD The world's draught horses – such as these Shires – are classed as coldbloods. They are typically tougher, less refined, and more statuesque than their hot-blooded counterparts.

COAT COLOURS AND MARKINGS

There are four basic coat colours; black, brown, bay, and chestnut. All other colour variations are formed by a mixture of these colours, or different shades or patterns of these basic colours. Many people have favourite colours as far as horses are concerned but, when judging a horse, the condition of his coat is a far more important consideration than its colour!

BAY A bright bay is a perfect coat colour for really showing a horse off. The black points define his outline yet the bay coat is light enough to show off his shape. The coat colour can vary from light bay to almost black.

DOES COLOUR MATTER?

Despite some old horsemen's beliefs, a horse's colour contributes nothing to his actual ability. Amongst many old sayings and beliefs is 'a good horse is never a bad colour'. There is a belief that chestnut mares are bad tempered and fiery, and that black horses have black tempers, but these often prove to be unfounded. Coloured horses have always been popular in the US but, in the UK, for many years they were very much discarded as not having any serious worth. More recently, they have become a 'must-have' colour among pleasure riders in particular, and are now specifically bred to meet demand.

BLACK

Although black is a dominant colour, truly black horses are not all that common. A black horse will have black coat hair as well as a black mane and tail. The black gene is easily modified by the genes that create bay and brown colouring, which is why these two colours are more common than pure black. However, black is dominant over chestnut, so if you mate a black and a chestnut horse, you will get a black foal. Some breeds have a greater tendency than others to produce black horses. The Friesian, for example, is only ever black – a characteristic that has made him popular as a funeral horse.

BROWN This is a more common coat colour than black, although it often takes close inspection to define the difference between the two. A brown horse will always have a brown mane and tail hair.

BROWN

A brown horse will have brown coat hair and also a brown mane and tail. He may have light tan colouring around his eyes, muzzle, and stifle. The coat colour is often dark enough to appear almost black but a close inspection will show it to be brown.

BAY

Bay horses have red-brown or brown coat hair, but they will have a black mane and tail and black hair on their lower legs. These are called black points. Bays can come in many shades: light, dark, bright, and mahogany.

CHESTNUT

Chestnut colouring covers a wide variety of shades from pale gold, through strong red, to dark liver-chestnut.

CHESTNUT In a chestnut horse, the mane and tail may be the same colour as the coat hair, or darker, or lighter. If lighter, it is called flaxen. Coat colour varies from light chestnut to dark liver-chestnut (chocolate colour).

BLACK This is a relatively rare colour but is very striking. It has always evoked dramatic images of such well-known horses as Black Beauty. The Friesian ancestry of Dales and Fell Ponies is the reason they are often black in colour.

WHITE

Pure white horses (albinos) are very rare. They are born with white hair and pink skin. Grey horses are far more common. The colour grey is the result of loss of pigment from the coat. So grey horses are always born any colour other than grey – they turn grey as their coat hair loses its pigmentation. There are different patterns and variations of grey but most grey horses become whiter as they get older. Lipizzaners are the world's most famous 'white' horses. They are, of course, really grey, but it is the older horses that famously feature in the Spanish Riding School of Vienna, so by this stage of maturity they look white.

ROAN

Roan colouring is a mixture of white hairs with any other basic coat colour. The end results can vary dramatically depending on the mix of white and coloured hairs but there are three main roan colours:
• blue or silver roan – a mixture of white with black hair. The mane and tail remain black.
• red roan – a mixture of white and bay hair.
• strawberry roan – a mixture of white and chestnut hair.
Usually the face, lower legs, mane, and tail retain much of the stronger basic colouring whilst the body shows more of the roan colouring.

PALOMINO

Palomino colouring ranges from pale cream, through gold to dark bronze. The mane and tail are often silver or flaxen. This colouring is now found in quite a range of breeds although, as is the case with coloured or spotted colouring, it is never found in Arabs or Thoroughbreds. In America, there is an actual Palomino breed. One Palomino horse found fame and fortune as a star of film and television. Trigger, the Quarter Horse x Thoroughbred, was partnered by Roy Rogers. When the horse died in 1965, his body was stuffed and, placed in its rearing position, was displayed at the Roy Rogers Museum.

DUN

Dun colouring varies from pale cream to gold, and can also be a blue or silver shade. The lower legs, mane, and tail, and sometimes the face, are often darker brown or black. These horses often carry a dark dorsal stripe as well.
   The stocky Fjord Pony from Norway is always dun in colour and carries a prominent dorsal stripe (a black line running from the tail, along the spine and up the neck). The Asiatic Wild Horse, or Przewalski's Horse, is also always dun in colour, often showing a primitive dorsal stripe as well as zebra-like striping on the legs.

GREY

ALBINO

FLEABITTEN

RED ROAN

STRAWBERRY ROAN

BLUE ROAN

PALOMINO

PALE

BRONZE

BLUE WITH DORSAL STRIPE

GOLD

CREAM

COLOURED (BROKEN COATED)

Coloured horses have large patches of white mixed with patches of another coat colour. The coat colour can be anything from black, brown, or chestnut through to roan or dun and the mix can vary dramatically from small splashes of white, to mainly white with patches of colour.
• Piebald – white with black patches.
• Skewbald – white with any other coat colour.
• Ovaro – dark coated with large patches of white.
• Tobiano – white coated with large patches of brown, chestnut or black.
The Pinto is the most famous breed of coloured horse.

SPOTTED

Horses with spotted coats were depicted in cave drawings as long ago as 20,000 years. Today, the Appaloosa is the most prevalent spotted horse. They were bred in the 18th century by a tribe of Nez-Perce Indians whose land bordered the Palouse river in Oregon, United States. Over time, their Palouse horses became known as Appaloosa horses.
Appaloosa coat patterns:
• Leopard – white loins and hips with dark, egg-shaped spots.
• Snowflake – spots all over body and especially prevalent over hips.
• Blanket – spots or flecks on body except over hips, which are white.
• Marble – small dark specks/sprinkles on a light base coat.
• Frost – small white specks on a dark base coat.

SKEWBALD

TOBIANO

OVARO

SPOTTED

LEOPARD

SNOWFLAKE

BLANKET

MARBLE

FROST

Coat markings

Horses have individual markings that make them unique. Some are obvious such as white markings on the face or legs but others, known as whorls, are quite subtle, but they allow every horse to be individually identified.

Whorls are usually circular patterns in the coat formed where the hair grows in different directions. When a vet has to identify a horse on a passport, he draws in all the hair whorls as well as any other colour markings.

Prophet's thumb mark
The Prophet's thumb mark is an indentation in a muscle, usually in the horse's neck but sometimes in the chest also. It looks just as if someone has pressed a thumb into the muscle and left a dent. Legend has it that the Prophet Mohammed blessed the foundation mares of the Arab breed by placing his hand on their necks. The mark of his blessing is said to be passed on to their best offspring, generation after generation.

White markings
White markings commonly appear on horse's faces and legs.

Old horseman's saying:
'One white sock, buy a horse.
Two white socks, try a horse.
Three white socks, look well about him.
Four white socks, do without him!'

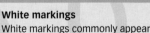
STAR STRIPE SNIP

ERMINE SOCK STOCKING
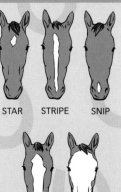
BLAZE WHITE FACE

CONFORMATION

How a horse is put together, in terms of his skeleton and musculature, is referred to as conformation. A horse with good conformation, i.e. one that is well assembled, is more likely to find his work easy, be well balanced, and be less prone to injury.

GOOD PROPORTIONS A well-made, well-proportioned horse will fill the eye as this lovely grey horse does. You don't need to be an equine expert to see that everything looks well balanced and well proportioned.

BUILT FOR THE JOB

Conformation varies between different breeds depending on what purpose the horse was being bred for. Work or draught horses will be thick set, powerful but stocky, whereas a racehorse is going to be longer, leaner, and more streamlined. The horse's conformation has an effect on how well he moves and jumps. His musculature will vary depending on how he is being worked, i.e. which muscles he is being asked to make most use of. Very few horses have perfect conformation but it is important to be sure that they do have enough good points relevant to the job you want the horse to do.

THE FRAMEWORK The horse's skeleton provides the framework which his muscles will develop around. On a well-conditioned horse it takes an experienced horseman to see 'under the skin' to assess the actual frame-work that he has to work with. The proportions and positioning of the horse's bones will dictate his athletic ability.

GOOD LEGS

The horse's limbs should be well aligned, well balanced, and well proportioned. A picture of perfection is hard to find: many highly successful performance horses have conformational faults and different horsepeople develop their own ideas of exactly what they are looking for in a horse. The legs should be well proportioned from shoulder to hoof, with a pastern and hoof angle of 45 degrees. Pasterns in particular should be well proportioned: too long and they put excessive strain on the tendons and

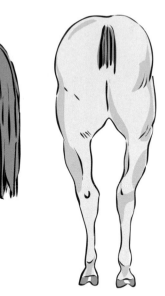

HINDQUARTERS The quarters should be well rounded and powerful and allow the hind legs to be well positioned, showing a balanced line from the point of the buttock to the hock and to the floor.

ligaments; too short and they produce too much concussion. Viewed from the side, the legs should not appear to tilt forwards (over at the knee) or backwards (back at the knee).

A GOOD HEAD

The horse's head should have a wide forehead. It should be well placed on a powerful, well-proportioned neck. The head should join the neck in a way that doesn't restrict the windpipe and therefore the horse's ability to breathe efficiently. The neck should be set on the shoulders in a way that will make it natural and comfortable for the horse to carry himself well. A low-set neck makes it harder for the horse to lighten and elevate his forehand. The shoulders should be at an angle of about 45 degrees. Too steep an angle limits the horse's ability to open out his stride.

GOOD CHEST

A broad chest indicates plenty of heart room and gives the horse more powerful movement of his front legs. The back should be straight and not too long or too short. Ideally, the measurement from wither to croup should be the same as the length of neck from poll to wither.

GOOD FEET 'No foot no 'oss' is an old saying. The hooves should have the strength, size, and shape to carry the weight of horse and rider.

HORSE CARE

Every horse owner finds out very quickly that far more hours are devoted to caring for a horse than are passed actually riding it. But this is time well spent as it allows the rider to build a relationship with the horse – to learn how he reacts to different situations and how he is best handled. This knowledge can then be used to good effect when riding and training the horse. Equally, for your horse to perform well for you, he needs to be kept fit, happy, and healthy – a big part of an owner's responsibility is to learn how best to do this.

IN YOUR HANDS The stabled horse is totally reliant on his owner for his care and wellbeing. A regular routine of feeding and exercise is essential to keep him happy and healthy.

HORSE OWNERSHIP

Finally owning a horse is a dream come true for many horse and pony lovers. But it is not a responsibility to be taken lightly. Riding a friend's horse, or turning up for your weekly lesson, is a world away from the hard work and expense of owning your own horse. Horses and ponies take up considerable amounts of time and money. They have to be cared for every day and are usually happiest when they are in a regular routine.

COMMITMENT
Even a horse or pony that is just going to live out in a field should be checked at least twice a day. So horse ownership requires discipline and commitment to the cause! It is also important that you have acquired a degree of competence in handling horses and sufficient knowledge as to the care they require. Horses are big, strong, and unpredictable – they have to handled and treated with care and respect. There are probably as many accidents that occur when

HANDLING Looking after your own pony is the best way of getting to know him properly.

handling horses from the ground as there are when riding horses. To be fair to yourself and the horse, some knowledge and practical competence are absolutely essential.

LIVERY
If you have your own land and stables, you will probably choose to fully care for your horse yourself. An

AT GRASS A horse living out at grass needs to be checked twice a day to ensure that he is safe and happy and has not harmed himself in any way.

alternative is to pay to keep the horse in a livery yard. Livery yards offer various options of care from simply providing you with a stable and paddock, to taking over the full care of your horse other than when you wish to ride him or choose to look after him yourself.

The advantages of keeping a horse in livery are that there is someone else around to ease the workload if you are very busy, there is plenty of company both equine and human, and there may be more facilities than might otherwise be available to you, such as an all-weather arena, horse walker, or cross-country course.

GETTING TO KNOW YOU

But, if you have the time, the facilities and the expertise, you will learn far more about your horse and yourself if you take on the full responsibility of his care. Horse and rider have to work as a team, and caring for your horse is a great way of getting to know him. In the same way as you feel more at ease with people you know well, your horse will feel more comfortable with you the more time you spend together.

COMPANIONSHIP One of the advantages of keeping your horse in livery is that there are plenty of people to socialize and ride with. Also, there is always someone to ask if you are not sure about something, and someone to help if you run into problems. It may even be possible to share transport.

Main costs of horse ownership

Some costs are unknown: you must budget for veterinary expenses. Despite their size and strength horses and ponies are quite vulnerable to injuries and illnesses. Insurance is available to guard against large veterinary bills, as well as death and theft, and is a worthwhile precaution if you can afford it.

INITIAL OUTLAY
■ Purchase price of the horse.
■ Pre-purchase vetting – a worthwhile precaution even if you know the horse.
■ Transport costs – it is usually the buyer's responsibility to transport the horse to his new home.
■ Tack and basic equipment – saddle, bridle, head collar, rugs, grooming kit, etc.

RUNNING COSTS
■ Weekly livery costs.
■ Feed – hay and concentrate feed.
■ Shoeing – every four to six weeks.
■ Routine treatments – vaccinations, worming, teeth rasping.
■ Additional tack and equipment – rugs, boots and bandages, protective travelling equipment, rider clothing, etc.
■ If you have ambitions to compete, do not underestimate the expense, including transport costs and entry fees as well as specialist equipment for horse and rider.

CHOOSING A HORSE

It is usually easier to buy a horse than it is to sell one! Some people happily make a living buying and selling horses, but most of us hope to obtain a horse that we will want to keep. The safest purchase is a horse you already know from someone you trust. If you have riding lessons, ask if any of the school horses are coming up for sale. Local pony clubs and riding clubs are good sources for 'recycling' horses and ponies.

WHERE TO LOOK

Equestrian magazines and local newspapers usually advertise plenty of horses for sale and sometimes it is possible to have a horse on trial or on loan before committing to purchasing it, which is ideal. It is good to buy locally if a suitable horse is available – a person is likely to be more truthful about the horse if he is selling to someone he is going to keep bumping in to. Reputable horse dealers are usually a good option. Firstly, they will have several horses you can try and, secondly, many of them will take a horse back and replace it with another one if you aren't getting on well.

KNOW YOUR LIMITATIONS

Whilst buyers often complain that sellers are economical with the truth about what they are selling, it is equally important that buyers are honest about their own ability, experience and aspirations. A better rider than you will always be able to show a horse off well. But *you* have to be able to ride the horse yourself! Never assume that because a horse goes well for one rider it will automatically respond in the same way for you. Be sure that you can get the performance that you want out of the horse.

PRE-PURCHASE VETTING

Ideally the horse you buy should be open to a pre-purchase vetting. Very few horses are perfect, most will carry signs of wear and tear, but a vet will be able to advise you, having examined the animal, as to whether or not it is fit to carry out the tasks for which it is being bought. Often, knowing the horse's history will tell you a good deal. If he

VETTING A HORSE A straightforward vetting will involve checking that the horse is sound in wind, limb, eyes, and heart. You can choose to have hooves and limbs x-rayed, but this will add considerably to the cost.

has been out and about competing season after season, then you can see that there aren't any suspicious gaps where he may have been laid up with injury for example. It is not the vet's job to decide if the horse is right for you in terms of temperament and ability! You need to have decided that before going as far as having him vetted.

INSURANCE

A horse can represent a large capital investment and you may wish to insure him. The cheapest insurance will cover death and theft but, with today's expensive veterinary costs, it is worth insuring for vet's fees if you can afford the extra premium. 'Loss of use' is a more contentious area. This covers the scenario where a horse is still able to do limited activities but is no longer able to do the job you bought him for. So if you bought an event horse and he suffered a serious tendon injury, he may recover well enough to be used for hacking but not for eventing. This is quite an expensive option and some insurance companies will insist on a lengthy 'recuperation period' in case there is any chance that the horse can recover sufficiently.

TRYING OUT A HORSE Wherever you look for your horse, it is always worth taking someone with greater experience than you along to advise you. Riding in an arena will allow you to assess his responsiveness, whilst a more experienced person looks on and judges his action and attitude.

Horse sales

There are numerous horse and pony sales in most countries. Some will be for down-to-earth, everyday horses and ponies, others will be for specialist performance horses, bloodstock sales, or stud sales. The advantage of sales is that there is a large number of animals to look at in one place. However, the opportunity to try them out and to find out much about them is limited and instant decisions have to be made. You really do need to know what you are doing and exactly what you are looking for if you intend to buy at a sale or auction.

THE HEALTHY HORSE

All horses have different characteristics and traits. Take time to stand and watch your horse in his stable and in his field. Learn to recognize what is normal for him in terms of behaviour and movement, then you will know instantly if something is wrong.

SIGNS OF A HEALTHY HORSE

A healthy horse should be sound; look well in his skin and coat; should be well conditioned, i.e. not too thin and not too fat; his eyes should be clear and bright; his nostrils clean; and his general outlook should be interested and alert. All horses and ponies have different characters; just like people some are nervy and anxious, others are bold and confident, and some are simply very laid back about life. Knowing your horse's character and recognizing when he is acting out of character is the best early warning system you can have.

If your horse lives out in the field with others, note whether he is normally sociable or whether he is a bit of a loner. Does he take an active interest in anything happening around him, or does he just glance over and then get back to eating? Knowing what is normal for him will make it easy for you to spot when something is wrong.

Physical warning signs that you should look out for are a general listlessness, a dull coat, and any discharge from the eyes or nostrils.

IN THE STABLE

A stabled horse is obviously easier to observe than a horse out at grass and, again, note if he normally has his head over the door looking at what's going on, or does he like to stand quietly at the back of his box? Is it normal for him to lie down a lot, or to roll frequently? Once again, knowing what is normal for him will help you identify when something is amiss.

Loss of appetite, drinking much more or less than normal, and any change in the number or consistency of droppings are warning signs that all is not well.

ROUTINE HEALTH CHECKS

It is important to know the horse's normal temperature, pulse rate, and respiratory rate. If you are able to report to your vet what these are when discussing any concerns about the horse, it will help him to assess the urgency of the problem (of course, he will make his own checks later).

Your horse's temperature should be about 38°C (101.5°F). His temperature is taken by inserting a thermometer into the rectum and holding it there for approximately one minute before taking a reading.

The pulse rate indicates the heart rate, which should be about 40 beats per minute (at rest). Count the pulse rate by pressing your finger against the artery that lies half way along the lower jawbone. Ask your vet on any routine visit to show you how to locate this so that you can check it yourself.

A healthy horse's respiratory rate is around 8 to 12 breaths per minute (at rest). Watch and count the rise and fall of the horse's flanks as he breathes.

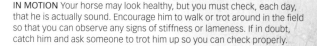

IN MOTION Your horse may look healthy, but you must check, each day, that he is actually sound. Encourage him to walk or trot around in the field so that you can observe any signs of stiffness or lameness. If in doubt, catch him and ask someone to trot him up so you can check properly.

Checking the feet and legs

Legs and hooves should feel cold and hard. Watch out for any heat in hooves, or for heat and/or swelling on the legs. Hooves can get bruised or infected and this will produce lameness and heat. Tendons and ligaments in the legs can get knocked and strained; these will show as heat and swellings. The horse's limbs and feet are one of the most common sites of injury. Make a habit of checking the feet for any problems or foreign bodies and feeling the horse's legs for any heat, filling, or lumps and bumps that are not normally there.

STABLE MANAGEMENT

A stabled horse needs a routine that allows him to be fed, mucked out, groomed, ridden, and ideally either turned out for a few hours or allowed a leg stretch on the horse walker or in hand every day. Horses and ponies were not designed to stand idle for hours with an empty stomach, and then be given a huge feed! In the wild, they would roam around all day grazing, so they would be continually moving and eating.

DAILY ROUTINE

Forage (such as hay or haylage), a concentrate feed (if needed), and fresh water should be given to your horse first thing in the morning. It is easier and healthier to muck out a stable without the horse in it, so this can be done while he has some daily turn-out or while he is on the horse walker. He shouldn't be ridden for at least an hour after he has had a concentrate feed, so his exercise routine needs to be worked around his feeding times. If he is to be stabled all day he should either have ad lib forage (i.e. forage that is accessible to him at all times), or be given more forage at lunchtime and again at teatime. Depending on how hard he is being worked, your horse may need a concentrate feed two, three, or even four times a day. Ideally, he should be groomed and either turned out in the afternoon, led out in hand, or put on a horse walker. At teatime in the evening he will have more forage, a feed if necessary, fresh water, and be rugged up for the night. A stabled horse should always be checked again a few hours after his teatime feed, as this is when digestive problems such as colic are most likely to occur (*see* p 47).

DUST-FREE ENVIRONMENT

Dust is as bad for a horse's health as it is for a human's. Every effort should be made to create as close to a dust-free environment as possible for the horse. Stables should be well ventilated and care should be taken to use bedding and forage that carries minimal dust and mould spores.

STABLES It is important to keep the working area around the stables clean and tidy. Horses have a knack of finding things to walk into, or get tangled up in. Keep all your mucking out kit stored against a wall when not in use. Ideally, hang up brooms and rakes rather than leaning them against a wall.

Mucking out

❶ Remove droppings by 'sieving' through the bed with a fork (to avoid throwing out clean bedding). Similarly, rake back the dry areas of bedding and remove any wet bedding.

❷ Sweep up the exposed areas of the stable floor and leave the bedding heaped up around the edges until the floor dries out. Scrub out water buckets and refill with fresh water.

❸ Spread the bedding back out over the floor of the stable. Add any fresh bedding needed to top up and mix it all together and relay the bed level, with banks around the edge if required.

OUT AT GRASS

Many people think that a grass-kept horse is a lot less work than a stabled horse, but this is not true. The main advantage to keeping a horse out at grass is that the routine can be more flexible than that of a stabled horse, but otherwise he still needs a fair amount of care and attention. His paddocks must be well fenced and the fences must be regularly checked for any damage and repaired as necessary. He needs access to fresh water and water troughs must be regularly cleaned out. He may also need supplementary feeding when grass growth is poor. To maintain good grass growth the land will need harrowing, rolling, and maybe fertilizing. Any poached areas of ground (where muddy areas have been rutted by the horse's hooves) will need to be levelled and reseeded. While there may not be a stable to muck out, droppings should still be cleared from grazing areas to prevent soiling of the grass and to reduce the risk of worm damage to the horse. His grazing must also be kept free of poisonous plants, such as ragwort.

Your horse's condition needs to be monitored year-round and action taken if he gains or loses too much weight. The horse should always be checked at least twice a day. Depending on his breed, condition, and general hardiness, he may need to wear waterproof rugs during the winter. A summer fly sheet may also need to be used to protect him from flies and midges in the

SEASONAL CARE In the winter, horses at grass need to be protected from the cold and wet. Hardier breeds will cope provided they have hedges to shelter behind or a field shelter. More finely bred horses will need to wear warm, waterproof rugs. In the summer, protection needs to be offered from the sun and flies. Fly fringes or fly masks will help protect the horse's face, but very sensitive horses may need to wear a fly sheet.

summer. If the horse needs to wear rugs, these will have to be changed regularly to prevent rubbing and to ensure they are not sodden. It's also worth remembering that when you do want to ride him, it will take longer to groom him in preparation than it does a stabled horse.

Beating boredom

A good routine with plenty of exercise, care, and attention should prevent a stabled horse becoming bored. But if boredom is a problem, there are various stable toys available to occupy his mind!

■ Horseballs are a popular horse toy.

■ Another alternative is a feed distributor. This is a gadget filled with feed which the horse rolls around and around with his nose to release the food through a specific opening.

■ Salt and mineral licks should also be made available to a stabled horse. A grass-kept horse will gain certain vitamins and minerals from the grasses he eats, as well as from licking the soil. A stabled horse is completely reliant on what you provide him with.

FEEDING

Horses have relatively small stomachs and their digestive system is designed for how they would have lived in the wild – eating little and often by wandering around grazing the grasses and herbs in their environment.

Once domesticated and put to work and leisure use, the horse had to be fed additional food to match his increased workload. And today's barn- or stable-kept horses are very far removed from their original lifestyle.

ESSENTIAL ROUGHAGE

Forage, either as grass, hay, or haylage, is a vital part of a horse's diet – it is what he was designed to eat as it provides the roughage that his digestive system requires. Depending on how much work the horse is in, and what his body condition is like, his diet can be supplemented with concentrate feeds. It is important to monitor the quantity and quality of your horse's grazing. In poor growing conditions, even a horse doing no work at all may need his diet supplemented with hay, haylage, or concentrate feeds. Similarly, during lush growing conditions, you may need to restrict the horse's intake.

FEED QUANTITIES

The daily food intake of a horse is equivalent to 2–2.5% of his body weight. As a general guide, a horse doing little or no work should get most of his feed requirements from forage. Horses in regular light work should be fed two-thirds forage to one-third concentrate feed. Horses in hard fast work can be fed two-thirds concentrate to one-

HORSES EATING HAY For most horses, a straightforward, well-balanced diet, good management, and correct training and handling, will be enough to keep them happy. Feeding hay on the ground is a more natural way to feed them than putting hay in a haynet.

Supplements

There is a huge range of dietary supplements available for horses and ponies, and it is very easy to be swayed by all the advertising claims and end up spending a small fortune over supplementing your horse's diet. If you are feeding a compound feed, it should already be providing your horse with the vitamins, minerals, and trace elements he needs. A blood test taken by a vet will show up certain deficiencies if they exist and then the diet can be supplemented specifically. Before being tempted by all that's on offer, ask first whether there really is a problem that needs to be fixed and secondly, can the product on offer really do what it claims.

Colic

Colic is the term used to describe any kind of abdominal pain, and is one of the most common ailments to afflict horses. It can be fatal and early symptoms or warning signs should never be ignored. The first indication of a problem is usually a reduced number of droppings, or droppings that are becoming dry and pellet-like. Most colics occur in stabled horses and so this is an easy sign to spot. The horse will usually start to drink less as well. If you spot these early signs, you should remove any food from the horse's stable so that he cannot add to his problems by continuing to eat. Walking in hand or on a horse walker is sometimes enough at this early stage to clear any discomfort in the horse's intestines. If the problem persists, the horse will start to look uncomfortable. He may keep looking round at his stomach, get up and lie down and appear generally restless, or start to roll violently as the pain increases. A vet should always be called out to check the horse and to assess the seriousness of the colic. Often everything will settle down with the help of some painkillers and muscle relaxants. However, in the most serious cases, surgery has to be carried out to remove any blockage from the intestines.

Sudden changes of diet or of routine are common causes of colic. And so colic often occurs as a result of some other problem that has necessitated a change in the horse's routine. If a horse in regular work suddenly injures himself and is confined to his stable without exercise, he will be vulnerable to colic. A vet will advise you on reducing the risk, such as feeding bran mash to help his digestive system, soaking his forage so that he is receiving adequate fluids, and leading out in hand if his injury allows. Picking grass to feed to a stable-bound horse is another good way of keeping his digestive system healthy.

---

third forage. This ratio can be altered for levels of work between these two extremes. A good horseperson will feed each horse as an individual, and adjust his ration accordingly, rather than stick to a set ratio.

FORAGE AND CONCENTRATE FEEDS

All food should be as free from dust and mould spores as is possible. Haylage is generally less dusty than hay, but both types of forage can carry mould spores. Buy from a reliable and consistent source so that your horse's diet can be as consistent as possible.

Although some people still like to mix their own concentrate feeds, specialist horse-feed manufacturers supply a wide range of ready-made concentrate feeds. These compound feeds are made from a blend of cereals and other ingredients to provide different levels of protein and carbohydrates to match the different requirements of horses and ponies. Barley, oats, and maize are popular ingredients, but they can vary in feed value so feed balancers can be added to home-mixed rations to ensure the diet is consistent and well balanced. Sugar beet, which has been soaked in water, is a good succulent source of energy and fibre and is added to many diets.

GOLDEN RULES OF FEEDING

Bearing in mind the limitations of the horse's digestive system, it is worth remembering a few golden rules.
1 Feed as much of the diet as you can as forage.
2 Feed concentrates little and often. Give his total ration as three or four feeds throughout the day.
3 Ensure fresh water is always available.
4 Do not work the horse immediately after a feed. Allow an hour to an hour and a half between feeding and exercise in order to give the food time to digest.
5 Match his feed intake to his work, i.e. reduce his concentrate feed if he is having a day off or is suddenly dropped back into light work.
6 Introduce any changes to the diet gradually over a few days to avoid shocking his system.

CONCENTRATE The contents of ready-mixed concentrate feeds may vary considerably from one brand to another. Feed companies often provide helplines and nutritionists to advise horse and pony owners on the best way to feed their particular animal.

GROOMING

Horses need to be groomed to keep their coat and skin clean and healthy, and to help improve their muscle tone. In the wild, horses actually groom each other using their lips, tongue, and teeth. If a horse is to be expected to wear any kind of tack, he should be thoroughly groomed first to avoid the sweat and dirt in his coat causing sores and rubs when it comes into contact with his saddle, harness, or rugs.

REGULAR BRUSHING

Daily grooming will keep your horse's coat and skin in good condition. Grease and sweat build up very quickly in the horse's coat and will soon lead to rubs and sores if not removed, so the horse should always be groomed before he is tacked up to be ridden. Pay particular attention to any areas that will come into contact with his tack. After exercise, if the horse has not been sweating, you can just brush him off again before turning him out or rugging him up and putting him back in his stable. But if he is hot and sweaty, he will need washing off properly. Use a bucket of water with some shampoo in it as this will help lift the sweat and grease out of his coat. With a large sponge, wash any sweaty areas with the soapy water. This will then need to be rinsed off. Most horses soon get used to being rinsed off using a hosepipe if one is available. Otherwise, sponge him off using a fresh bucket of clean water. Then use a sweat scraper to remove the

TETHERED HORSE This horse is being secured by cross-ties while he is being groomed. Some horses will panic if tied in this way, so they should always be used with caution.

excess water from his coat. Towelling him off as well is a gesture he will appreciate. He should then be walked off to dry (or put on a horse walker). If the weather is cool, you should put some sort of absorbent rug on him such as fleece, so that he doesn't get cold as he dries off.

BONDING
Grooming is also a good way of bonding with your horse and gives you a chance to double check for injuries,

sores, or signs of stiffness. Horses groom each other quite happily if given the chance, so when you groom your horse it should be a relaxing and pleasant experience for him. As you brush him, take note of whether his muscle tone is even or not. This will help you spot any areas of weakness or strain that may need attention. Similarly, if he is stiff or sore anywhere he is likely to flinch when you groom him so, again, this indicates an area that should be investigated.

Grooming kit

A grooming kit usually includes a range of brushes and combs to perform various tasks. The kit itself needs to be cleaned regularly.

HOOF PICK Mud and stones will get tightly packed in the horse's feet if he is out hacking or turned out. A hoof pick should be used to clean them out carefully.

Grass-kept horses

If a horse is living out in the field, the grease that occurs naturally in his coat will act as added protection against the wet and cold. So he shouldn't be groomed and washed as vigorously and frequently as a stabled horse. Use a curry comb and dandy brush to remove the mud and loose hairs from his coat and leave it at that. For a special occasion, he can be washed and shampooed, but try not to do this too often.

CURRY COMB This can be used to clean thick mud from the horse's coat and from his mane and tail. It is also used to clean dirt out of the other grooming brushes.

DANDY BRUSH This is a stiff brush to remove the worst of the mud and dust from the horse's coat. Most horses find it too scratchy to use on sensitive areas of the face.

BODY BRUSH A softer brush for use on sensitive areas such as the face, stifle, and stomach. It will lift the dust and grease out of the coat. Clean it using the curry comb.

WATER BRUSH This is a very stiff brush that can be dipped in water and used to scrub the heels and hooves if they are very muddy. Take care not to scratch the horse's skin.

MANE COMB A small comb for use on the mane. If the mane is very muddy or tangled, it is better to wash and condition it first. Then comb through it once it is dry.

TAIL COMB This is a wide-tooth comb that can be used on the tail to remove tangles. It is usually best to wash and condition the tail first to get rid of the worst tangles.

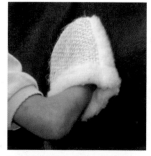

GROOMING OR MASSAGE MITT This sheepskin mitt is used to groom bony parts of the horse such as knees, hocks, and elbows, or used to massage all over.

SPONGES Use two different coloured sponges: one to clean the eyes, nose, and mouth; and the other to wash around the sheath and under the dock of the tail.

SHOWING OFF

If you are going to compete your horse or take him out hunting, you are expected to make an extra special effort to be smartly turned out. Your own clothing should be clean, neat, and tidy and your horse should be thoroughly well groomed and, if appropriate, have his mane and tail plaited. Attention to detail, such as adding quarter markers and oiling the hooves, makes a world of difference to the overall picture.

FINISHING TOUCHES

Nothing beats good grooming and the genuine well-being of the horse for really showing him off at his best, but you can add to the overall picture of glowing good health by using a few finishing touches. For example, chalk can be rubbed into any white markings to make them appear really bright white. Baby oil, rubbed into the palm of your hands and then gently smoothed over the muzzle, will give a lovely, soft velvety shine to the skin. Similarly, hoof oil brushed onto the hooves is not only good for their condition, but also makes them look great.

LOOKING GOOD
Pride in appearance is part of the discipline of the horse world. A well turned out horse shows respect to the host of the venue.

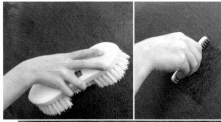

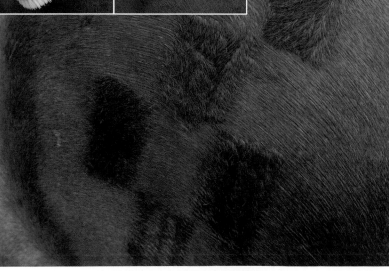

Quarter markings

Quarter markers are simply patterns that are brushed or combed onto the horse's coat. They are usually put on the well-rounded muscular area on top of the hindquarters, or on the flat area down each side of the hindquarters. You can buy ready made stencil patterns, or you can easily create your own quarter markers using a brush and comb.

❶ Brush over the area where you want to make the pattern with a damp, clean brush. This gives you your blank canvas to work on!

❷ Using a small comb, and working in a different direction to that in which the hair grows, comb a small rectangular shape.

❸ Leave a similar size rectangle of hair next to it and then 'back comb' another square shape. Continue in this way to form a chess board pattern.

Plaiting the mane

❶ Dampen the mane and split it into equal bunches using elastic bands. The size of the bunches will determine the number of plaits.

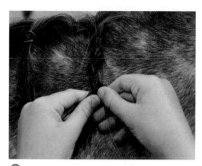

❷ Work your way through all the bunches, plaiting them neatly and evenly, until the whole mane, and the forelock are all plaited.

❸ Roll or fold each plait back up into the crest. You can then either secure it with an elastic band or use a needle and thread.

Plaiting the tail

❶ Take two sections of hair from the top of the tail, one from each side. Take a third section from the middle of the tail. Make sure each section of hair is of the same thickness.

❷ Cross the left section over the middle section, then cross the right section over the middle also. Hold this in place and pick up another section of hair from each side to form the next plait.

❸ Continue down, taking a new section of hair from either side, and picking up more hair from the middle. Keep each section the same size and plait it in as tightly as you can.

❹ Once you reach the end of the dock, stop taking hair from either side and simply continue to plait the three sections of hair that you are left with, so that you form a long plait. Fasten the end securely with an elastic band.

❺ Now fold up the long plait and tuck the end in behind the point where it started. Secure it in place with another elastic band.

❻ Put on a tail bandage or tail guard to protect it and hold it in place. Remove it carefully – if you use a tail bandage you will have to unwind it rather than just slide it off!

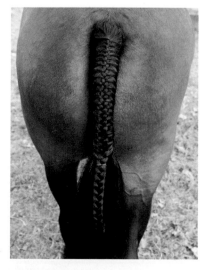

WAITING AROUND Always remember to consider your horse's needs as well as your own. At a show, you may want to stand and watch the action – just make sure your horse is as warm and comfortable as you are.

CLIPPING

Horses in regions with a cold winter climate will grow thick winter coats as protection against the weather. If the horse is to be kept up in work, then this thick coat will cause him to sweat excessively. He runs the risk of catching a chill, in the same way as you would if you stood around outside in damp clothes, and is likely to lose weight through excess sweating. So it is far more comfortable for him to have this heavy coat clipped off.

HOW MUCH TO CLIP

How much of the coat is clipped off depends on whether the horse is stabled or turned out, or a mixture of both, how much work he is doing and whether he is likely to lose or gain condition. There are a variety of different types of clip, ranging from a full (or hunter) clip, which removes all the coat apart from a saddle patch and the legs, to a bib clip, which just takes off the hair under the throat, on the underside of the neck, and off the chest. The variations in between range from the blanket clip, which leaves hair on the legs, back, loins, and quarters, to different degrees of trace clip, which takes hair off the underside of the neck, chest, belly, and the lower half of the hindquarters.

STABLED OR TURNED OUT

If your horse is turned out at grass rather than being stabled, then a partial clip, combined with wearing a turnout rug, will leave him with some natural protection against the elements whilst keeping him cool in those areas from which he is most likely to sweat, i.e. the neck, chest, belly, and stifle.

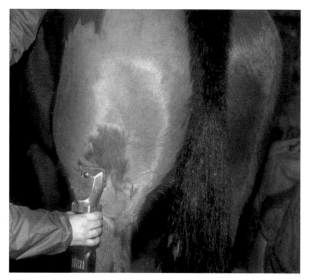

HORSE BEING CLIPPED To produce a clean, tidy clip, the horse's coat needs to be clean and dry. Work in a well-lit area and put on a riding hat to clip the ticklish areas under his belly in case he kicks out at you. Use chalk to draw the lines you want to clip along so that you end up with an even clip on both sides of the horse.

BIB CLIP Often used for ponies that are turned out but are still in work. It involves removing the hair from under the throat, down the underside of the neck, and off the front of the chest. It can also be extended along the belly.

TRACE CLIP This comes in a variety of forms but all based on the same theme. Differing amounts of hair are removed from the underside of the neck and belly and also from the lower half of the hindquarters.

BLANKET CLIP This clip helps keep the muscles of the loins and hindquarters warm as the hair is left on the back, loins, and quarters. Again, the size of the 'blanket' can vary depending on how much hair you want to keep or lose.

A horse in regular work who is stabled most of the time will benefit from a full or blanket clip in combination with stable rugs. This will enable you to keep the horse warm in the stable, but cool during his work.

BE PREPARED

Most horses are quite happy to be clipped or, if they have never been clipped, should have nothing to fear if they are introduced to the idea properly. If you have never clipped a horse before, then you must be sure to have someone with you who knows what they are doing. A well-clipped horse can look stunning but if it is done badly it will look patchy and messy. And, just like a bad hair cut, it will take a long time to grow out! Before you start, make sure that you have everything you need: clippers, brush, towel, something to stand on to reach the high bits, a riding hat to wear for clipping underneath his belly, and oil to keep the clippers lubricated. If you do not know the horse's history, or if he has definitely never been clipped, take the time to just stand by him letting the clippers run so that he gets used to the noise. Then place the clippers against his neck or shoulder so that he gets used to the vibration.

CAREFUL CLIPPING

If all seems well, then you can start to clip him. Run the clippers in the opposite direction to the hair growth. Use long, smooth, sweeping strokes, keeping a firm pressure against the skin so that the clippers are always working at the same level. For the face, stifle area, and girth/elbow area, it may be better to use smaller trimmers as they are less ticklish and quieter. When you have finished, brush the horse off to remove any loose hairs. Use a warm, damp towel to rub all over the horse's coat to remove any grease or dust. Rug the horse up well afterwards.

HUNTER CLIP The full, or hunter, clip usually involves removing all the hair apart from the legs and a saddle patch. This particular horse has had some hair left on his face. This may be done through choice for warmth, or if the horse is particularly wary of his head being clipped.

SHOEING

A wild horse's hoof is strong enough to withstand the terrain that he travels across. But a domesticated horse is asked to work on harder surfaces, at greater speeds, and is also expected to jump and perform intricate movements, all of which puts more wear and tear on the foot than it would experience in the wild. So metal shoes are generally fitted to the feet to allow the domesticated horse to carry out the tasks we require of him.

FIT FOR THE PURPOSE

It is worth noting that, in the wild, the evolutionary law of the survival of the fittest ensured that only horses that had naturally strong, sound feet and limbs survived to breed and produce the next generation. Today, quite wrongly, horses with all kinds of weaknesses and deficiencies are bred from,

THE FARRIER A good farrier will study how the horse's feet are developing before deciding exactly how to shoe him.

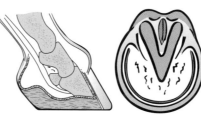

THE HOOF The pedal bone, navicular bone, and short pastern bone sit inside the hoof. The v-shaped, rubbery 'frog' on the sole of the foot acts as a shock absorber.

which means modern horse owners then spend a great deal of money on supplements, vets, and remedial farriers to keep weak-footed horses sound! It is not absolutely essential to shoe all horses, and there is a growing trend to work horses 'barefoot' provided they have strong enough feet to withstand the demands of their work.

ANATOMY OF THE FOOT

A horse's foot is protected by a hard outer casing of horn that forms the hoof wall. The outside of the foot is tough, but inside the foot are many delicate structures. The foot bones are surrounded by the sensitive laminae tissues that carry the nerve and blood supply to and from the foot. The 'white line' is a visible line on the sole of the foot, running between the insensitive hoof wall and the sensitive inner structure of the foot. The underside of the foot is protected by the sole and frog. The sole protects the inner foot but is also relatively sensitive and can become bruised or punctured. Horses with particularly weak, thin soles can have protective pads fitted under the shoe to reduce the risk of damage to the sole.

Horse boots

An alternative to horse shoes are horse boots. These can be put over the bare hooves to protect the feet during certain types of work. A horse being worked in an arena may be comfortable barefoot, but on a road he may need the protection of the boots.

AN EXPERT JOB

A qualified farrier should be used to shoe a horse, as untold damage can be caused by bad shoeing and foot trimming. In many countries, it is illegal for anyone other than a qualified farrier to shoe a horse. The horse's hoof is continually growing and should be trimmed and/or reshod every four to six weeks. The farrier will remove the old shoe, trim and rebalance the foot so that the weight-bearing surface is evenly distributed across the frog and around the wall of the hoof, and then fit a new shoe. The shoe is heated up and shaped to match the shape of the horse's hoof. A good farrier will fit the new shoe in such a way as to encourage the hoof to grow in the desired shape whilst offering as much protection to the underside of the foot as possible. Another important factor is the correct foot-pastern axis – ideally the angle of the pastern and the hoof should match the angle of the slope of the horse's shoulder. In a well-put-together horse,

Foot care

It is vital to take good care of a horse's feet. Start by using a good farrier who will be diligent about keeping the shape, balance, and length of the feet correct. Ensure that you book him in to shoe your horse regularly – every four to six weeks. Correct diet helps to encourage the growth of strong hoof horn and there are many supplements available to aid hoof growth as well. Moisture retention is important to prevent the hoof becoming dry and brittle, which results in it breaking up badly. Wetting the hooves and then applying hoof oil to retain the moisture is a good practice.

this should be approximately 45 degrees. The shoe is fixed to the foot with nails, which must be accurately placed so that they remain within the hard hoof wall and do not puncture the sensitive part of the foot.

Shoeing a horse

❶ To remove the old shoe, the farrier has to lift the clenches (the turned-over ends of the nails). He then uses a set of pincers to lever off the old shoe, complete with nails.

❷ He then uses a trimmer to clip off any excess hoof wall. This stage is vital as it allows him to rebalance the foot so that the weight-bearing surfaces are all level.

❸ A rasp is then used to level off the trimmed areas. Whilst he works, he should be constantly checking that the horse's foot will be level and balanced as a result of his trimming.

❹ The new shoe is heated up and placed against the trimmed foot to see that it matches the required shape. While the shoe is still hot, it is easy to reshape to produce a perfect fit.

❺ Once the shoe is the correct fit, it is fixed to the foot with nails. These must be carefully and correctly positioned so that they do not enter the sensitive tissue inside the hoof.

❻ The end result is a securely fitted shoe. Shoes can have wedges and extensions fitted to counteract problems in the feet and limbs. This shoe has an extension on one side only.

HORSES ON THE MOVE

Transporting horses by road, sea, and air is becomingly increasingly common, whether it be transportation to a competition, or the importing or exporting of horses to different countries. Most of us will only ever be involved with transportation by road. If a horse has to travel by air or sea, there are specialist companies with the necessary expertise required to organize international transportation as safely as possible.

PROTECTION

Most horses are quite happy to travel, but it is important to protect their limbs in particular from damage during transportation. Preparation for any journey is important as becoming lost or breaking down with a horse on board is quite stressful for all concerned.

If you are going to compete regularly, keep a permanent check list of everything you need to take with you.

MODERN TRAILER Modern design and technology has brought great improvements to horse lorries and trailers; trailers are now available complete with living accommodation for the rider.

BE PREPARED

■ Take more food and water than you think you need for the horse in case of a delay or breakdown.
■ Take a variety of rugs so that you can keep the horse's temperature as constant as possible during transportation.
■ Always carry a well-equipped first-aid kit.

RUGS Always carry a selection of clean rugs in a range of light- and heavyweight materials. Throughout the day, you should keep checking how warm your horse is and change his rugs accordingly.

■ If you are travelling to a competition, pack all your kit and equipment the night before to save last-minute delays. Take the schedule, rule book, and directions with you.

■ Pack buckets, sponges, and sweat scrapers so that you can wash the horse off properly after his competition.

BE PREPARED On route to a show, be sure to bring maps and schedules; plus a mobile phone and contact details in case you are delayed.

SHOW KIT

It is worth keeping some equipment especially for shows so that it is always clean and in good condition. Some good grooming brushes and a favourite travel rug are good things to keep for various outings.

FRESH AIR

Fresh air and good ventilation are vital to a horse's health, whether at home in his stable or when travelling. Keep as many windows open as possible in the transporter. It is better to put an extra rug on the horse to keep him warm but have all the windows open. Put some bedding down on the floor so that it will absorb any urine produced by the horse. Urine contains ammonia, which will irritate his respiratory system, so it is far healthier if it can be soaked up by some bedding.

On arrival at your destination, let the ramp down straight away to let as much fresh air in as possible. Take the horse out for a leg stretch, and whilst he is out of the lorry, clean out any wet bedding and muck. Give the horse a good walk around to ease any stiffness and to let him fill his lungs with clean air. Check that he still has all his shoes on: it is quite easy for the horse to step on his own foot and pull a shoe off while he is travelling. Put him back in the lorry, check that he is not too hot or too cold and, if necessary, change his rugs accordingly. Offer him some water and wipe out his mouth with a wet sponge. Check throughout the day's activities, and on the journey home, that he is not getting too hot or cold again.

FRESH AIR
Once you are at the show, make sure the horse can get plenty of fresh air. Open the ramp and any other doors and windows.

UNLOADING THE HORSE When unloading a horse, give him time to see how he has to negotiate the ramp. Keep yourself to one side of him as some horses will jump down the ramp. It is worth keeping travel boots on the horse to protect his legs whilst loading and unloading him.

FIRST AID AND COMMON AILMENTS

Despite their size and strength, horses seem to be especially prone to accidents, injury, and illness. This is partly due to their nature and quick reactions: their first instinct when faced with something they don't understand is to flee from it, so they often run themselves into danger. But the fact that we have removed them from their natural way of life also means that any shortcomings in their management and care can lead to health problems.

FIRST-AID KIT
If in any doubt at all, a vet should always be your first port of call. However, there are some minor conditions that can be treated if you have the necessary knowledge and the right equipment. You can buy ready made up first-aid kits or, alternatively, ask your vet to advise you on the main things you should have so that you can put your own kit together.

ROUTINE CARE
All horses should be routinely wormed, vaccinated, and have their teeth rasped. Horses pick up worms from the pasture that they graze. These parasites can cause damage to a horse's internal organs, and the more horses there are grazing a particular area, the higher the worm burden will be unless pastures are well managed and *all* the horses are routinely wormed. Different types of worms are prevalent according to the time of year, and oral wormers carry different active ingredients to tackle particular types of infestations. Wormers are usually administered every eight weeks, although some of the more modern drugs work for longer. Another option is to have a specialist laboratory carry out a worm count on your horse's droppings and advise you on specific problems and suggest a tailor-made worming programme.

VACCINATIONS
Different countries will have different health hazards, but horses are generally vaccinated against such diseases as tetanus and equine influenza. Additional vaccinations against specific threats that occur from time to time, such as African Horse Sickness, may be necessary as well. Official competition bodies such as the International Equestrian Federation (FEI) and the Jockey Club insist that all registered horses are correctly vaccinated. An initial course of three injections has to be given; the first two must be at least four weeks apart, followed by a third injection six months later. After that, an annual booster is required. All this is recorded in the horse's passport or vaccination certificate.

First-aid kit

- **THERMOMETER** Insert the thermometer into the rectum. Hold it there for one minute; wipe it clean and take the reading.
- **MELONIN PADS** These absorbent pads can be placed over a wound as a dressing to keep it sterile and encourage healthy tissue to grow.

- **VETRAP** This is a self-adhesive stretchy bandage that can be used to secure a poultice or wound dressing in place.
- **SOFBAN** A soft absorbent bandage that acts as a padding over a wound dressing such as melonin. It will soak up any fluid.
- **STICKY TAPE** This is used to secure the ends of bandages. Extra-wide sticky tape is especially useful for securing a foot poultice and padding.
- **GAMGEE** Soft padding that is used under a bandage to protect a wound or tendons and ligaments from undue pressure.
- **ANTISEPTIC CREAM** Used on minor scratches, a good antiseptic cream helps to cleanse a wound and encourage healthy tissue growth.

- **WOUND POWDER** A fine antiseptic powder that can be dusted on to minor scrapes. Do not use on deep wounds that should be kept moist.
- **SCISSORS** First-aid scissors for animal use should have blunted ends to reduce the risk of them causing injury.
- **POULTICE** A poultice can be used either hot to draw out pus and infection or cold to relieve bruising. They must never be more than 'hand-hot.'
- **COTTON WOOL** Use cotton wool soaked in warm water to clean out wounds. Keep using plenty of fresh pieces to avoid reintroducing germs into the wound.
- **HIBISCRUB** An antibacterial agent added to warm water and used to clean wounds or skin that is to be the site of any injections.

TEETH RASPING

A vet or equine dentist should check the horse's teeth at least once a year. He will rasp off sharp edges and ensure that the horse can eat his food properly and is also comfortable in his mouth so that he is comfortable when wearing a bit and bridle.

LAMENESS

The feet and legs are one of the most common sites for injury. The feet can suffer from bruised soles or from an infection building up inside. The ligaments and tendons of the limbs are prone to injury particularly in high-performance horses such as event horses and racehorses. The problem area may be indicated by heat in the leg or foot. Lameness can also indicate laminitis – a painful and severe inflammation inside the hoof wall.

TEETH RASPING A metal gag is used to hold the horse's jaws open so that the vet has easy and safe access to the surfaces of the teeth. As well as levelling off sharp edges, the vet will also check for abnormalities.

How to poultice a foot

The purpose of poulticing is quite simply to use a heat source to increase the blood supply to an injury site to help promote quick healing. A poultice will also help to draw out any pus (the result of infection) that may be in the wound. An infection within the hard shell of the hoof rapidly becomes painful as the hoof cannot expand to accommodate it. The vet or farrier will usually cut carefully into the site of the infection to make a hole for it to drain through. The poultice is then applied and this acts to draw the pus out through the hole. If left untreated, the infection will eventually force its way out somewhere, usually through the soft tissue of the coronet band, causing considerable discomfort and leaving an open wound.

❶ Use a scrubbing brush and plenty of water to thoroughly clean the whole sole and frog area. If you leave any mud it will be drawn back into the wound and may reinfect it.

❷ Use a piece of poultice soaked in warm water. Squeeze out excess water and place the poultice over the wound. You can put some kitchen foil over this to help retain the heat.

❸ Place some gamgee or suitable padding over the poultice and foil, and secure it all in place with some vetrap. Wide sticky tape over the top will give extra protection.

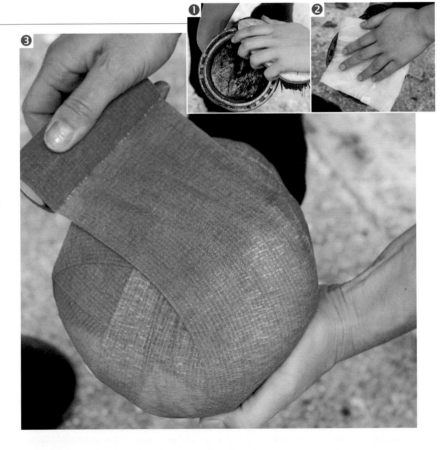

ASSESSING THE PROBLEM

If you trot up a lame horse, he will lift his head and neck as the lame foot touches the ground, and nod his head down again as the sound foot touches the ground. He lifts his head and neck in an effort to keep the weight off the painful limb. If you suspect the lameness is in a hind limb, watch the horse trot away from you – the hindquarter of the lame leg will drop lower than that of the sound leg.

Checking your horse's legs each day may allow you to pick up early warning signs of trouble before too much damage is done. Soft swellings and heat along the lines of the tendons and ligaments are an indication of damage to that area. If the horse continues in work, even if he is only showing a tiny degree of heat or swelling, the

WATCH THE HORSE WALK To check for lameness, you can either watch the horse trot up in a straight line or you can lunge him to assess the problem. Some lamenesses are more obvious on a turn than on a straight line.

Laminitis

An early sign of laminitis is intermittent lameness and, as the feet become more painful, the horse will stand with his front feet out in front of him in an effort to take the weight off them. Laminitis can be managed by diet, expert foot-trimming, and by the use of anti-inflammatory drugs. Prevention is better than cure, so it pays to restrict grazing when grass growth is lush.

damage can be made dramatically worse. Immediate box rest and the application of a cold compress or ice to reduce the heat and swelling as quickly as possible will all serve to minimize the damage until the vet arrives to fully assess it. Bandaging, either as a way of giving support to the injury or as a method of holding a dressing or poultice in place, may be a vital part of the treatment programme.

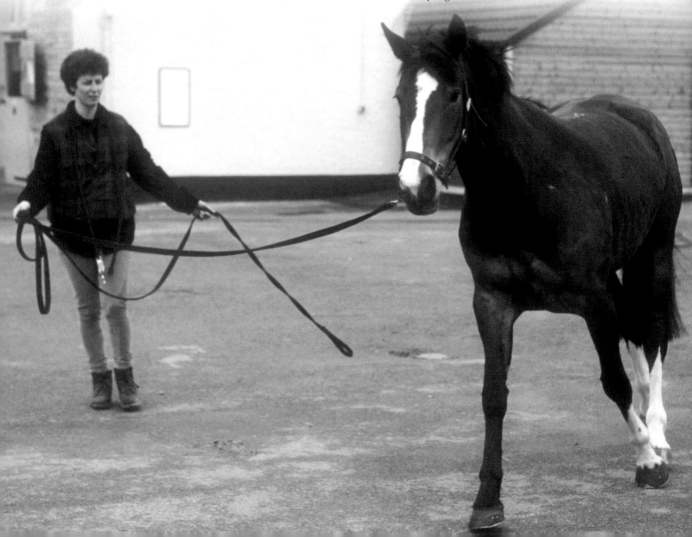

How to apply a stable bandage

❶ Hold a bandage pad securely around the leg. The pad should extend from below the knee or hock, down to the coronet band so that it encompasses the fetlock joint.

❷ Tuck the free end of the bandage inside the overlap of the pad. Bandage the leg, keeping the pressure even all the time.

❸ Work your way up and down the leg until you run out of bandage. Make sure the pad beneath remains smooth and flat. The bandage may be secured by Velcro or tapes.

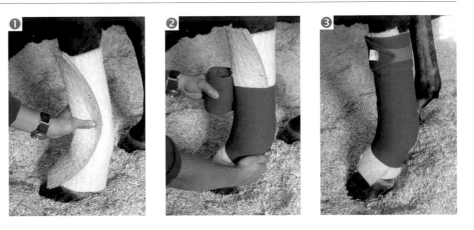

How to bandage a hock

❶ Hold a piece of bandage pad or gamgee around the hock joint. Secure the top of the pad by running the bandage around it a couple of times. It helps to have someone hold the pad while you apply the bandage.

❷ Using a figure-of-eight pattern, work the bandage from above the hock to below the hock, leaving the point of the hock clear.

❸ Secure the bottom of the pad by running what remains of the bandage around the bottom of the pad and then securing it.

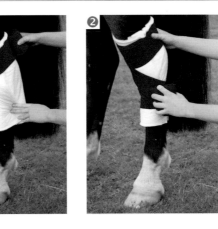

How to bandage a knee

❶ Hold a pad around the knee. Secure the top of the pad by running the bandage around it a few times. Then use a figure-of-eight pattern to encompass the knee joint, leaving part of the back of the knee clear.

❷ Run the bandage around the bottom of the pad a few times and then secure it in place. Keep checking the bandage pressure to ensure that it isn't too tight or too loose.

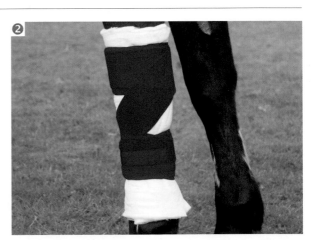

BREEDING

Breeding a foal from your own mare can be a rewarding exercise although, sadly, from a financial point of view, it is often cheaper to buy in a horse bred by someone else as a two-, three- or four-year-old, than it is to breed and raise one of your own – bearing in mind the mare itself is also costing you time and money! If you do decide to breed from your mare, you must pay careful attention to your choice of stallion and stud farm.

TO BREED OR NOT?

There are two types of breeders: the commercial breeder who probably runs several mares and is breeding to sell the offspring at a profit, and the single-horse owner/breeder who takes the decision to breed a foal from a mare that has been used for riding and/or competing, to act as a replacement for that horse in the future. The commercial breeder has to breed 'profitably' and will therefore make non-sentimental decisions about his programme. Single-horse owners should also base their decision to breed on common sense and with a view to producing a better class of offspring rather than on a feeling of sentimentality. Ideally, you should only breed from a horse if there are compelling good reasons to want to reproduce the traits of that particular horse, such as excellent conformation and temperament, exceptional ability or paces, etc.

CHOOSING A STALLION

A stallion should be chosen to enhance the mare's good points and to try to reduce or eliminate any bad points. So if the mare is a bit light of bone, you would choose a stallion with good bone; if she has a good hindquarter but is not so correct through the shoulders and neck, you need a stallion with an exceptionally good front; and so on. Some stallions pass on certain traits more strongly than others. Some are, rightly or wrongly, labelled as having tricky temperaments. Others are renowned for passing on a good jumping technique or spectacular movement. All these things have to be taken into account when choosing the right match for your mare. The likely size of the offspring must also be considered – if your mare is just the right size for you and you are hoping to breed a replacement for her, it is no good choosing a stallion of markedly different height or build. Equally, temperament and ability must also be matched to the intended end use of the offspring. If you are planning to sell the youngster you produce, note which breeds and crossbreeds are particularly popular with buyers.

Stallions are generally kept on commercial stud farms where specialist staff and facilities are available to provide the safest environment for both the mare and the stallion during mating or 'covering'. A fee has to be paid to the stud, based on the quality and success of the chosen stallion. There will also be veterinary and livery charges because it is normal for the mare to stay at the stud to be mated more than once during the same heat period, to optimize the chance of a successful mating.

MARE IN FOAL You must carefully monitor the condition of the mare during her pregnancy. Allowing her to become too fat or too thin can be detrimental to both the mare and foal. Ask your vet for advice as the mare's pregnancy progresses and this will allow you to correct anything before it is too late.

CHOOSING A STUD

You need to be happy with the choice of stud at which the stallion is stood: take advice from your vet, or other local horse-breeders. Find out whether the stallion runs free with the mares or whether the covering takes place under control, with someone holding the mare and the stallion. The latter is safer, although the former can be more successful as it is more natural. A mare who is not ready to be served will kick out at a stallion if he tries to cover her and he is likely to retaliate, risking injury to both parties. You should also ask what a particular stallion's fertility rate is. It is usually possible to achieve a successful mating, but it can be expensive if several attempts have to be made.

Your mare can either foal at your premises or she can be sent back to the stud farm to foal. If you are inexperienced or time constraints mean that you would be unable to keep a close watch on her as foaling becomes imminent, then it is a safer option to return her to the experts.

STUD FARM As the mare's owner, you need to be happy with the choice of stud farm as well as the stallion himself. It is especially important to note how well the grazing is fenced and managed, as your mare will be turned out during her stay.

Reproduction cycle

Mares reach puberty at approximately two years old, but they wouldn't normally be bred from until they are three. The mare comes 'on heat' about every three weeks during the mating season, and her heat period lasts for five to seven days. It is in this short window of opportunity that she has to be covered by the stallion if breeding is to be successful.

The warmer weather and longer daylight hours bring the mare into season and the birth of the foal the following spring coincides with abundant grass growth and warmer weather.

In the wild, the mare would be mated by the stallion in late spring or early summer. However, in the high-powered and expensive world of bloodstock breeding for horse racing, mares are often encouraged by artificial means to come into season early in the spring so that the foals are born as early in the year as possible. This is because all racehorses (in the northern hemisphere) are officially aged from January 1st of the year in which they were born, irrespective of their actual birth date. So foals born early in the year have a significant advantage on the track over their later-born rivals. Foals in the southern hemisphere are aged from August 1st.

CARING FOR THE OLDER HORSE

Like people, horses are generally managing to remain healthy and active for longer. Good nutrition, preventative care, and advances in medicine have helped to ensure that many horses continue to compete through their teens and even into their twenties. Obviously, some horses will age faster than others and, as with people, some will struggle to maintain their fitness, although this shouldn't stop them being suitable for an easier but still active life.

OLD-AGE PROBLEMS

All the while a horse is looking and feeling well, and handling his workload, there is no need to treat him any differently as he ages. Once he starts to show signs of ageing then his management needs to be altered to help him as much as possible.

Difficulty in maintaining body condition is one of the more common problems afflicting ageing horses. He will find it harder to withstand extremes of temperature as he ages and lack of body condition will make him particularly vulnerable to the cold. It may be worth clipping him in the summer as older horses usually have a thicker coat even in the warmer months and, in the winter, he should be well rugged up. It is particularly important that his rugs fit well and are changed regularly as he will be more susceptible to rubs and chafes as he ages. Because of his vulnerability to heat and cold, it is even more crucial now that he is older that he should have adequate shelter in his field and easy access to water if he is turned out. Remember, too, that if he is turned out with other horses, he is likely to slip down the pecking order as he gets older and weaker, so it is important that he doesn't have to fight for his food, water, or shelter.

TEETH

Another cause of appetite and/or weight loss can be poor dentition. All horses should have their teeth regularly rasped – annually at least – but older horses should have their teeth checked every six months.

At some stage, the teeth may prohibit adequate chewing of his food. He can be helped at this stage by soaking his feed so that it forms a soup. Concentrate feed can be given in this way and he can receive adequate fibre by soaking grass or hay cubes as well as sugar beet.

TEETH An older horse will need more regular attention paid to his teeth. As he ages, the teeth become longer and it becomes harder for the horse to align his jaws to chew properly. An indication of this is that he may start to 'quid' his food – lumps of semi-chewed food will drop out of his mouth.

NUTRITION

As the horse ages, his ability to digest his food efficiently is reduced so he is receiving fewer nutrients from the same amount of feed input. Any changes to the diet should be made slowly as it will take his digestive system longer to react. There are a good number of commercial brands of veteran feeds that will be well balanced, and either extruded or micronized to maximize digestibility.

Feeds should be high in protein, fat, and fibre. You can add cooking oil, such as corn oil, to each feed to increase the fat intake – up to a cupful per feed. Calcium levels should be reduced and phosphorus levels increased. Good quality hay or haylage should be fed.

ARTHRITIS

Years of wear and tear, and particularly the stresses and strains of a competitive life, are likely to result in stiffness of the joints and often chronic lameness. There are various anti-inflammatory drugs such as phenylbutazone, as well as joint supplements to help alleviate these

conditions. Good foot-trimming and shoeing is essential, especially as older horses are prone to problems with the navicular and pedal bones. Alternative therapies such as massage, chiropractic treatment, and even acupuncture may also help.

Try not to restrict the horse's opportunity to move around. Turn him out as much as possible and make sure that his stable is large and has a thick, secure bed to make it easy and comfortable for him to get up and down and to lie down to rest.

EUTHANASIA

For those of us who keep an older horse, a hard fact of life is that nature is rarely kind enough to allow him to simply die peacefully in his sleep. A decision usually has to be made by the owner, at a stage where it is believed that the horse's quality of life is diminishing. It is a hard decision, but usually one that is best made too early rather than too late. Deciding to give an old horse another chance and see if he can live through another cold winter or scorching hot summer may backfire if his condition deteriorates rapidly. Ideally, a horse's last few months of life should be relatively comfortable and enjoyable, not full of pain and misery. As his owner, it is all too tempting to keep delaying the inevitable, but the ultimate responsibility lies with you and you have to find the strength to make the right decision for the horse when the time comes.

OUT TO GRASS Retiring a horse by simply turning him out to grass is only an option if you are prepared to ensure he receives the care and attention he will need to keep him happy and comfortable in his old age.

SADDLERY AND EQUIPMENT

The first man to ride a horse was taking a leap of faith into the unknown. Given how basic his equipment would have been – optimistically aiming to control the creature with some form of rope bridle, and probably nothing to sit on – imagine his amazement if he could see the modern horse and rider festooned in all kinds of elaborate kit! To be fair, tack and equipment have evolved along with the demands that are made of horse and rider. The working horse had workmanlike tack and equipment; the sporting horse of today has the benefit of new technology to allow him to perform in optimum comfort to his maximum potential.

FANCY SADDLERY Western tack evolved to allow cowboys to ride for long hours in comfort, whilst carrying their 'survival kit' with them. Today, this once workmanlike kit is now often highly decorative and elaborate.

SAFETY FIRST

Whilst there is a large element of fun to be had with horses, you must never forget the dangers – they are strong, powerful animals with far quicker reflexes than us. Safety considerations should be paramount.

BEING AWARE

Horses rarely intend to hurt anyone, but accidents happen when riders are either thrown from the horse, or when someone on the ground finds themselves in the firing line when the horse reacts to a situation or something that he isn't happy about. It may be something as simple as kicking out at something tickling him – such an insect or even you grooming him – or it may be a full-blown panic when his fight-or-flight instinct kicks in and he tries to escape from a situation he deems to be dangerous. If you find yourself in the way, you are vulnerable to injury. An awareness of all that is going on around you and the horse will help keep you one step ahead. If you are able to second-guess what is likely to happen next, you may be able to take action to avoid trouble. Watch out for things that might spook the horse in the road – oncoming traffic, other animals such as dogs or farm livestock – and also the terrain ahead – slippery patches on the road, or rabbit holes or wire on the ground, etc.

Remember that as many accidents occur on the ground when handling horses as they do when riding!

You have to learn to ride or handle the horse whilst still taking in all that is happening around you in just the same way as a car driver has to drive the car whilst also reading the road ahead and interpreting the intentions of other road users!

LUNGE WORK Even in the relatively safe environment of an arena, it is vital that you wear protective clothing. In this case, both the rider and handler are correctly dressed. If something goes wrong and the rider is thrown off, the handler is left to control the horse and needs to be well protected.

RIDING KIT

There are good reasons why a 'uniform' of riding clothing has been established over time – even for everyday riding. Breeches and jodhpurs are designed to give freedom of movement, and are robust enough to stand up to the wear and tear of working with horses, but without rubbing or chafing. A top that has long sleeves to protect the arms and is relatively close fitting so that it doesn't flap about when riding is also a good idea.

A correctly fitted riding hat, with a properly adjusted harness, is essential. Many riders are tempted not to wear a hat when riding a horse they believe to be quiet or when riding in an arena, but accidents can happen to anyone – and anywhere. If we could all foresee when we were likely to be thrown off or kicked, we would all, presumably, take action to avoid the situation. The problem is that most accidents happen when we are least expecting them, so be prepared and properly dressed!

Choose a hat designed to meet national safety standards. There is unwarranted prejudice in some circles against helmets with ventilation holes or slots, on the grounds that something might pierce the rider's skull through these holes. The main purpose of these holes is to help dissipate the shock and pressure that the head is subjected to as a result of a severe blow, which far outweighs the minimal risk of a sharp object managing to penetrate the rider's head through one of these holes.

Stock

A properly fitted and tied stock around the neck offers some protection against whiplash as well as looking very smart. For the protection it offered, it was traditionally worn on the hunting field but many cross-country riders still wear one.

BODY PROTECTORS

Body protectors are compulsory for most racing and cross-country riding competitions, but it is well worth wearing one whenever your ride. There are various different designs, weights, and thicknesses available, but they are all relatively similar in design. What is most important is choosing one that is light and flexible enough not to restrict your movement, balance, and reactions. A more recent innovation is the BodyCage – a metal framework that acts as a protective cage around your upper body. If you are thrown from a horse, you should try to curl up in a ball and keep rolling if possible. Be sure that your body protector allows you to do this.

LEGS, FEET, AND HANDS

Gloves are always advisable for riding and handling horses as they give better grip on the reins and also offer

BE SEEN AND BE SAFE Fluorescent clothing for horse and rider is highly advisable if you have to ride on the roads. In poor light, it makes you more visible but it has also been shown to cause drivers to slow down anyway, even in broad daylight.

Neck strap

An old stirrup leather can be used as neck strap to be worn around the horse's neck. It's there for you to grab hold of in an emergency as well as helping a rider to keep his hands low and still when jumping over a fence.

some protection against rope burns and grazes if the horse pulls away from you as you lead him.

Footwear should be reasonably stout with a non-slip sole and a low heel to reduce the risk of your foot becoming trapped in the stirrup irons. Steel toe caps are also an option and, if you have ever had a horse stand on your toe, you will appreciate the protection they offer.

HIGH-VISIBILITY CLOTHING

Fluorescent jackets, waistcoats, and hat covers are available for riders, whilst exercise sheets and leg and tail wraps are available for the horse. Fluorescent leg wraps are particularly effective as the movement instantly attracts attention – in the same way that a flashing light would.

RIDING KIT

If you decide to take your riding seriously and begin to compete in any of the disciplines that are available to horse and rider, you will need to invest in the appropriate clothing, tack, and equipment for your particular discipline. Equestrian sports all carry the ethos of tradition and discipline with them and, as a competitor, it is easy to find out what you are expected to wear for your chosen sport. The basic turnout is known as 'ratcatcher'.

DRESS FOR THE JOB

At the lower levels of the main disciplines of dressage, showjumping, eventing, and showing, the 'ratcatcher' turnout of a hacking (tweed) jacket, shirt and tie (or stock), a crash helmet with a dark blue or black cover, and breeches and boots will see you through. This turnout is also perfectly correct for hunting. However, there are a few unwritten rules which, although only tiny in detail, mean a great deal in terms of correctness

DRESSAGE UNIFORM At the higher levels of competition in both pure dressage and the eventing phase, the rider is expected to wear a top hat and tails. Without a chin strap of any sort it is essential that the top hat fits correctly!

and acceptability! In eventing, and out hunting, for example, ladies wear beige breeches rather than white, whereas in showjumping and dressage, men and ladies wear white breeches. A coloured stock should be worn with a tweed hacking jacket, but a white or cream stock should be worn with a blue or black jacket.

CHANGING TIMES

Traditionally, riding kit has been kept as plain and uniform as possible, but in recent years fashion has led to more colour and design entering the field. Showjumping jackets in particular are now any number of colours and riding is beginning to lose some of its more conservative nature.

SHOWJUMPING KIT It used to be that ladies wore blue or black jackets and men could wear red jackets. In a move to become more spectator or television friendly, riders can now wear a variety of different colours – ladies are even allowed to wear red!

CROSS-COUNTRY KIT For cross country, the riders wear a coloured sweatshirt, or similar, under their body protector. Most riders have their chosen set of colours and will have their body protectors made to match. A coloured hat cover completes the picture.

BRIDLES

When horses were first ridden by man, they were simply a means of transport. The only control needed was the ability to stop and turn the horse, so the earliest bridles were simple rope headpieces, although there is archaeological evidence of rope bits being used very soon after horses were first domesticated. Where bitless bridles were used, control was asserted by applying pressure to the nose via a rope noseband.

MODERN DESIGN

As riding techniques became more sophisticated, and the horse was used more for leisure and competitive pursuits, more subtle control was required. Over time, bridles have evolved into precision-designed leather creations which, in combination with a bit, allow subtle pressure to be applied to the poll, nose, and bars of the mouth. Modern bridle designs offer padded nosebands and headpieces to make them more comfortable, and newer designs have cutaway headpieces to alleviate any irritation to the sensitive areas at the base of the horse's ears!

FITTING A BRIDLE

A bridle needs to fit the horse's head correctly for it to offer the right degree of control and comfort. There should be room to fit two fingers between the horse's throat and the throatlatch. The noseband should be snug but not overly tight, as this can make the horse tense. You should be able to fit a finger under the noseband. The cheekpieces should hold the bit at the correct height so that it just wrinkles the corners of the horse's mouth. The browband must be roomy enough not to pull the bridle forward against the horse's ears.

DOUBLE BRIDLE
This bridle has two bits, each with a separate rein attached for precise control. The bridoon bit helps to raise his head and the curb bit encourages him to flex his poll and lower jaw.

BASIC BRIDLE This pony is wearing a basic snaffle bridle. The bit is an eggbutt snaffle, which is less likely to rub the corners of the mouth than the alternative, a loose-ring snaffle.

Schooling aids

Schooling aids are 'gadgets' that allow the rider to help teach a horse to use and carry himself properly. They are used in the short term to show the horse the correct way of going; as his balance and muscles start to develop in the right fashion he should be able to work correctly without the schooling aid. The rider's aim is to teach the horse to carry and use himself in a correct manner. The horse's power should come from his hind legs powering underneath him, and he should remain straight and upright. As his training progresses, he should carry more of his weight on his hind legs so that his forehand is light and elevated. The aim of all training is to achieve this, and the purpose of a schooling aid is to help the rider achieve this aim.

DROP AND FLASH A drop noseband (*main picture*) is effective in keeping the horse's mouth closed, and applies some pressure to the poll to encourage flexion. A flash noseband (*inset*) has less effect but the flash strap does help keep the mouth closed.

MARTINGALES

A standing or running martingale is a leather attachment that is fixed to the girth, runs up through the horse's front legs, and is attached either directly to the noseband (standing martingale) or has rings on it through which the reins pass. The purpose is to prevent the horse from raising his head so high that he can evade the rider's control. An Irish martingale is a simple leather strap with two rings attached that the reins pass through. It helps prevent the reins coming over the horse's head if they are pulled out of the rider's hands for any reason.

MARTINGALES These are commonly used to prevent the horse raising his head so high that the rider can no longer control him.

GRACKLE Also known as a cross noseband or Mexican grackle, the grackle helps prevent the horse not just from opening his mouth, but from crossing his jaw also. Horses do both these things in order to evade the action of the bit.

BITS AND BITTING

The bit acts on different parts of the horse's mouth and head depending on the type of bit used, and whether it is being used in conjunction with a particular type of noseband and/or martingale. The horse's mouth is a very sensitive area and that is the way it should remain. It is every rider's responsibility and goal to learn to ride well enough that it is not necessary to hang on to the reins (and in turn the horse's mouth) to maintain balance.

BITTING

A well-balanced, secure seat will allow the rider to use the seat and legs effectively to control and influence the horse, in combination with the hands and bit. It is a fault of many riders to rely too much on the hand and bit, instead of learning to use their seat and legs as well.

If a horse is happy and comfortable in his mouth, he will be a lot easier to work with and train. It is also worth remembering that different bits have different actions and purposes. Whilst your horse's training is progressing, you may need to change the type of bit you ride him in depending on what you are trying to achieve at any particular stage in his training. The bit is only as kind or harsh as the hands on the end of the reins. If the bit your horse is in allows him to pull or lean on it, and the rider ends up hauling on the horse's mouth to stop him, it is not comfortable or correct for horse or rider. Equally, if the rider is unbalanced and pulls on the reins in order to stay on, the horse will become uncomfortable in his mouth.

POSITION AND BALANCE

As a rider, you have to take responsibility first for becoming secure and balanced enough in your seat and position that you can use your hands independently of whatever else is going on. This, combined with ensuring you are also using your seat and legs to ride the horse correctly, will allow you to then experiment and find the best bit for your horse and the particular job that you want him to do.

RESTRICTIONS

There are restrictions in some disciplines on the type of bit you are allowed to use, so this needs to be borne in mind whilst training the horse. In dressage, for example, the horse can only be ridden in a snaffle bit, and at higher levels, in a double bridle.

TYPES OF BIT

Most bits fall into one of five categories: snaffle, curb, Pelham, gag, and nose.

SNAFFLE

There is a huge variety of designs of snaffle, the mildest being a straight bar snaffle (with no joint). The jointed snaffle has a nutcracker action across the lower jaw, making it sharper than a straight bar. When the horse works with a low head carriage, the snaffle puts upward pressure on the corners of the lips. As the head carriage becomes more elevated, the bit works across the lower jaw.

HOW THE BIT WORKS The action of different bits affects different parts of the mouth: the corners of the mouth, lower jaw, bars (gums), tongue, curb groove, poll, and roof of the mouth. This jointed snaffle, for example, can act on the corners of the lips, the tongue, and the lower jaw.

CURB

A curb bit and a snaffle (or bridoon) bit are both employed in a double bridle. Each bit has its own rein. The snaffle bit/rein is in primary use, encouraging the horse to raise his head. The curb bit/rein is used when necessary to ask the horse to flex at the poll and to soften his jaw.

PELHAM

The Pelham comes halfway between the snaffle and the double bridle in that it has only one mouthpiece but it still has a curb action and can be used with two reins, although commonly leather roundings are used to link the top and bottom rings of the Pelham so that a single rein can be used. The mouthpiece can be straight or jointed and the bit acts on the poll and curb groove as well as on the mouth.

GAG

The gag is an adaptation of the snaffle that offers a far higher upward action and is used on horses that try to lower their head and neck to evade the rider. There are two main types. One group, which includes the American gag, has long shanks that offer greater leverage to the rider. The second group, which includes the Cheltenham gag, achieves the same effect by using gag 'roundings', which pass through holes in the bit ring, attaching at one end to the cheekpiece of the bridle and the other end to the reins.

NOSE, OR BITLESS, BRIDLE

Nose bridles do not have a mouthpiece, and act by putting pressure on the nose, poll, and curb groove. Horses ridden in bitless bridles are often easier to manoeuvre by using neck reining than by trying to 'steer' conventionally.

EGGBUTT SNAFFLE The jointed mouthpiece has a nutcracker action over the lower jaw but is still a relatively mild bit. The 'eggbutt' joint on the rings is gentler on the corners of the mouth.

TWISTED SNAFFLE Athough the snaffle action in itself is fairly mild, the twisted mouthpiece is uncomfortable on the tongue and corners of the mouth if the horse tries to ignore it.

FRENCH LINK The central link in the mouthpiece sits comfortably on the tongue and reduces the nutcracker action. The loose rings will make it a little sharper on the corners of the mouth.

HAPPY MOUTH SNAFFLE The straight flexible mouthpiece gives the bit a very limited action, but many horses settle happily in it as there is very little to 'fiddle' with or fight against.

FULMER CHEEK SNAFFLE The long cheekpieces help keep the bit central in the horse's mouth. It will also aid with turning as the cheekpieces put pressure on the side of the mouth.

PELHAM A straight bar vulcanite Pelham is the mildest version of this bit. There is only a single mouthpiece but the curb action encourages the horse to flex his poll and soften the jaw.

BALDING GAG A gag bit should help the rider to raise the horse's head and is used mainly on horses that try to gallop off by putting their heads down and leaning on the bit. The cheekpieces of the bridle go through the bit rings and attach to the reins.

THREE-RING GAG This is basically a snaffle mouthpiece, but a strong downward pressure on the poll can be applied by attaching the rein to one of the two lower rings.

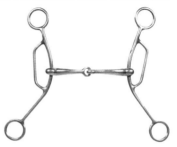

AMERICAN GAG The mouthpiece can slide upwards higher into the horse's mouth as the rider applies pressure with the reins. Again this bit is designed to help raise the horse's head and the long shanks offer considerable leverage which should be used with care.

SADDLES

A saddle was an unheard of luxury when man first sat upon a horse, and when he did decide to make life more comfortable for himself, his 'saddle' would have been a simple blanket or animal skin, held on with a girth and breaststrap.

Today's saddles are hi-tech masterpieces, with different designs for different riding disciplines. The saddle usually represents the most expensive piece of equipment that the horse owner has to purchase.

EARLY SADDLES

The Scythians, nomadic horsemen who originated in southern Russia around 3000BC, developed the first saddle that was more than just a blanket strapped to the horse. The saddle comprised two oblong pads either side of the horse's spine, joined front and back by a wooden arch. As with the modern saddle, this allowed the rider's weight to be carried and evenly distributed on either side of the spine. Archaeological evidence suggests that the Scythians were also the first to use a basic stirrup of a hook hanging from a chain.

SADDLE FIT You should be able to slide the flat of your hand under the girth. Always smooth the skin under the girth after tightening.

CHECKING THE NUMNAH Always ensure that the numnah is lifted clear of the horse's withers and that there is sufficient clearance between the saddle and the horse.

The stirrup iron, as we know it today, was invented in northern China. The Terracotta Army (200BC), more than 8,000 life-size statues of foot soldiers and horsemen discovered in northwest China, depicted warriors using stirrups. Stirrups were first invented as a means of mounting the horse in the form of a long single stirrup, but it didn't take long for riders to appreciate the stability and balance that a pair of stirrups could give them. Stirrups even influenced the face of fashion – in the 1500s, European nobility wore heels attached to their shoes to help keep their feet in the stirrups. Heeled shoes and boots became fashionable and the term 'well-heeled' was coined, referring to those who could afford such footwear!

FITTING THE SADDLE

The fit and design of the saddle is important to both horse and rider. The saddle must sit comfortably on the horse's back without creating any pressure points, and its shape must be such that it does not restrict the freedom of the

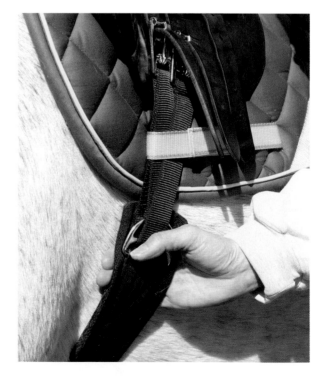

CHECKING THE GIRTH The girth is vital in keeping the saddle securely in place. You should still be able to slide the flat of your hand between it and the horse. Always smooth the skin under the girth after tightening it.

GENERAL PURPOSE A saddle for the everyday rider should allow you to sit centrally and upright for basic flatwork, and still have enough forward cut to allow a shorter length of leg for jumping.

DRESSAGE Purpose designed for flatwork, the dressage saddle helps the rider sit upright and ride with a long, straight leg, keeping the legs very close to the horse's sides.

JUMPING SADDLE A forward cut saddle allows riders to shift their centre of balance back and to ride with short stirrups. The knee roll helps stop the rider's leg shifting from its secure position.

shoulder or press too far back on the loins. For the rider, the saddle must facilitate sitting close to the horse, without being tipped forwards or back, and it must be the right size to accommodate the length of the rider's leg.

BREASTPLATES AND GIRTHS

Saddles are secured in place with a girth and/or a breastplate or breast girth. Girths are made from various materials such as leather, webbing, or synthetics. They usually incorporate a degree of elasticity to make them comfortable, and may be shaped to avoid chafing.

Breastplates and breast girths are designed to prevent the saddle from slipping too far backwards. They are most commonly used for rigorous sports such as cross country, racing, and polo. A crupper, a leather loop that tethers the saddle to the root of the horse's tail, is used mainly on low-withered ponies to prevent the saddle from slipping too far forwards.

TREE OR TREELESS

For many years, the saddle tree (the metal and wood framework inside the saddle) has been promoted as the most comfortable design for the horse, as its rigidity keeps the weight of the rider off the horse's spine. But new technology has seen a rise in popularity of treeless saddles, which are designed to protect the horse's spine whilst offering greater flexibility and comfort for the horse. Some modern saddles also incorporate air pockets that can be adjusted to provide the perfect fit. Great claims are made for new saddle designs, particularly as to how they may improve the horse's way of going. But quick fixes are rare, so 'try before you buy' is the best advice!

NUMNAHS

A soft cloth of some kind is usually worn underneath the saddle to prevent the saddle rubbing the horse, and to absorb sweat. They are either rectangular shaped (saddle cloth) or cut to match the shape of the saddle (numnah). Different colours, materials, and thicknesses are available in both designs. Moulded pads are also available to improve saddle fit if one saddle has to be used on a number of horses.

NUMNAH A numnah is designed to match the shape of the saddle. You can buy different shaped numnahs to fit dressage, jumping, and general-purpose saddles.

SADDLE CLOTH An oblong saddle cloth can be used under a conventional saddle such as this, and also under a Western saddle. A thick, folded blanket is frequently used as a numnah in Western-style riding.

BOOTS AND BANDAGES

Boots and bandages are used on the horse's lower legs to protect them from external injury and to offer support to the joints, tendons, and ligaments. Boots are designed in different shapes and with differing degrees of pads and protection depending on the specific purpose they are intended for. All boots and bandages need fitting carefully, particularly with regard to how much pressure they apply to the legs; uneven pressure can cause injury.

BOOTS

'Brushing' describes the action of the horse brushing the inside of one leg with the hoof of the opposite leg. If a horse's leg action isn't absolutely straight this may occur in all or some paces. So for everyday riding and schooling, many horses wear brushing boots, which fasten with straps on the outside of the leg and have a protective pad on the inside of the leg.

More specialist boots are available for different disciplines or problems. Before deciding which boots to use for a particular horse, you need to understand which parts of the leg are most at risk as a result of the work you are planning to do.

BRUSHING BOOTS These offer protection against the horse 'brushing' the hoof of one leg against the inside of the opposite leg. They also protect against scrapes and scratches when hacking.

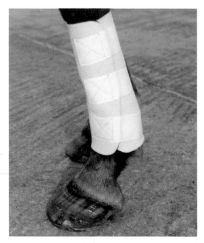

EXERCISE WRAP A soft, stretchy, but quite robust wrap offers similar protection to bandages but is quicker and easier to put on. It is fastened with Velcro to help achieve a snug fit.

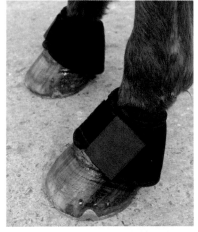

OVER-REACH Fastened around the front feet, over-reach or bell boots protect the heel from being struck by the back feet – commonly used for cross-country jumping.

TENDON BOOTS These are used mainly by showjumpers, as they offer protection to the vulnerable tendons at the back of the leg, whilst ensuring a horse feels the knock if he hits a pole.

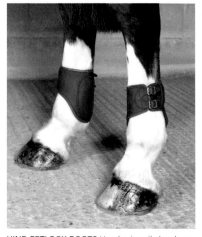

HIND FETLOCK BOOTS Used primarily by show-jumpers, these protect the inside of the fetlock from being knocked by the opposite leg, whilst leaving the cannon bone area exposed.

SPECIALIST BOOTS

Everyday brushing boots offer little protection to the tendons or the cannon bone. Both these areas are at risk when jumping solid cross-country fences. The cannon bone is vulnerable if the horse hits a solid fence, and the tendons and ligaments are at risk because of the speed and turns involved. So a specialist cross-country boot should be shaped, and offer enough protection, to cover both these areas. Dressage work puts strain on the joints and, to a lesser degree, on the tendons, although there is always the risk of the horse striking into his front tendons with one of his back feet. But, as much of the horse's work is done on an artificial surface, the materials used in the surface can often cause boots to rub, so bandages or supportive wraps are often preferred.

In showjumping, the tendons need to be protected, but it is considered unwise to offer too much protection to the front of the cannon bones. The showjumper has to learn to be careful and avoid hitting the poles with his legs, so too much padding would prevent him from even realizing that he has hit a fence.

New materials and technology have vastly improved the comfort, safety, and effectiveness of boots. Materials used now will mould themselves to fit the shape of the horse's leg as they warm up. Stretchy straps and Velcro fastening allow a much more snug fit to be achieved without the risk of exerting too much pressure on the tendons.

BANDAGES

Exercise bandages can be used instead of boots. They particularly suit horses with sensitive skin, which can be rubbed by boots. Correct application of bandages to get an even tension all down the leg is vital. Too tight and they can cause injury to the tendons, too loose and they will slip down and unravel, which again can cause injury through uneven pressure, or a fall if the horse trips on them. Exercise wraps are designed to offer the same softness and support as bandages, but are quicker and easier to fit.

Putting on an exercise bandage

❶ An exercise bandage extends from below the knee down to the fetlock joint. The bandage padding needs to be the right length to meet this requirement.

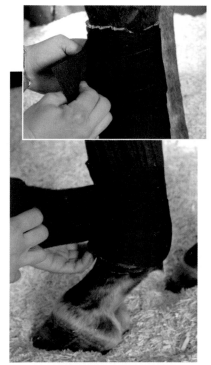

❷ Tuck the end of the bandage into the overlap of the bandage pad and bandage the leg, encompassing the fetlock joint neatly and overlapping each turn by one third.

❸ Apply even pressure throughout the exercise bandage. There should be a tiny overhang of padding at the top and bottom to prevent any part of the bandage being directly against the leg.

WESTERN RIDING

Western riding equipment for both horse and rider was designed to cope with the harsh practicalities of life faced by the early cowboys in a wild and inhospitable land. The cowboy was completely reliant on his horse for survival, and every item of equipment had to serve at least one purpose. His saddle had attached to it everything from his water bottle, his blanket for sleeping, to spare ropes, knives, and guns. His horse had to be calm and patient.

RIDER CLOTHING
The Western rider's uniform starts with his Stetson – the hat named after John Betterson Stetson who started to sell them from his shop in Philadelphia in 1865. Designed to last a lifetime, the Stetson provided protection from the elements, and could also be used to scoop up water to drink.

WESTERN OUTFIT Western dress is designed to be comfortable and practical. But every cowboy is a showman at heart, hence the decoratively fringed chaps and often elaborate leatherwork on boots and saddles!

BOOTS
Cowboy boots are shaped to sit securely in the stirrup – the pointed toe is easily directed and the high heel prevents the foot slipping through. The heel also allows the wearer, when on the ground, to 'dig-in' and brace against a roped animal. The boots themselves were often long to protect against deadly snake bites when on the ground. The low-hanging spur jangles as the cowboy walks, ensuring his cattle are aware of his presence amongst them.

CHAPS

Leather over-trousers, called chaps, are worn over jeans. The chaps are robust enough to protect the wearer from thorns and brambles, or can be sheepskin lined to protect against the cold. They usually feature decorative fringing.

A ROBUST SHIRT

A shirt, usually a check pattern, is worn as a top, sometimes with a leather waistcoat. A bandanna (neck scarf) was the choice of the working cowboy as it could protect the mouth and nose from the dust raised by the cattle's hooves. It could also be used to strain river water to drink.

THE WESTERN BRIDLE

Young horses are often started off in a hackamore (bitless bridle), which uses pressure on the nose. As the horse's education continues, he will then be ridden in a long-shanked bit, usually without a noseband. The bridle has two styles: the split-ear, which has a headpiece with slots that secure over both ears; and the one-ear bridle, which, as its name suggests, has a loop over a single ear. The reins are held in one hand and are not joined as they are for 'English' riding. This is to avoid the risk of the horse putting his foot through the reins when his rider has to jump off to see to something.

WESTERN SADDLE The wide girth (cinch), sturdy pommel, and elaborate engravings are all characteristic of the Western saddle.

WESTERN OR STOCK SADDLE

The saddle is larger and heavier than a normal saddle, is comfortable and practical enough for long hours of riding, and carries much of the cowboy's kit. A thick, folded blanket is used as an under pad, and the saddle's large weight-bearing area makes it comfortable for the horse. The horn at the front is prominent and strong enough for a lassoed steer or Mustang to be anchored to. The saddle is secured by a cinch (girth) fastened to the saddle rigging, and is often decorated with patterns carved into the leather.

SKID BOOTS

A more recent innovation in Western-style riding is the use of skid boots. These are worn by the horse to protect the backs of his fetlocks when he performs the dramatic sliding halt – a popular feature of modern Western riding, performed during rodeo shows.

Fitting a Western saddle

❶ A thick, folded saddle blanket is laid on the horse's back. It should lie flat without any wrinkles that might rub or irritate the skin.

❷ The heavy saddle must be lifted carefully, ensuring it does not move the blanket, and then it is lowered gently onto the horse's back.

❸ The saddle is secured by a broad cinch (girth) attached to the rigging. It must be tight enough to prevent the saddle slipping if the rider mounts from the ground.

❹ The bridle is fitted and adjusted. The reins are draped over the horse's neck or the pommel until the rider picks them up.

THE WORKING HORSE

Although the horse was first domesticated in order to provide food and skins, it didn't take early humans long to realize they could harness the power and strength of this creature for all manner of tasks. Soon he was being ridden or driven, carrying people far greater distances than they had ever dreamed of, and transporting their possessions to new lands. Exploration brought conflict and the horse served us as faithfully in war as in peace. Today, in many parts of the world, he still does his day's work – testimony to the great partnership that humans have forged with the horse.

HARD WORK A working horse's life can be arduous but it is interesting and active for him. When the horse is relied upon for work, his care and wellbeing are of great importance to his owner.

DOMESTICATION

The human relationship with horses began in prehistoric times when the horse was simply seen as a source of food. So 50,000 years ago, the prehistoric hunter, with no hope of running as fast as the horse and with no means to kill him from a distance, is thought to have chased the unfortunate creatures over a cliff to kill them.

HUNTING HORSES Cave paintings, such as the African example shown above, provide clues to primitive hunting practices. Deer, horses, and buffalo were herded using fire and noise, until the panicked animals would stampede over cliffs to their doom and their meat and hides were collected.

FIRST HERDERS

By 4000BC, humans had started to herd horses in the same way as they had other farm animals. Horses were faster and more reactive, and therefore harder to control than the more placid sheep, cattle, and goats, and it would have taken time for humans to work out how best to

ANCIENT GREEK CHARIOT This sculpted image depicts an early Greek chariot. They were designed to carry two men – a driver and an archer – and would be pulled by up to four horses. As better ways of fighting battles were devised, horses and chariots took on a new role in the exhilarating but dangerous sport of chariot racing.

manage their new friends. The first horses were thought to be domesticated by the nomadic tribes inhabiting the steppes of Eurasia. The horse provided meat, milk, and skins, and soon his usefulness as a pack animal was realized, first by simply loading things on his back, and then by building simple sleds to be pulled by horses.

There is some debate as to whether horses were ridden before they were driven. It was originally assumed that they were first used as draught animals, but more recent archaeological discoveries indicate that they may have been ridden very soon after they were first domesticated. Wear patterns found on horse's teeth dug up in Kazakhstan appear to have been made by rope bits and bridles – these date back to 5,000 years ago.

THE HORSE AS TRANSPORT
As soon as man sat upon a horse, his horizons expanded hugely. He could travel faster and further than ever before, and soon he was exploring new territories. Sadly, this would soon lead to man and horse going to war. Horses were first used in battle to pull chariots, but as riding techniques improved, the mounted cavalry unit was developed.

A fascinating insight into early horse management and training is provided by the Kikkulli Text of 1350BC, which is recorded on four clay tablets. The text was written by Kikkulli, the horsemaster appointed by the Hittite King Suppililiuma to train his war horses. He used interval training: working the horse for a period of time, resting him for a short period, and then working him again; as fitness increases the working periods are increased and the rest periods reduced. Young horses were led from another horse or from a chariot until they were strong enough to take a rider or pull a chariot themselves. After work, the horses were washed off in warm water and wrapped in warm rugs. They were fed three to four times a day, and the exact rations for each feed were recorded. In 1991, an Australian university duplicated the Kikkulli method and found it produced extremely sound horses.

THE HORSE AT WAR
Many warring tribes became infamous for their fearsome mounted warriors. The Scythians, for example, were nomadic horsemen who originated in southern Russia. Mounted on fleet-footed little horses, they were armed with swords, daggers, and bows and arrows, and invaded and occupied vast areas, finally arriving in Egypt during the 7th century BC. They were the first riders to use a simple saddle and also wore trousers, a far more practical garment than the flowing robes generally worn at the time.

The horse was hugely important in terms of communication. As early as the 5th century BC, the

Persians were using relays of mounted couriers to dispatch commands throughout their mighty Empire.

THE HORSE IN AGRICULTURE AND INDUSTRY
By the 8th century AD, the horse was in common use in Europe as an agricultural animal, when the development of the horse-collar harness allowed the true power of the work horse to be utilized. The Chinese were way ahead of Europe in inventing and improving harness equipment: they were using driving shafts and a horse collar hundreds of years before such ideas developed in the West.

The horse began to take over from oxen as the power source on the land and, by the 18th and early 19th century, he was an integral part of a rapidly developing industrial scene. Horses and ponies were employed in myriad roles in mines, on canals, in grinding mills, and in passenger transportation. The use of the horse for sport and leisure was also becoming an increasingly important and popular aspect of society.

Today, in poor and developing countries, the horse still forms the backbone of the workforce, particularly on the land. In the developed world, he has held his own as the interest and enthusiasm for horse ownership and horse sports has continued to grow.

The first book of horsemanship

The Greek historian and philosopher Xenophon wrote the first known book on horsemanship. He lived from 430 to 354BC and his book was called *The Art of Horsemanship*. He advised forming a partnership with the horse based on mutual trust and respect. The horse should be rewarded when he is right and corrected when he is wrong. He should learn to associate everything he likes with humans; that way he will be happy to co-operate. His beliefs are still followed by horsepeople today and the book is the oldest surviving text of its kind.

WAR HORSES

As soon as man had learnt to ride, he used the horse to help him fight. The types of horse used in war have changed through the ages, as the equipment and tasks required of them altered. The early nomadic warrior tribes, such as the Scythians, Ancient Egyptians, the Mongols, and the Arabs, used small lightweight horses.

NOMADIC WARRIORS
The early nomadic horsemen had little in the way of tack and equipment – their weapons being bows, light spears, or javelins – so speed and agility counted for more than power and weight bearing. The small, light horses of the Orient that were the forefathers of the Arab and Akhal-Teke breeds had speed, agility, and great powers of endurance. These horses were used for raiding parties, light cavalry, reconnaissance, and communications. As different fighting techniques and heavy weaponry developed, stronger horses were needed. Chariots that could carry two or three fighting men are one example, bearing in mind also that soldiers were now starting to wear early forms of body armour for protection. The largest and heaviest of these medium-sized horses were sometimes called Destriers, and possibly resembled the Irish Draught breeds of today.

ARMOURED HORSES
The invention of the stirrup completely altered how effective a rider could be in the saddle. It allowed the rider to brace himself in the saddle and thrust powerfully with a lance or sword. Along with the invention of body

CAVALRY CHARGE The superiority of a fighting man on a horse over a foot soldier is obvious, provided each side has the same weaponry. A middleweight horse such as this could carry a lightly armoured warrior.

armour, this led to the use of heavily armoured men, mounted on large, powerful horses, and so the medieval knight on his great charger came into being, particularly in Europe during the Middle Ages. These horses, which were big and powerful enough to carry a knight in full coat of armour, were sometimes called 'the Great Horse'. These horses were the forefathers of the Shire Horse.

The more recent warfare of World War I and, to a lesser degree, World War II, saw a demand for

FRENCH CHASSEUR This drawing depicts members of a Napoleonic Chasseur regiment. Napoleon made great use of mounted troops in battle.

MOUNTED ARCHER Early warriors were lightly armoured. The Scythians were infamous for pretending to flee their enemy before twisting round on their horses and firing a hail of arrows.

a middleweight horse that could be used for light cavalry duties as well as horse-drawn artillery. Today, thankfully, their work is limited to ceremonial duties. Mules and donkeys were also commonly deployed as pack animals, carrying equipment and supplies for foot soldiers. They are calmer, hardier, and cheaper to keep than horses.

TRAINING WAR HORSES

Horses had to be trained to cope with the harsh and frightening environment of war. War horses had to learn to trust their riders and not to be ruled by their own natural instincts, which would be to flee from noise and danger. The horse had to learn how to remain balanced whilst his rider twisted and turned in the saddle during combat. Balance, agility, and responsiveness were crucial requirements of the war horse. The origins of the modern-day discipline of dressage were founded in the need to teach the horse these skills. Similarly, many of the High-School movements demonstrated by the famous Lipizzaner horses of the Spanish Riding School are based on manoeuvres required on the battlefield. Horses used in close combat would have been encouraged to bite, kick, and strike out at the enemy.

FIREARMS

The development of light firearms from the late Middle Ages brought the fast, agile cavalry horse back into vogue. The Spanish *conquistadores* used horses and fire power to great effect, enabling them to conquer the Aztec and Inca empires when they came to America in the 16th century. Horses had been extinct in the Americas for the last 10,000 years, but many of the Spanish invaders' horses escaped, forming wild herds (the Mustang herds of today), which were soon captured and made use of by the indigenous peoples. The Native American tribes famously became great mounted warriors, eventually proving to be an effective and vicious enemy of the new American Pioneers.

WORLD WAR

Light cavalry remained an integral part of war campaigns right up until World War I. Horses were still in use in World War II, but the harsh lessons learnt in the previous war meant the usage was far more limited. Up until the start of World War I in 1914 the cavalry regiments of the army on both sides reigned supreme. Britain and Germany each had, at this stage, a cavalry force numbering over 100,000 men. Many senior army ranks were held by cavalry forces, hence the naive belief that the cavalry would ride to the rescue once again. No-one could have foreseen the horrors or limitations of the trench warfare that characterized the war. The trenches, along with razor-wire barriers and machine guns, made successful cavalry charges almost impossible. In March 1918, one such cavalry charge of 150 horses and men resulted in only four horses surviving – the rest being gunned down by German machine guns. As a viable tactic of war, the cavalry charge was becoming obsolete. However, large numbers of horses and mules continued to be used to carry and pull weapons, machinery, and supplies. Alongside the massive loss of human life, it is a sad and sobering fact that over 8 million horses died on all sides fighting in World War I. About two-and-a-half million horses were treated in veterinary hospitals, with the majority being successfully treated and returned to duty.

World War II still saw large numbers of horses and mules employed in the war effort, although far fewer were used in direct combat. The poorly equipped Polish army relied

MOUNTED GUARD Cavalry units are retained by many regiments but their duties are mainly ceremonial (below is the change of the guard at the Royal Palace in Madrid, Spain). However irrelevant they may seem today, the contribution of the horse in war deserves to be remembered.

heavily on the Polish Cavalry to defend itself against the advance of the Germans. Both the German and the Soviet armies used horses to transport ammunition and equipment, and used mounted units for reconnaissance. In India and Asia, the British Army used mules as pack animals for military equipment and the United States deployed some cavalry units. Some officers consider that the campaigns in North Africa would have been more successful if cavalry divisions had been more widely deployed.

The formidable firepower and brute force offered by tanks led to the demise of the mounted soldier as a serious weapon of war. However, mounted fighters still operate in parts of the world, the militia groups in Sudan being one example. Even American and British special forces sometimes resort to horse power on harsh terrain in campaigns where a horse will also attract less attention than other forms of transport.

ARMY PACK MULE, ARGENTINA Mules are strong, hardy, and surefooted, making them excellent pack animals in harsh and rugged terrain. They are able to pull heavy guns and ammunition, and often served to transport badly injured men back from the front line to field hospitals for treatment.

HORSES IN AGRICULTURE

Despite the seemingly obvious suitability of horses for farmwork, it was many hundreds of years before they earned their place as the power source on the land. To begin with, horses of sufficient size and strength had yet to be bred, and agricultural methods and machinery were not nearly advanced enough to take advantage of the power they had to offer.

WOOD WORK Horses continue to hold their own in forestry. Horses can transport felled timber far more efficiently than tractors can. They are more manoeuvrable, cope with rough terrain, and do less damage to the soil, and to the environment in general.

AGE OF OXEN

By the 8th century AD, horses were being used on a small scale for agricultural work in Europe. The breeding of stronger horses for war in the early Middle Ages meant that horses of sufficient size and strength were now available. Just as importantly, the inventiveness of the Chinese, who were centuries ahead of the West in the development of wheeled vehicles and harnessing systems, slowly filtered through to Europe and the age of horse power could begin.

The simple harnesses that had been developed for oxen did not allow the horse to use his strength effectively. Also, whilst agricultural methods remained slow and basic, the ox was

WORKING ON THE LAND Powerful horses were needed to cultivate heavy soils. The relatively simple harness in use here is based on the horse collar, which allows the horse's full strength to be utilized.

TO MARKET In many countries, horses are still a vital part of the agricultural scene, whether it be working the land, acting as pack animals, or transporting produce and people into town.

more than up to the task and was cheaper to keep and easier to handle than the horse. But advances in farm methods and machinery brought about in the 18th century, combined with the effectiveness of the horse-collar harness, saw the ox rapidly replaced by the horse throughout Europe and America. The vast plains of America needed to be transformed into productive farmland, and the Americans were quick to develop and master the use of multi-horse farm implements. Some of the huge combine harvesters, drills, harrows, and ploughs that were in use needed teams of 36 or 42 horses to power them.

Horse power on the land was not so prevalent in the Mediterranean and the Middle East – the lighter horses that had evolved in these regions could not compete with donkeys and oxen in terms of strength or hardiness. The lighter soils meant there was no need for the heavy draught horse that was becoming prevalent in Europe.

GIANT BREEDS

Up until the early 20th century, horse power was essential for agricultural and industrial output. In western Europe, the breeding of the larger heavy-draught breeds allowed nations to develop and improve their agricultural practices.

In France, Germany, Holland, Belgium, and Scandinavia, the native heavy breeds were gradually enhanced, producing the predominant draught horse breeds: the heavyweight Brabant (Belgium Heavy Draught) and the versatile Percheron, also used as a coach horse. During the late 1800s and early 1900s,

Percherons were extensively exported to the United States, Canada, Australia, South Africa, and South America. Thousands were used in the military during World War I.

Eastern Europe was slower to modernize its farming industry, and the smaller farms and lighter soil types led to a lighter-weight farm horse. Such a horse was cheaper to keep than the heavy-draught breeds and more versatile – he was big enough to pull a simple cart to market and yet he was small enough to be ridden.

Horse-drawn carts were used to deliver milk and bread in the towns and cities. Farmers used a horse and cart to deliver their own produce to local markets. The farm horse was very much a part of the family.

From the early 20th century onwards, the traction engine rapidly replaced horse power; the motor-powered machinery could work more quickly and efficiently than horse-drawn implements. However, in parts of Eastern Europe and poorer countries, horses are still vital farm tools.

MOVING CATTLE Horses are still used to a large extent to herd and manage cattle. They need to be adaptable enough to turn and control a stampeding herd on the open plains, as well as to quietly guide them through towns and villages to market or to fresh grazing.

COWBOY In large open countries such as parts of the United States, Argentina, and Australasia, there is still enough space for large herds of stock to roam, be they horses or cattle, allowing the romantic image of a man and his horse riding the plains to live on.

THE HORSE AT WORK

It is ironic that whilst the massive move to mechanization in the Industrial Revolution eventually put the workhorse out of a job, in this period of unprecedented growth and development, the demand for horses to power industry grew and grew. Breeding became more specialized – refining the heavy horses using breeds such as the Thoroughbred, to produce middleweight horses as well as pony crosses and breeds to undertake varied tasks.

COMMUNICATIONS

Business and personal mail was carried, in most countries, by mounted postboys or in mail carts and coaches. America deployed the legendary Pony Express before moving on to mail coaches; dreamt up by William H. Russell, the service began in 1860. The route covered over 3,000 km (nearly 2,000 miles) and passed through six states. The journey was covered in ten days by relays of riders utilizing 400 ponies. Armed with a pistol and rifle, they had to make their way through hostile Indian territory; each man rode 100 km (60 miles), stopping along the way at the 190 relay stations where the mail, fresh ponies, and supplies were stationed. The Pony Express operated for just two years but that was long enough for its romantic image to earn its place in history.

In Britain and America, the mail carts paved the way for passenger coaches, running to a regular timetable and offering speeds of 16–19 kph (10–12 mph). Older

PACK HORSES Hardy ponies, donkeys, and mules are still used as pack animals. They learn to walk in a line – sometimes tethered to each other, sometimes free – and are often left to walk the route unattended once they know it well enough.

civilizations had long made use of teams of pony riders to carry messages across their empires. As far back as the 6th century BC, the Persians had a message relay system that covered 2,400 km (1,500 miles) in 7 to 14 days. Similarly, the Mongol Empire deployed relays of message carriers, often riding up to 240 km (150 miles) per day.

Coal was a vital source of fuel during the Industrial Revolution. Ponies, such as the Shetland and Welsh breeds, worked down the mines, turning the wheel that drove the hoist, and hauling the heavy carts of coal to the surface. The pit ponies were also stabled underground. Ponies were being used in British mines, in declining numbers, until as recently as 1972.

Transportation of any kind relied on the development of a network of hard roads. Horse-drawn buses, and later trams, transported passengers through towns and cities. Even fire engines were drawn by teams of horses. Milk, bread, and beer were delivered by horse-drawn vehicles. The milkman's horse soon learnt to move on from one house towards the next house whilst the milkman was walking to the door of the first house. This intelligence led many to argue that the horse-drawn milk float was far more efficient than the electric float that followed it.

CANALS AND RAILWAYS

A network of canals was established throughout Britain and Europe during the 18th century. The barges carried cargo and passengers and were towed by horses. The canal horses had to be versatile and intelligent, dealing with bridges, tunnels, gates, and stiles along the way. The late 18th century saw the introduction of a highspeed passenger and light-freight boat. It was drawn by two horses, one of which was ridden, and the pace was a smart canter. By frequently changing horses, an average speed of 19 kph (12 mph) could be maintained.

PULLING THEIR WEIGHT Horses are still used in some cities to make local deliveries. In some cases they are more economically viable, as well as more environmentally friendly, than lorries. Big brewery companies in particular are great supporters and sponsors of horse-drawn deliveries.

Rail carriages and trams were horse drawn, and horse-drawn carts brought the supplies to and from the railway stations. A horse-drawn railway service operated in Northern Ireland up until 1952 – and at Newmarket (the flat-racing capital of Great Britain), a railway horse moved horseboxes around the sidings up until 1967. An indicator of the importance of horses to the railway industry is borne out by the fact that, even in the 1920s, the railway companies of Britain owned well over 9,000 horses.

Police horses

Many cities around the world employ police horses. They undergo specialist training to ensure they remain calm in all situations and are without parallel in crowd control – a calm, powerful presence in often noisy and volatile situations. With police forces in many large cities complaining that they feel alienated from the public they are meant to serve, some have reintroduced mounted officers. They provide a very visible presence and officers say that members of the public are far more willing to talk to them when they are mounted. The Royal Canadian Mounted Police are a world-famous unit that was formed to police the vast landscape of that country. Since World War II they have, sadly, been limited to ceremonial duties only.

THE SPORTING HORSE

There is nothing quite like the great partnership and loyalty that can develop between horse and rider. Horse sports, in particular, have allowed that bond to thrive. The years of training and preparation involved in producing and competing a sports horse act to cement that bond. Trust and co-operation are paramount, and riders or trainers have to work hard to understand the mind of the animal they are working with in order to get the best out of him. Fortunately for the horse, the fun that he affords us should safeguard his future.

READY FOR ACTION It can be said that there is no finer view of the world than that seen from the back of a horse, although this horse thinks that the view would be a lot better if he could overtake the one in front!

SPORTING HISTORY

Knowing man's natural competitiveness, it has to be highly likely that, as soon as men could ride, they would have been testing themselves and their steeds against each other. Certainly horses helped men to hunt; although this was a matter of survival, it is not hard to imagine a scenario where they would race each other home, for example, or honour the most successful hunter among them!

CAVE ART Cave paintings clearly illustrate the use of horse to man in the task of hunting. What started out as a necessity became, over time, a great way for horsemen to enjoy an exhilarating day out. The sport of hunting continues to thrive in many countries.

ANCIENT OLYMPICS

The Ancient Greeks embraced horse sports in the form of horse races and chariot racing. The first documented horse race was held at the Olympic Games in 648BC. Mule racing and loose-horse racing were also Olympic sports for a short time. Chariot racing was extremely popular. The chariot was originally designed as a weapon of war; a soldier could be transported in it at speed, and he could fire arrows from it. Chariot racing was included in the

FOUR-HORSE CHARIOT Chariots were used in spectacular and dangerous racing competitions. The modern equivalent is harness racing which, fortunately, is not nearly so dangerous.

Ancient Olympics of 680BC; there were races for two- and four-horse chariots. The hippodrome was large enough to allow 60 chariots to race together. It was a dangerous sport – death and injury to man and horse was commonplace. The races were held over a relatively tight circuit, with earth banks and pillars marking the inside track. The tight turns tested the skill of the charioteer as it was easy to overturn or collide with competitors or the pillars and banks. The races were run over about 6.5 km (4 miles).

When the Romans defeated the Greeks in 146bc, they quickly adopted the sport. The main venue in Rome, the *Circus Maximus*, could hold 150,000 people. Roman chariots were usually driven by slaves although the prize money went to the owner of the horses and chariot! The modern-day equivalent is harness racing.

HUNTING
Hunting on horseback has long been enjoyed as a pastime, particularly in Europe. Early prey would have included hares, wolves, bears, deer, and wild boar; the latter two both still being hunted in France today.

France has the oldest history of organized hunting; in Britain, the sport dates from the time of the Norman Conquest (1066). Hunting for pleasure was very much a sport of the wealthy – if some poor peasant caught a wild animal and killed it for supper he could well be hung for poaching! In Britain, the 17th century saw the start of fox hunting. This version of the sport endured in the United Kingdom until an unprecedented hunting ban was brought into force by the Labour government banning hunting with dogs from February 2005. The sport of fox hunting is reliant on the goodwill of landowners to allow countless horses and riders to career across their land, often inflicting great damage, in the thrill of the chase.

POLO
Polo was played in Persia as long ago as 600BC; a sport enjoyed then, as today, by women as well as men. From Persia, the game spread to China, Japan, Tibet, and Manipur. Until the late 1800s, the game had never been played outside of Asia. But British Army officers and tea planters introduced the sport to the West. In 1859, the first polo club for white men was formed in Cachar with its own set of rules, which originally allowed for nine players per team. This was later reduced to seven and finally to four.

The first polo match was played in England in 1869. Some years later a visiting American, James Gordon Bennet, saw the game played and introduced the idea to America. From there it was quickly adopted in Argentina, Australia, New Zealand, and then France. Today, it is played at all levels, from Pony Club to international championships.

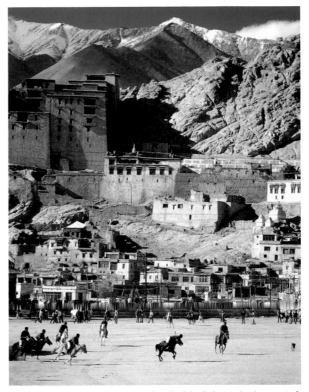

POLO PLAYING IN LADAKH, INDIA Played originally in Persia, the sport of polo spread throughout the world. It now embraces considerable wealth and glamour, with matches played at prestigious venues around the globe.

GYMKHANA
Gymkhana games were originally an excuse for adults to have some fun – a break from the more serious polo matches and formal regimental duties. Gymkhana is an Anglo-Indian word meaning a 'field day on horseback', and British soldiers based in India in the late 19th century quickly got into the spirit of things. Athough the main aim was to have fun, it did help keep soldiers and horses fit and supple, as well as encouraging regimental loyalty and team spirit. Camels, donkeys, mules, and bicycles were used as well as horses and the games included 'Kiss the Girl', Tent Pegging, Cushion Polo, and Grab the Hat! When the officers returned to Britain, they brought the idea of mounted games with them. They were enthusiastically received by children in particular, whose small, quick-turning ponies made perfect mounts for the games. The Pony Club, formed in Britain in 1929 (but now international), saw the benefits of these games as a way for children to improve their riding, balance, and co-ordination, and foster team spirit. They have supported and encouraged mounted games ever since.

MODERN HUNTING

Hunting today is very much a country sport as opposed to a means to find something for supper. Organized hunting involves a pack of hounds kept to hunt a particular quarry – the upkeep of the hounds and the cost of employing a huntsman and hunt staff are met by the mounted followers and supporters of the hunt, and through local fund raising.

THE HUNTSMAN

The pack of hounds is controlled by the huntsman, and he is assisted by one or more 'whipper-ins' whose job it is to keep all the hounds up together during the hunt. A Master of Foxhounds (or more often than not in these cash-strapped days, a group of joint Masters) is in overall charge of the hunt and the hunt staff. Often, he also acts as Field Master – the person that all the mounted hunt supporters (the field) must follow and obey during the

FOXHOUNDS The modern foxhound has been carefully bred over many generations. Most of the main hunts have successful bloodlines, which are used by other hunts to improve their own lines.

HUNTSMAN AND HOUNDS The Boxing Day Meet at Badminton Estate in England is renowned. Venue also for the famous Badminton Horse Trials, this estate is also the home of the famed Beaufort Hunt.

day. He will have spoken to all the farmers whose land the hounds are likely to cross and he will know areas that they have been asked to avoid or where to take extra care. The huntsman takes the hounds ahead of the field, and 'casts' them into an area of land (covert) to pick up the scent of the quarry. All being well, the hounds pick up a good scent and set off in pursuit of their prey. The Field Master follows, keeping the field far enough back so that they can't interfere with the work of the huntsman and hounds but close enough that they can see hounds working and enjoy 'the chase'. For the privilege of seeing hounds at work, and of following them in often exhilarating fashion across the countryside – where possible jumping whatever crosses their path – the hunt followers are happy to pay a subscription, which goes towards the cost of maintaining the hunt. It is these mounted followers that have been the target of 'hunt saboteurs' for decades, with hunts often marred by violence between the two sides.

Great Britain and Ireland have long been considered the hunting 'capitals' of the world. In these countries, the fox is the most popular quarry, although stag and hare hunting also takes place. Hunting with dogs was banned by a Labour government in the United Kingdom in 2005. Dogs can still hunt rabbits – an exception that led to much confusion as many Members of Parliament, as well as members of the public, were incapable of telling the difference between the two when challenged during the furious rounds of debate that led up to the ban! Hunts in the United Kingdom have managed to survive by offering trail hunting – the hounds follow a previously laid scent rather than chase a live quarry – or by using hounds to flush foxes out to be shot by gunmen. The rights and wrongs of the ban would fill an entire book, but it is fair to say that banning hunting has done nothing to save the fox – he can still be killed by other means, such as shooting or trapping. Fox hunting has always stirred strong emotions; the famous English poet and playwright Oscar Wilde described it as 'the unspeakable in pursuit of the uneatable'. And the most vociferous supporters of the ban seemed more concerned with preventing riders on horseback enjoying themselves by galloping across the countryside, than ever they were with the welfare of the fox. He remains a legitimate target of gamekeepers and farmers.

HUNTING AROUND THE WORLD

In other parts of the world, hunting continues to grow in popularity. In Europe, France heads the table of enthusiastic hunters. France still enjoys the advantage of vast tracts of rural landscape where wildlife and hunting co-exist. Deer and wild boar are popular quarry, but the element of cross-country jumping – such an intoxicating part of English

Drag hunting

Drag hunting is a popular sport for those riders keen to gallop and jump with little interruption, rather than endure the often steady and circuitous progress that hunting a live quarry entails. Drag hunting involves a small pack of hounds following a pre-set scented trail. The organizers obviously have complete control of where the 'trail' goes, so they can ensure it includes plenty of jumping whilst avoiding known hazards. The pace of a drag hunt is much faster than true hunting as the trail is laid on a straightforward line, without employing the natural cunning of a hunted animal.

and Irish hunting – is not generally part of a day's hunting in France. America, Canada, and Australasia also have organized hunting – the grey fox and coyote being the principal quarry in those countries.

Organized hunting involves each pack of hounds being registered with a Hunting Association. Individual hunts are allocated boundaries within which they may hunt; the land they hunt over is known as the Hunt Country, and the hunt is usually named after its own local town or region.

HUNTING AND CONSERVATION

The fact that hunting and conservation work together is a confusing issue for many people. But hunting is about controlling a species of wildlife – usually because the quarry in question no longer has a natural predator to do the job that nature once took care of through survival of the fittest. The aim of a hunt is not to eradicate the local population of deer, hares, foxes, or coyote – but to help ensure numbers are kept at an acceptable level. Many hunts plant and manage areas of natural habitat that benefit not only their quarry but also any other local wildlife.

POLO

Polo has always been an expensive sport to indulge in, with each player needing a string of polo ponies. Having originated in Persia about two and a half thousand years ago, the game spread worldwide. The first of many polo clubs was London's Hurlingham in Great Britain, whose rules were later universally adopted.

THE GAME OF POLO

Polo is played on a grass or snow pitch 274 m (300 yd) long by 183 m (200 yd) wide. There is a 7.5 m (8 yd) wide goal at each end. Two teams of four players take part.

No. 1 player takes forward passes and shoots at the goal. If he doesn't have the ball, his aim is to keep the opposing team's back player (their No. 4) away from the goal to allow one of his team mates (usually No. 2 or No. 3) a clear shot. No. 2 player is also up at the front, working closely with the No. 1 player to keep trying to send the ball forwards towards the goal. No. 3 player is the link between the two forward players and the back player, and it is his job to try to turn the play from defence to attack. He must be able to defend, attack, and score goals. No. 4 player is the back player charged with defending the goal, although he must also be a good hitter to send the ball far and hard up the field to give his front players a chance of scoring.

SNOWBALL Polo is also sometimes played on a snow-covered pitch. A larger, bright red ball is used for visibility, and the ponies wear special attachments on their shoes to stop the snow balling up inside.

WEALTH OF TALENT Polo continues to enjoy a glamorous image today. Many teams are backed by a wealthy patron, which allows talented, but not necessarily wealthy, players an opportunity to ride for a team.

Each polo match is divided into six seven-minute periods called chukkas; one pony plays a maximum of two chukkas (not consecutively), hence the need for a string of polo ponies for each player to call upon. Players use a mallet (a bamboo stick with a wooden head) to hit the ball down the field and, hopefully, through the goal posts. Obviously, the opposing team are doing their best to defend their goal and send the ball back the other way to give them a chance of scoring. Each polo player is graded by being given a 'handicap', which varies between -2 goals to +10 goals, reflecting his value to the team. Teams are also given an overall handicap that determines the level at which they may play: high goal, medium, intermediate, or low goal.

A player has to master four main playing strokes: offside forehander, offside backhander, nearside forehander, nearside backhander, along with eight subsidiary strokes.

A game of polo is very fast. Ponies learn to read the game and often anticipate where they need to be next before their riders have. There is no longer a height restriction for polo ponies but, whatever their size, they are always referred to as ponies. Ponies and riders wear plenty of protection during a match; ponies' legs are bandaged and tails are taped up to avoid getting caught in the mallets. Riders wear knee pads, helmets, and sometimes visors.

OTHER BALL GAMES

Horseball and polocrosse are also mounted team ball games and are growing in popularity as sports for both adults and children. One of their main attractions is the fact that a string of ponies is not a necessity!

   Horseball resembles a cross between rugby football and basketball on horseback. Two teams of four players oppose each other on a pitch 70 m (76 yd) long x 30 m (33 yd) wide, allowing it to be played indoors also. A football with six leather handles is thrown from player to player; if it falls to the ground, riders have to be able to reach down and scoop it off the floor. A goal is scored by tossing the

POLOCROSSE International polocrosse is another fast and furious game. Its popularity has spread rapidly as it is far cheaper to take part in than polo, as a whole string of ponies is not required!

ball through a suspended hoop with a net attached to it. Polocrosse is based on polo and lacrosse and involves two teams of three players (from a full team of six). A large pitch is required, a bit bigger than a rugby pitch, with a 2.5 m (8 ft) goal at each end. The ball is thrown and caught using a long racquet with a net on the end. A soft rubber ball is caught and passed from player to player either by throwing or bouncing it.

HORSEBALL Another popular sport, particularly in France, horseball is played by both adults and children. The ball is tossed through a suspended hoop and net (like a basketball net) to score a goal.

A PHYSICAL SPORT Polo is a very physical contact sport, played at speed with men and women wielding wooden mallets and whacking a very hard ball. Protection for both pony and rider is essential.

FLAT RACING

Horse racing was included in the Ancient Olympics, and the nomadic tribesman of Central Asia certainly raced the horses that were to be the forefathers of the Arab breed. The enormous racing industry of modern times owes its existence to the development in England, during the early 17th and 18th centuries, of the Thoroughbred – the racing machine that we know today.

ORIGINS

Arab Horses, which had been brought to England by knights returning from the crusades, were coveted for their speed and spirit. Enjoying royal patronage then, as it does today, horse racing was held in Newmarket throughout the 1600s during the reign of King James and Kings Charles I and II. Today, Newmarket remains the 'capital' of British flat racing.

Horse racing in its recognizable form started during the reign of Queen Anne (early 1700s). Races were staged between groups of horses, and spectators could bet on the outcome. Racecourses were developed for this popular sport, including Ascot, founded in 1711.

In 1752, the Jockey Club was formed – the organization that still exists today and that governs the sport of horse racing. Today, racing thrives around the world, but its organization is based on the British pattern. In Europe, England, Ireland, France, and Italy are all major players, whilst America, Hong Kong, New Zealand, and Australia, amongst many others, have all embraced the sport.

THE DERBY, EPSOM As a Group One Classic race for colts, it is the dream of racehorse owners and trainers from around the world to win the Derby at Epsom, in Great Britain.

Eclipse

Considered to be the greatest racehorse of all time, Eclipse was born in 1764, the year of the great eclipse. He was a thick-winded, bad-tempered creature, but in 1769 and 1770 he won every race he entered. Early flat races were over much longer distance than they are today; Eclipse often ran in four-mile races. He was retired to stud in 1771 because no-one was willing to race against him. He was hugely successful at stud, his bloodline featuring predominantly amongst Derby winners. He died in 1789 and then part of the secret of his success was discovered: he had an exceptionally large heart weighing 6.5 kg (14¼ lb).

Each country has its own General Stud Book in which the pedigree of every Thoroughbred foal is recorded. Britain has the oldest stud book, dating back to 1793. All racehorses must be registered Thoroughbreds and they are trained by licensed trainers. There are very strict rules and regulations, which are overseen by the Jockey Club.

Flat racing is operated as a Pattern system: a series of races are organized over set distances that are appropriate to test the ability of the best horses. Because of the fast-maturing trait of Thoroughbred horses, they can start racing at two years old. The highest level of racing includes the Group One Classics: the most prestigious races being the Derby (colts) and the Oaks (fillies) at Epsom; the 2000 guineas (colts) and 1000 guineas (fillies) at Newmarket; and the St Ledger (Doncaster). Whilst the Classics capture the imagination, there are races for all levels of ability and ages, run on grass or all-weather surfaces and, in America, on 'dirt' tracks. The racing industry and the gambling bandwagon that goes with it are worth billions of dollars, hence the need for strict regulation.

ARAB RACING

The success of the Arab's descendant, the Thoroughbred racehorse, nearly brought an end to Arab racing. Arabs were the original racehorses in Britain and, for a time, they continued to be raced against the Thoroughbred breed; but as breeding of the Thoroughbred became more refined, his greater size and speed meant the Arab could no longer match him on the racecourse. By the 1900s, Arab racing had come to an end. But in 1978, members of the Arab Horse Society obtained permission from the Jockey Club to organize amateur flat races for Arabs.

HANDICAPPING

Horse racing uses a handicap system in many of its races: in a handicap race, the best horses have to carry the most weight. The official handicapper monitors the progress of every racehorse and decides whether he should go up or down in the handicap. Racehorses vary enormously in the natural ability they are blessed with and also with how well, or otherwise, they are trained. Without a handicap system, it is argued that the same horses would win everything. Sadly, it does mean that the best horses reach a point at which they cannot win under the burden of the handicap imposed. After a few poor runs, they will be dropped in the handicap and may find success again.

ARAB RACING Arab racing enjoyed a resurgence from 1978, when the Arab Horse Society obtained permission from the Jockey Club to run amateur flat races for Arab horses. The sport had died out in Britain by the end of the 19th century, but is now thriving.

DIRT TRACK Dirt-track racing is very popular in America. Some horses love this surface, which creates 'kickback' (dirt that gets in the faces of the horses and riders). But some horses hate it – and who can blame them?!

JUMP RACING

National Hunt racing and point-to-pointing were both born out of hunting, so it is not surprising that Great Britain and Ireland remain the heartland of these sports. Steeplechase and hurdling are the professional arm of the sport, whilst point-to-pointing has retained its amateur status. Great races include the Cheltenham Gold Cup and Aintree's Grand National.

STEEPLECHASING AND HURDLING

National Hunt racing, as it is known in Britain and Ireland, covers steeplechases, hurdle races, and bumpers (flat races for young National Hunt horses). Steeplechases are held over distances of between 2 and 4½ miles (3.2 and 7.2 km) and involve jumping a series of National Hunt fences (large, sloping brush fences that are over 4 ft/1.2 m high). Some racecourses also have water jumps as part of the course. The horses must be registered Thoroughbreds and they must be trained in yards run by licensed trainers. They are ridden by professional (and sometimes amateur) jockeys.

Thoroughbred horses that are bred and trained for National Hunt races are generally later maturing than those that are bred to race on the flat, and do not usually start racing over fences until they are four or five. They are sometimes given an easier introduction by running in bumpers (flat races specifically for National Hunt horses). They can run in these from three years of age, and for this age group the distance to race would usually be 1½ miles (2.4 km). They then either progress straight to a steeplechase race, or they may run in hurdle races. Hurdles are much smaller and softer than National Hunt fences, and collapse if the horse hits them. Some horses remain hurdlers all their racing lives.

HANDICAPS

The complicated system of handicaps, penalties, and allowances has a huge influence on the likely success or otherwise of a racehorse. Once a horse has run in at least

How steeplechasing was named

It is said that the sport of steeplechasing was born on a day in 1752 when two Irishman, O'Callaghan and Blake, raced their hunters over 4½ miles (7.2 km) of natural country between the churches of St Buttevant and St Leger, in County Cork, Ireland. The race was to settle a wager over who had the better hunter – the answer was Blake. Whilst Great Britain and Ireland are the forerunners of the sport, it has been adopted by other countries but not to the same extent as flat racing. France has the famous course at Pau, the Czech Republic hosts the Gran Pardubice, and America hosts the Maryland Cup.

Hunter chases

Hunter chases are races held at National Hunt racecourses, but are open to point-to-pointers even though their trainers aren't licensed. It is an opportunity for the amateur trainer and jockey to have a taste of the professional arm of the sport. The prize money is much higher than for a point-to-point race and the two biggest prizes to be won are the Cheltenham and Aintree Foxhunters – the latter giving the amateurs a chance to experience the awesome Grand National fences!

three races, he is given a handicap rating based on his performance. Some races are run on level weights, i.e. every horse carries the same weight, whilst other races start with a level weight for each horse, but then a series of allowances and penalties are taken into account to arrive at the weight each horse finally has to carry.

POINT-TO-POINTING

Point-to-points are amateur jump races held on unofficial courses all over the country – each one being organized by the local hunt. The races vary from 2½ to 4 miles (4 6.4 km) and start at Maiden level (for horses that have never won a race), progressing through Restricted and Intermediate races (the horse moving up a level as soon as he wins at the previous level), to Open level.
The fences are only slightly smaller than those found on a proper National Hunt racecourse. All horses taking part have to be registered Thoroughbreds apart from in a 'Member's Race', where you can still enter any horse provided he has hunted. Despite its amateur status and the fact that trainers are not licensed in any way, the sport is taken very seriously.

DESERT ORCHID The legendary Desert Orchid (*left*) battles it out with Norton's Coin at Cheltenham, Great Britain. The four day Cheltenham Festival features the coveted Gold Cup race for steeplechasers.

DRESSAGE

The word dressage is used to cover both the competitive sport of that name, and also the general use of flatwork training to produce a supple, responsive, obedient horse, whatever his role in life. A horse that has never been ridden soon finds his own natural balance, but as soon as he has to carry a rider, he has to learn how to rebalance himself to cope with the rider's weight and demands.

DRESSAGE HISTORY

The art of dressage is to help the horse find the correct balance, to improve his suppleness, power and expression of his paces, with the end result that the horse can easily and willingly obey his rider's most subtle instructions (aids). The long-term aim of dressage is to teach a horse to carry more of his weight on his hindquarters so that his forehand (head, neck, and shoulders) is light and elevated.

FLATWORK Correctness of training is the key to dressage and the rider needs to have a 'feel' for how the horse is using his body and muscles. Putting time and effort into the flatwork training of the horse can reap benefits in whatever discipline you then choose to specialize in.

SPANISH RIDING SCHOOL DISPLAY The Lipizzaner stallions of the Spanish Riding School beautifully demonstrate the higher levels of dressage in their High-School (*Haute-École*) work.

This not only helps him to excel in the dressage arena, but also makes him a far better horse for any activity, be it hacking out, hunting, racing, or jumping. The horse's hindquarters are his powerhouse or engine, so the more use that can be made of them, the more the rider can utilize the horse's natural strength to his advantage.

In the 16th century, a succession of European horsemen, including Frederico Grisone and François de la Guérinière, laid the foundations of classical riding and training. Much of the training was done from the ground on long reins, without the weight and sometimes hindrance of the rider to unbalance the horse. In Great Britain, hunting and cross-country riding were much preferred to what was seen as the soft option of dressage. After the Napoleonic wars, some of Britain's spirit drifted across to Europe, where the excitement of hunting and racing across country started to take over from the more refined art of dressage. But the beauty and skill of classical riding was not lost for long, and the late 19th century saw the founding of two great riding establishments that remain the envy of the world today: the Spanish Riding School of Vienna, Austria, and the Cavalry School at Saumur, France. Dressage competitions began as early as 1873, and the first truly international competition was held in Turin, Italy, in 1902. The 1912 Stockholm Olympics featured dressage for the first time; Swedish riders won gold, silver, and bronze!

NADINE CAPELLMANN AND ELVIS, AACHEN A judge (higher levels use three judges) gives the horse and rider a score out of ten for each movement and a final set of scores to reflect the overall impression, correctness of training, and the rider's position, balance, and correct use of the aids.

Over time, the influence of the great riding masters of Europe spread throughout the world, making dressage today a truly international sport.

COMPETITIONS

The international sport of affiliated (official) dressage is governed by the FEI (International Equestrian Federation). But it is a relatively easy competition to organize, so many countries also have unaffiliated classes for amateur riders.

Dressage tests are ridden in a marked out arena measuring 40 m x 20 m (130 ft x 65 ft) for the more novice tests, and 60 m (197 ft) x 20 m (65 ft) for more advanced tests. A dressage test comprises a series of set movements that are performed within the arena, using lettered markers as the point at which each movement starts and finishes. Dressage tests start at Preliminary level and progress through Novice and Elementary to Medium and Advanced tests. At the lower levels, the riders can have the test read out to them as they ride it, but at higher levels, and in all international competitions, the test must be ridden from memory. Dressage to music is another sector to the sport where riders devise their own test, which must incorporate a number of set movements as laid out in the rules for each test. The test is ridden to recorded music, which the rider will have put together to best match his horse's rhythm, paces, and character.

These competitions are particularly popular with spectators. The sport enjoys a great range of competitions, from local unaffiliated classes through to regional, national, and international championships.

ATTRIBUTES

The rider must have the temperament and self-discipline that will allow him to use endless patience as he quietly and calmly corrects the horse when he is wrong, and rewards him when he is right. Training really is that simple if you have the feel, the patience, and the discipline. The rider will be striving to continually improve his own balance and suppleness as well as that of the horse, to ensure that the horse is not restricted in any way by the rider's lack of balance or loss of position. All horses benefit from dressage training, but obviously some horses are better suited to it than others. A trainable temperament, correct conformation, and naturally big, expressive paces are all advantageous, but 'star quality' or presence is also important and can provide the winning difference between a test that is accurately and correctly performed and one that demands your attention and says: 'Look at me, this is the winning test!'

CROSS-COUNTRY RIDING

Aside from the sport of eventing, in which cross-country riding is one of three phases of the competition, there are other sports dedicated to the art of cross-country riding.

They are hunter trials and team chases. Both these competitions offer horse and rider the opportunity to show off their skills over a course of natural obstacles.

HUNTER TRIALS
Hunter trials involve tackling a course of cross-country obstacles and hazards, either in pairs or as an individual. Different classes offer differing heights of fences and levels of difficulty, but most competitions have sets of fences ranging from 0.75 m (2½ ft) to 1 m (3½ ft). The course may include water, banks, steps, and ditches as well as single and combination fences. The organizers decide upon an optimum time, although the precise time is not revealed to the competitors until the end. There is usually an additional timed section within the course, which often has a gate or slip rail to be negotiated (without jumping it!). The winner is the horse and rider who finish closest to the optimum time – if more than one competitor achieves this, then the winner is decided by the fastest through the timed section.

Pairs classes are often used to give a less experienced or nervous horse (or rider) the chance to gain confidence by having another horse to jump with. Pairs classes usually include several 'dressing fences' which are wide enough for both horses to jump side by side. Judges will award marks at these fences for style, togetherness, and general

CUTTING CORNERS Cross-country riding requires horse and rider to attain a good balance and rhythm. They must have confidence in each other to tackle what are often daunting obstacles. This fence is being jumped at an angle, which helps save valuable seconds.

impression and turnout. The winners are the pair achieving the highest marks, and who also complete the course without any jumping penalties.

ATTRIBUTES
Horse and rider need to be bold, confident, and determined to successfully tackle cross-country fences, as well as the often undulating terrain that the course may cover. The rider needs to have a good sense of pace, and must be able to balance and present the horse at each fence in a way that the horse has time to organize himself to measure and jump it safely and correctly.

The horse must also be careful, because if he is reckless or rushes his fences without concentrating properly, he is likely to fall as the fences are solid. He must also be obedient enough to slow down and allow the rider to manoeuvre him correctly to open and close a gate without having to be dismounted. Equally, in a pairs class, he must not become overexcited and try to race the other horse. To summarize, the sport demands, quite rightly, all the attributes one would look for in the perfect hunter.

SCHOOLING Cross-country schooling courses allow horse and rider to practise over cross-country fences without the pressure of competition. They usually have sets of fences of increasing height so you can start with the smallest and work your way up.

EQUIPMENT

The fact that cross-country fences are solid and won't fall down if hit by the horse does mean that both horse and rider need greater protection than for some other disciplines.

Riders should wear a proper safety helmet and harness, and also a body protector. Many riders will also wear a hunting tie (or stock) as this gives some support and stability to the rider's neck. Riders usually compete in either their normal hunting kit (tweed or dark jacket, breeches, and boots) or in a cross-country style sweatshirt or polo shirt, with breeches and boots.

The horse should wear some form of protective boots or bandages on all four legs. A breastplate or breast girth reduces the risk of the saddle slipping back, and some riders like to use an over-girth (or safety surcingle) as an added precaution in case the normal girth or girth straps should snap. The rigours of the terrain mean everything has to be that bit more robust and secure than it would for everyday riding. Some riders like to put grease down the front of the horse's legs to help him slide over a fence should he catch a leg on anything. It is important to know you have control of the horse when he is jumping cross country. It is one thing to ride forwards in a bold, attacking manner, but that doesn't mean just galloping flat out at everything. The rider must know that he can slow down and shorten the horse's stride for the more complicated fences, and also for turning on tricky terrain.

TEAM CHASING

Team chasing involves a team of four riders tackling a cross-country course together. Speed is of the essence as the competition is won by the fastest team to complete. Only three of the four riders have to complete the course, so the time is taken from the moment the team sets off to the moment the third team member crosses the finish line. Each team usually has a 'lead horse' who habitually sets off in front and is a bold, safe jumper who will give the others a good lead. The lead combination also have to have a good sense of pace, as they will be setting the gallop for the others to match. If the lead horse encounters a problem, there has to be another horse in the team that can take over the lead. No penalties are given for falls, stops, or runouts, but they affect the time it takes for the team to complete the course. There are usually one or two places on the course where the rules dictate that all the team have to have jumped over a certain obstacle before they can jump out over the next fence. This is to try to ensure that the riders tackle the course as a team rather than as four individuals each at their own pace.

TEAM EVENT Team chasing is a thrilling spectacle to watch, as everything is down to speed – the team that has the fastest three horses and riders that complete the course together will win. This team is competing in traditional hunting dress.

SHOWJUMPING

Showjumping involves horse and rider tackling a course of artificial jumps within an arena, which can be either grass or have an artificial surface. The fence poles are not fixed, and will fall down if the horse knocks them with his legs, so whilst it is not without its thrills and spills, it is not as risky an occupation for horse and rider as cross-country jumping.

JUMPING PRACTICE Gridwork involves jumping over a line of fences set at differing distances. The aim is to improve the horse's gymnastic ability and to teach him to cope with shortening and lengthening his stride between fences. The fences can start small, making it a good introductory exercise.

HISTORY OF THE SPORT
Leaping or 'lepping' competitions were being held in countries such as Ireland, Russia, and France in the late 1800s. America also held high-jump classes at a National Show in Madison Square Gardens in 1883. Showjumping was first included in the Paris Olympics in 1900, and in 1907, the first International Horse Show was held at London's Olympia. Showjumping quickly developed into

PONY CLUB CHAMPIONSHIPS This partnership are showing a really good technique. The pony is lifting his forearms and tucking his lower forelegs up tightly. The rider has remained in a good, secure, well-balanced position.

PUISSANCE SHOWJUMPING The Puissance is a particularly popular and dramatic class. Riders tackle a short course of fences, which includes a wall that is always higher than the rest of the course. Each rider that jumps clear comes back to jump the course again with all the fences raised. The class continues until no-one is able to jump clear over the wall.

an international sport and remains highly popular, particularly throughout Europe and America. Classes are judged on jumping performance, with faults or penalties being awarded for knocking poles down, running out or refusing, falling off, and, in timed classes, for exceeding the optimum time.

SHOWJUMPING COMPETITIONS

Showjumping as an affiliated sport is governed by the FEI, but there are also many unaffiliated competition venues offering an easily accessible sport to riders of all abilities. The simplest type of unaffiliated competition is clear-round jumping. Each rider pays to jump round a course of fences. A rosette is awarded if the combination jumps a clear round. This class is often used as an introduction for young or inexperienced horses and/or riders. Organizers are usually very tolerant, often lowering a fence if someone is struggling. Another advantage of this type of class is that if you jump a fence badly you can circle round and jump it again, so that both horse and rider can learn immediately from their mistake and hopefully make a better effort second time round.

ATHLETIC HORSE The showjumping horse must be very well balanced, supple, athletic, and responsive. But, perhaps more than anything, he must be determined to clear the jump.

The next level of competition includes a timed jump-off for all those who jump a clear round. Unaffiliated classes can start at whatever height the organizers choose and usually go up to a maximum of 1.2 m (4 ft). Affiliated classes usually start at around 90 cm (3 ft), and go up to well over 1.85 m (6 ft) at the highest level.

Derby competitions involve a mixture of showjumps and cross-country obstacles, which can include ditches, hedges, banks, and walls. The most famous Derby course is at Hickstead, England, which features the awesome Derby Bank, where horse and rider have to slither down and then clear a jump just a few strides from the base of the bank.

ATTRIBUTES REQUIRED

Showjumping courses are often set up in a relatively small area, requiring horse and rider to be able to jump, land, and turn quickly and smoothly, still in balance, to the next fence. Flatwork training is important as this improves the horse's balance, suppleness, and responsiveness. Gridwork, involving lines of jumps set up at different distances to each other, is used as a gymnastic exercise to help the horse's agility and speed of reactions.

The rider needs to ride in a balanced rhythm to each fence and to have a good enough position to stay in balance with the horse over the fence. If the rider cannot control the horse's stride, they may find that the point of take-off is too close to the fence. This means the horse doesn't have the time or space to get himself up in the air to clear the fence. If he is too far from the fence on take-off, he may be unbalanced as he lands. However, the most vital requirement is that the horse must want to clear the fence.

EVENTING

Eventing is a compete test of all-round ability in horse and rider. It combines aspects of the three separate disciplines of dressage, show-jumping, and cross-country riding – and so requires more riding kit than the other sports.

ORIGINS

The sport began as a test devised for cavalrymen to keep them fit and their skills honed. It was called 'The Military' and included the three phases we know today. The dressage phase tested the horse's obedience and suitability for parade duties; the cross-country phase showed he could quickly and safely cross any country to seek out, attack, or escape the enemy; and the showjumping phase proved that, after the rigours of battle, the horse was still fit, well, and obedient enough to continue with his duties. Eventing was included in the Olympics in 1912, and was restricted to military riders. The sport spread from country to country through inter-regiment competitions, and soon attracted the attention of civilian riders and spectators. Eventing developed originally on the continent of Europe and today can boast a large international cast of competitors, but Great Britain is the centre of the world of eventing. Britain's Badminton three-day event is today one of the most prestigious and coveted prizes in the sport, and is one of only five events held at this level throughout the world.

BURGHLEY To tackle a four-star course, horse and rider will have worked their way up through the system, learning to tackle different obstacles as they progress. There are only five four-star events worldwide: Badminton and Burghley (GB), Lexington (US), Luhmuhlen (Germany), and Pau (France).

COMPETITION STRUCTURE

Eventing involves two main types of competition: one-day events, which can be national or international, and three-day events, which are usually international. Professional riders use one-day events as preparation for three-day events, but many amateurs compete only at one-day events.

At a one-day event, all three phases are completed in one day: a dressage test, followed by the showjumping, and finally the cross-country phase. Horse and rider must be allowed a minimum of half-an-hour rest between each phase. The scores for each phase are added together to find the winner.

In three-day events, each of the three phases will be more technical and demanding than it would be at a one-day event. The dressage test is ridden on day one, followed by the cross-country phase on day two, and finally the showjumping on day three. The showjumping is run in reverse order of merit, so the overnight leader after the cross-country phase will be the last one to enter the ring

EVENT HORSE The event horse has to be bold and fast enough to tackle the cross country, controllable and calm enough for the dressage, and careful and athletic enough for the showjumping.

to showjump. This produces a tense finale, with the winner not being known until the last horse has jumped.

ATTRIBUTES

Correct training based on the principles of rhythm, balance, confidence, and responsiveness will take horse and rider a long way in all three phases. Probably the key requirement for both horse and rider is temperament. The rider has to be disciplined and correct in teaching himself and the horse the different aspects of the sport. The horse has to accept, and learn from, the training required to achieve proficiency in all three phases. This is made harder by the fact that the event horse has to be fitter than a pure dressage or showjumping horse, and yet must be able to handle the same pressures and requirements of both these disciplines.

WATER Water jumps are a real challenge and water is always one of the main feature fences at every event. The horse will have been introduced to the idea from an early age, trotting through puddles and streams out hacking, to ensure that he is completely comfortable with this hazard.

Speed and endurance

The cross-country phase at a three-day event used to be known as the speed and endurance phase, as it included several additional elements. Riders used to set out on what was called Phase A: a section of roads and tracks that had to be ridden in a set time (otherwise time faults were incurred). This phase acted as a warm up for the Steeplechase, where horse and rider had to gallop round a course of steeplechase fences, before setting off on Phase C, another section of timed roads and tracks which acted as a recovery phase. There was then an obligatory 10-minute rest period before tackling the main cross-country course. In the early 2000s, the speed and endurance phases were dropped from the cross-country phase. Much of the reason was the amount of ground these additional phases took up and there was pressure, particularly at Olympic level, to limit the resources that were required for what is still considered a relatively minor sport. The 'short format' as it became known, was adopted at the 2004 Athens Olympics and it was inevitable then that the rest of the sport would follow suit.

ENDURANCE

Over the centuries, humans and horses have undertaken many long and arduous journeys: some in the name of war and conquest; others for exploration and settlement in new lands; and some simply as a challenge, to see how far and wide they can travel.

AMERICAN ORIGINS

Endurance riding as a sport started in 1955 in California. Wendell T. Robie wanted to prove that modern-day horses and riders could still measure up to the arduous undertakings of their forebears. He and a group of friends rode 160 km (100 miles) of old mining and emigrant tracks and trails from Squaw Valley, through the Sierra Nevada range, and finishing at Auburn. This ride was to become the first official endurance ride and remains a coveted prize in the sport today – it is the Western States Trail Ride. The winner received the Tevis Cup, named after the president of the 19th-century Wells Fargo Company, whose Pony Express riders were legendary in their day for their courage and stamina.

VET CHECK The back-up team play a vital role in looking after the comfort and wellbeing of horse and rider. They have a short opportunity at each vet check to refresh them both and to present the horse in the best possible health for the vet's inspection.

ENDURANCE TODAY

Modern-day endurance riding is a competition of speed and stamina over a set route and against the clock. The sport has had FEI status since 1982. Competition rides vary in length, but an international event run over more than one day (up to two or three days in total) would cover 80–100 km (50–60 miles) per day. Championship events have adopted the one-day ride format and these usually cover 160 km (100 miles), with a winning riding time usually between 10 and 12 hours. Each ride is split into phases of approximately 40 km (30 miles) each. At the end of each phase, the horse is checked by a vet for soundness, sores on his back or mouth, over-reaches, and general wellbeing. The horse's heart rate is checked (if it is over 64 beats per minute at any vet check, the horse is eliminated). There is a small window of time at each vet check for the back-up team to do everything possible to ensure the horse is presented to the vet fit and well. The rider relies heavily on a back-up team that follow the competitors' progress and are on hand to refresh horse and rider at each vet stop, changing tack, equipment, and clothing if necessary. The rider's judgement of pace and in-depth knowledge of the horse's wellbeing are essential if he is to complete the ride fit and well.

TAKING A BREAK The rider has to ensure the wellbeing of the horse throughout the ride. This may mean walking with the horse to rest its back, or to help him tackle particularly strenuous terrain.

Endurance riding is particularly popular in Europe, America, Australia, and Dubai. One of the attractions of the sport for riders at championship level is the chance to ride through some of the most spectacular scenery around the world.

ATTRIBUTES

The endurance horse obviously has to be tough and have stamina. Good limbs and feet are an absolute must, as much of the terrain will be rough and rugged. Temperament is also important, as the horse needs to be able to remain calm and relaxed throughout the ride to conserve energy. The horse's action and paces are also important; a light, ground-covering stride is going to make life easier for horse and rider than a heavy, short, choppy stride. The accumulative effects of concussion on the horse's feet and joints cannot be underestimated, so conformation and a way of going that alleviates this as much as possible is a considerable advantage. The horse has to learn to settle into a relaxed trot or canter, to balance and carry himself with

Trail riding

Another form of long-distance riding is trail riding. Unlike endurance riding, this is not a race but simply the opportunity for horse and rider to tackle long-distance rides whilst still testing their horsemanship and judgement of pace. The aim is to complete the ride with your horse still in good condition. Trail riding has veterinary checks in the same way as endurance riding, ensuring that a horse that is unfit or uncomfortable is not allowed to continue.

GOOD CHOICE Arabs or Arab crosses have dominated endurance riding since its inception. Their inherent toughness and stamina, combined with a light, floating action, makes them ideally suited to the rigours of the sport.

minimal interference from his rider, and to be confident enough to face the many natural hazards that he will encounter. The sport involves long hours in the saddle, and specialist equipment and clothing for horse and rider has been developed. Most riders use specially designed endurance saddles and gel pads and numnahs that reduce any chance of saddle sores. Bitless bridles are popular, as many horses find them more comfortable. Boots tend not to be worn, as the possibility of rubs or sores is quite high. The riders wear lighter-weight clothing than for other equestrian disciplines.

EARLY MORNING START The endurance horse and rider will tackle all kinds of terrain and meet untold hazards and weather conditions. They also get to ride through some of the most spectacular scenery in the world.

MOUNTED GAMES

Mounted games are played in many countries either through the affiliated international organizations of the Pony Club or the Mounted Games Association, or on a more impromptu basis amongst any group of riders with the requisite degree of agility and competitiveness who want to have a go for fun. For the mounted games specialist there are national and international competitions to compete at.

LIGHT RELIEF Mounted games started out as games for adult riders, usually soldiers, to hone their riding skills, promote team spirit, and provide light relief from their more serious duties. This group of Afghan horsemen are playing Buzkashi, where two teams battle for possession of a dead goat!

ADULTS AND CHILDREN

The main advantage of the mounted games is that, certainly at the lower levels, there will be a game to suit every pony and rider, whatever their riding ability, and the games are an excellent way of gaining confidence and producing a good partnership between pony and rider. The most famous children's mounted games

FLAG RACE The International Mounted Games Association encourages adults to continue the tradition of playing mounted games. This combination are taking part in a flag race, which requires a fast and agile pony that is able to turn quickly and sharply.

competition is probably the Prince Philip Cup which is held annually by the Pony Club in London, England, at the International Horse of the Year Show.

NATIONAL AND INTERNATIONAL GAMES

The International Mounted Games Association caters for both children and adults. There is no upper age limit for riders but there are limitations as to the weight of the rider relative to the size of their pony or horse. Ponies must be 15 hh (1.5 m) or under. There are individual, pairs, and team competitions and over 25 different games to play. The aim of the games is to test the accuracy of the rider and the co-operativeness and responsiveness of the horse, rather than simply a test of pure speed.

As well as national competitions there is also an annual World Mounted Games championship, with categories for individual, pairs, and team champions.

THE GAMES

The simplest games, such as musical chairs, musical mats, and musical statues, are for young children who are being led. Then there are the races such as bending, egg-and-spoon, and sock race. In a bending race, all the ponies line up and then race away, bending in and out of a line of poles. Other races involve racing off to grab an item and racing back to deposit it in a bucket. Some of the races are run as relays with teams of four riders taking part one after the other.

The annual Prince Phillip Cup competition sees ever-more inventive and exciting games developed to challenge the best teams in the country. Some, such as the spectacular Dragon game, involve elaborate obstacles; others, such as Chase me Charlie, involve jumping.

ANOTHER PONY CLUB RACE The Pony Club Mounted Games have done much to encourage all that is best about riding. They promote team spirit, co-operation, fitness, and agility, as well as the ability to accept winning or losing in the same spirit of fun.

ATTRIBUTES

If you want to be a serious team contender, then your pony needs to be fast and agile yet remain obedient, as there is much stopping, starting, twisting and turning involved. He must stand stock still when required, to allow his rider to grab an item and accurately deposit it somewhere. The pony must be brave enough to face up to strange objects and obstacles. A quick start will win a vital advantage, as will the ability to only have to slow down and turn at the last minute. The rider needs to be fit and agile and will often choose a pony that, for most other sports, would be considered too small, making it easier to reach down and grab items, as well as being easier and quicker to stop, start, and turn, and to jump on and off. The pony must be robust enough and tolerant enough to not mind the hustle and bustle.

SACK RACE The sack race is guaranteed to involve various runners and riders tripping over themselves. One suspects that both the legs of each competitor should be in the sack, but otherwise this interpretation of the rules should give them an advantage!

HEAVY HORSES

The heavy-horse breeds were, for a time, the backbone of the workforce in farming and industry in many countries. But by the early to mid-20th century, tractors and lorries had made their mark and signalled the end of the road for most working horses. However, there are still niche roles for them; in some cities it is commercially viable to use them for local deliveries of goods, and they still play an important role in forestry work.

BOULONNAIS This gorgeous portrait of a Boulonnais, a French heavy-horse breed (*see* pp 132–33), shows that despite being bred for hard work, many draught horses still retain a certain elegance and noble bearing. In this particular breed the large, expressive eyes are evidence of its Arab ancestry.

Ardennais

ORIGIN France/Belgium
ENVIRONMENT ▲
BLOOD ◌
USES 🐎🐴
HEIGHT 15.3–16.1 hh (1.60–1.65 m)
COLOURS Mostly roan, but also grey, chestnut, bay, brown, and palomino

BROWN   CHESTNUT   GREY   BAY   PALOMINO   ROAN

The relatively short but incredibly powerful Ardennais is named after its homeland, the rugged Ardennes region on the French/ Belgian border. It is an ancient breed; its ancestors were praised for their stamina and toughness by Julius Caesar 2,000 years ago. The heavy type is known as the 'carthorse of the north'.

ORIGINS

The Ardennais is believed to be the direct descendent of the Solutrian Horse: a prehistoric, snub-nosed horse that lived over 50,000 years ago whose skeletal remains were discovered at Solutré, southeast France. Evidence suggests that the Solutrian horse stood at about 15 hh (1.50 m), as does the smaller type of Ardennais. These horses roamed in a cold, mountainous region and they evolved to be surefooted and tough.

RIDING HORSE

Prior to the 19th century, the breed was not as massive and thickset as it is today, and it was used for riding as well as for draught work. Some were ridden in the crusades and, when Arab horses were brought back to Europe during the crusades, their finer blood was crossed with that of the Ardennais. During the 17th and 18th centuries, much use was made of the breed in battle. It is said that Napoleon owed his safe return from the Russian campaign to them.

In the early 19th century, more Arab and Thoroughbred blood was introduced, as well as some Boulonnais and Percheron. The relatively small Ardennais that proved his worth as a cavalry and artillery horse is now quite rare but Ardennais blood is very evident in other breeds. The demands of

RED ROAN The most common and popular colour for the Ardennais is roan, particularly red roan. Iron grey is acceptable but not dapple grey, and chestnut, palomino, bay, and brown are also allowed.

agriculture for a strong workhorse led to outcrosses to the larger Belgium Draught. This produced the more commonly found heavy Ardennais, and influenced the development of the Trait du Nord (*see* p 170), sometimes known as the Ardennais du Nord, and the Auxois (*see* p 130).

CHARACTERISTICS

The Ardennais is short and stocky, with a thickset neck, a short back, and muscular loins. His limbs are short with plenty of bone. The feet are relatively small but strong. There are thick, wavy feathers on the lower limbs, although the original, smaller Ardennais has slightly lighter bone and less feathering. The head is short and blunt. The Ardennais is kind, willing, and gentle. For such a massively powerful beast, he is surprisingly energetic and active.

FARM WORK The Ardennais has stud books in a number of European countries and efforts are made by its breed societies to encourage the horse's use in farming and forestry work.

Auxois

ORIGIN France
ENVIRONMENT 🌾
BLOOD 💧
USES 🐂
HEIGHT 15.3–16.2 hh (1.60–1.67 m)
COLOURS Mostly roan, but also bay and chestnut

CHESTNUT	BAY	ROAN

The Auxois is closely related to the Ardennais (*see* pp 128–29) to the extent that he is considered by some to be a 'type' derived from that breed. Taller than the Ardennais but not so heavily built, he is similarly strong and docile. Few of this old breed remain, although efforts are being made in the Yonne and Saône-et-Loire areas of France to maintain his existence.

ORIGINS

The Auxois originates from the Burgundy region of France, and is descended from the Burgundy Horse that was known in the Middle Ages. During the 19th century, in an effort to produce a larger, stronger workhorse, Percheron, Boulonnais and Ardennais outcrosses were used. Since the beginning of the 20th century, only Ardennais blood has been allowed to improve the breed. Due to its rarity, the breed is now protected by the *Syndicat du Cheval de Trait Ardennais de L'Auxois*.

CHARACTERISTICS

Although very similar in appearance to the heavy Ardennais, the Auxois is taller over all but less massively proportioned in the quarters and limbs. Neither are the limbs as heavily feathered as they are in the Ardennais. It is broad through the back, with a long, sloping, muscular croup, and a low-set tail. The head is relatively small and broad, with sharp alert ears.

POWERHOUSE A picture of power and strength, the Auxois has proven to be an exceptional workhorse whose gentle nature makes him easy to manage and work with. The short, thick neck, muscular forearms, and broad chest give him tremendous pulling power.

AGILE HORSE Although built for power, the Auxois is no slow-coach! His good shoulders, powerful croup, and lighter limbs allow him to move surprisingly freely and quickly.

Black Forest Horse

ORIGIN Germany
ENVIRONMENT
BLOOD
USES
HEIGHT 15.0–16.0 hh (1.50–1.60 m)
COLOURS Mostly chestnut, but also grey

CHESTNUT	GREY

The Black Forest Horse is a small, hardy draught horse that evolved as a workhorse and riding horse that could withstand the long, cold winters of its homeland, the Black Forest in Baden-Württemberg, in southern Germany. He is also known as the Schwarzwälder, St Märgener, and Wälderpferd, and, locally, due to his colouring, as the Black Forest Fox!

ORIGINS

The Black Forest Horse was developed from the old Noriker breed that came from the mountainous region of Austria. Efforts were made in the late 19th century to increase the size of the breed by only allowing heavy Belgium Draught stallions to be used, but the farmers of the area continued to secretly use native stallions, even forging the breeding papers. The use of Belgium Draught blood soon ended when it became obvious that it was not producing a horse that was suitable for the steep, wooded terrain of the region. The farmers were able to continue producing the stamp of horse they knew they wanted. Hence the Black Forest Horse was able to retain its neat size, and nimble and lively character.

CHARACTERISTICS

The Black Forest Horse resembles a large Haflinger (*see* p 328). He is a well-made, strong little horse with a particularly good active trot. Hardy and surefooted, he is well adapted for work on farms and forests in hilly areas. The breed is still used in the Black Forest today for clearing wood, and is increasingly popular as a riding horse as well as for light draught and carriage work.

FOX The characteristic reddish brown coat with 'fox-coloured' mane and tail gave rise to the local name of Black Forest Fox. Another sought-after colour is a dark silver dapple.

Boulonnais

ORIGIN Northwest France
ENVIRONMENT 🌾
BLOOD 💧
USES 🐎
HEIGHT 15.0–16.2 hh (1.50–1.65 m)
COLOURS Predominantly grey, but also bay, black, and chestnut

| BLACK | CHESTNUT | GREY | BAY |

The Boulonnais, sometimes called the White Marble Horse, is the most elegant of the heavy horses, largely due to Arab influence in their bloodlines. Once widespread in France, the stock was devastated in the World Wars. All Boulonnais have an anchor-shaped brand on their necks to honour their coastal origins.

ORIGINS

The heavy type of Boulonnais that exists today is a direct descendant of the knight's charger. A smaller, lighter type, known as the Mareyeur (horse of the tide) was used to haul the heavy carts of fish from Boulogne to Paris. The journey covered 322 km (200 miles) and could be made in under 18 hours, allowing fresh fish to be delivered in time for breakfast in Paris. The breed's strength, endurance, and speed made him the ideal transporter. An annual race, the *Route du Poisson*, is still held today to commemorate the horse. The smaller type has all but disappeared and, whilst the large Boulonnais does find some employment in agriculture, he is mainly produced for his meat.

Much is being done to preserve the Boulonnais, however, including the creation of the American Boulonnais Horse Association, which works with French breeders to develop a breeding population of Boulonnais horses in the United States.

CHARACTERISTICS

The Boulonnais has a good rounded rib cage, a perfectly set shoulder, and well-placed withers. There is very little hair on the powerful limbs with their solid clean joints, open hocks, and short cannon bones. The neck is thick and muscular, with a thick double mane. He has a short, elegant head with a wide, flat forehead.

EXPRESSIVE FACE The Oriental blood in his ancestry shows in the large, dark eyes, expressive face, and sharp, mobile ears. He has a gracefully arched neck and good sloping shoulders.

GOOD PACES The Boulonnais has exceptionally good paces for a heavy horse. His action is straight and long, and his paces swift and energetic. His limbs are strong but not as heavily feathered as they are in many draught breeds.

Brabant

ORIGIN Belgium
ENVIRONMENT
BLOOD 🜄
USES 🐴
HEIGHT 16.2–17.0 hh (1.65–1.70 m)
COLOURS Colours vary across the lines, including, chestnut, dun, grey, and roan

CHESTNUT	DUN	GREY	ROAN

Also known as the Belgian Heavy Draught, the correct name of Brabant comes from the main breeding area in Belgium. This historic breed has been widely used in the improvement of many other heavy breeds, such as the Shire (*see* pp 164–65), Suffolk Punch (*see* pp 166–69), and Clydesdale (*see* pp 138–39).

ORIGINS

The Brabant is descended from the primitive Forest Horse, known during the reign of Julius Caesar and renowned as a calm, willing workhorse. The same primitive foundation stock was responsible for the development of the Ardennais (*see* pp 128–29). By the Middle Ages, the breed of heavy horse that had been developed in Belgium was known as the Flanders Horse. Often described as the 'Great Horse', these were the horses that first carried knights in armour into battle. Careful control and refinement of the breed led to the development of the definitive Brabant breed of today.

The role of the fertile pasturelands of Belgium cannot be underestimated in the development of such a large and powerful draught breed – there

INTELLIGENT FACE The Brabant has a relatively small, plain head but with a kind eye and intelligent expression. The neck is short and powerful and set into massive shoulders.

was no shortage of grass, hay, and grain with which to feed him. During the 1800s the Belgians recognized the importance of their native draught breed and did much to promote and control breeding and exportation. The horses were judged and inspected at a series of shows, culminating in the National Show in Brussels. Inspectors also examined and approved any horses standing at stud. Such was the demand for the breed that in 1891, Brabant stallions were exported to the Government Studs of Russia, Italy, France, Germany, Austria, and Hungary. A breed society was set up in Indiana, United

EXERCISE WHEEL A handsome pair take some gentle exercise. Despite his size, the Brabant is generally economical to keep. His body is relatively short, deep-girthed and compact, with powerful, rounded hindquarters. By nature he is gentle and easy to handle.

States, in 1887. Foundation stock were imported, which fortunately meant that, when the outbreak of World War I stopped all exports from Belgium, the Americans had sufficient breeding stock to go it alone. By the end of the 19th century, three strains of the breed had been developed: the *Gros de la dendre* line were mainly bay horses, the *Gris du Hainaut* type were mainly grey, red-roans, and bays, and the most powerful type was the *Colosses de la Mehaique*. The three types are no longer definitive and all are now known as Brabants.

CHARACTERISTICS

Selective breeding has also helped ensure soundness in terms of limbs and general constitution. The limbs are strong and hard, with medium size, well-formed feet, with plenty of feathering. His massive strength is,

CAREFUL BREEDING Occasional but careful in-breeding and the exemption of any foreign blood has all been part of the Brabant's successful breeding strategy. A number are kept at the Kentucky Horse Park and some mares have been used to breed Mammoth Mules!

fortunately, coupled with an amenable temperament. The strict breeding policy enforced in Belgium has produced a horse that is very true to type. The breed is still used on small farms in parts of Europe and retains its popularity in the United States.

Breton

ORIGIN France
ENVIRONMENT
BLOOD
USES
HEIGHT 15.0–16.2 hh (1.52–1.67 m)
COLOURS Mainly chestnut, but also roan, bay, and grey

| CHESTNUT | GREY | BAY | ROAN |

The Breton is a relatively small but heavily built, hardy draught horse. In the Middle Ages, one strain was popular for riding due to its comfortable trot – or ambling – pace. Its 'squarish', stocky build is accentuated by its tail, which is traditionally docked.

ORIGINS

The Breton probably evolved from the steppe horses of the Breton Mountains. These horses were used as mounts for Celtic warriors and later, after the crusades, would have been bred to the Arab and Oriental horses brought back to Europe. The early product of this crossbreeding was called the Bidet Breton. By the Middle Ages there were two distinct types, the Sommier and the Roussin (Cob). The Sommier was bred in

ACTIVE WORKER Despite the Breton's short neck and shoulder, he has a fast, active walk and trot, making him popular for both agricultural work and as a coach horse.

North Brittany and was used mainly as a pack horse or in agriculture. The Roussin, from the south of the region, was more refined and was particularly popular with military officers as a riding horse.

CHARACTERISTICS

By the 19th century, the three types that are recognized today had developed. The Small Breton Draught Horse is thought to most resemble the original Breton type, and has a dished face. The Large Breton Draught Horse is bulkier and more plain as a result of Ardennais crosses. The Postier Breton is the most elegant of the three, with light, easy paces. The Postier's more refined build and paces are due to the use of Norfolk Roadster blood during the 19th century. The Draught Breton is used to a small degree in farming but his main use today is for meat. The Postier is still popular as a coach horse and is exported to Africa, Spain, Italy, and Japan to help upgrade their native stock.

MOVEMENT The Breton is renowned for his free and easy gait. He is still used as a workhorse on small farms and is prized for his remarkable power, hardiness, and energy.

STOCKY BUILD The Breton has a short, bulky neck; a compact, stocky body; broad, square quarters; short, strong legs; and small, hard feet. There is relatively little feathering on the legs.

SQUARE HEAD The Breton has quite a square head, with low-set ears. His wide-set eyes are kind and suggest quite correctly his co-operative and engaging character.

Clydesdale

ORIGIN Scotland
ENVIRONMENT
BLOOD
USES
HEIGHT 16.2–17.0 hh (1.67–1.73 m)
COLOURS Commonly bay, but also black, brown, grey, roan, and chestnut

BLACK	BROWN	CHESTNUT	GREY	BAY	ROAN

The Clydesdale proved a popular heavy draught breed and was extensively exported from his native Scotland. He is described by the Clydesdale Horse Society as being 'handsome, weighty, and powerful, with a gaiety of carriage and outlook…. The impression given being of quality and weight rather than grossness and bulk.'

ORIGINS

The Clydesdale as a recognized breed came into being in the 19th century but was most likely descended from a type of draught horse being developed during the 18th century. During that time a horse breeder called John Paterson from Lochyloch in Scotland, bought a big black Flemish horse from England to cross with the local native stock of pack horse. The stallion stamped his stock well and the Lochyloch bloodline became much in demand. The horses he bred were similar to the modern Clydesdale and were often marked with a lot of white. In 1808, a stallion called Thompsons Black Horse, or Glancer, was in popular use and he was believed to be of Lochyloch blood. Glancer can be traced in many Clydesdale pedigrees. Shire blood (*see* pp 164–65) was also used to create what we now recognize as the Clydesdale. Often referred to as Scotland's Shire Horse, the Clydesdale is less massively built and is a better mover than the Shire. In 1877, the Clydesdale Horse Society was launched but even

DRIVING HORSE The Clydesdale's gaiety of character and movement makes him a popular choice as a driving horse. Thanks to this, and a continuing enthusiasm for showing the breed, he has a more assured future than some of the other heavy draught breeds that have found themselves mainly unemployed since the middle of the last century.

SOUND
Clydesdales are selectively bred for good limbs and feet, giving the breed a reputation for soundness. It is acceptable for this breed to have 'cow hocks' – hocks that point inwards.

WHITE MARKS Broad, white face markings are a characteristic of the breed, along with plenty of white on the legs and often splashes of white around the belly. Big, kind eyes and big ears add to the attraction of this gentle giant.

before this large numbers of Clydesdales were being exported as far afield as America, Australia, and New Zealand. Many Clydesdales were conscripted for army use in World War I. As with all the heavy breeds, his place of power on farms and in cities was quickly usurped by tractors and lorries as the mid-19th century woke up to engine power.

CHARACTERISTICS

The Clydesdale Horse is a picture of power without bulk. His neck is longer than that of the Shire, giving him a slightly rangier look. The withers are well defined and the powerful shoulders gently sloping. An attractive characteristic of the Clydesdale, which adds to his showiness, is the abundance of white markings on the lower limbs, sometimes extending right up the legs and around the belly, and the characteristic white face. He has fine feathering on his lower limbs and round, open feet. Renowned for his soundness, the Clydesdale is currently enjoying a revival of interest and remains popular for showing, driving, farm work, and even riding.

Comtois

ORIGIN France/Switzerland
ENVIRONMENT ▲
BLOOD ⬙
USES 🐴
HEIGHT 15.0–16.0 hh (1.52–1.63 m)
COLOURS Generally chestnut, but may sometimes be brown

BROWN   CHESTNUT

The Comtois is relatively lightly built for a draught horse but has earned his reputation over the centuries for hardiness, strength, and agility. These qualities are a result of the rugged environment in which the breed evolved: the Jura mountains on the French/Swiss border. This sociable breed has a distinctive appearance characterized by a flaxen mane and tail.

ORIGINS

The Comtois is thought to descend from cob-type horses brought to the region by settlers from northern Germany. They were employed extensively from the 16th century onwards as cavalry and artillery horses. During the 19th century the breed was further developed by introducing blood from Percheron and Boulonnais draught horses, as well as the Norman Cob. In the early 20th century Ardennais. blood was also added to produce a stronger horse. The Comtois is still used for draught work, particularly for timber hauling in the pine forests of the mountainous Massif Central, in the hilly vineyards of the Arbois area of France, and often for pulling sleighs in ski resorts.

CHARACTERISTICS

Although nothing like as heavily built as many draught breeds, the Comtois has a stocky, powerful body and very well-muscled hindquarters. They

QUICK ACTION The Comtois' light, quick action made him a popular choice as a cavalry horse. The breed was used extensively for cavalry and artillery by both Louis XIV and Napoleon.

FLAXEN MANE The most common coat colour is any shade of chestnut. The flaxen mane and tail are thick and shaggy, although the legs are clean and not feathered.

have particularly strong feet and legs, but they do not carry any feather on their limbs. They are exceptionally surefooted and well balanced – attributes that have helped to keep them employed in hilly, rugged conditions where they can still triumph over motor power.

As a breed they are renowned for their good temperament and 'trainability'. Though mainly used for draught and carriage work, some are also ridden.

Døle Gudbrandsdal

ORIGIN Norway
ENVIRONMENT
BLOOD
USES
HEIGHT 14.2–15.2 hh (1.47–1.57 m)
COLOURS Predominantly brown, black, or chestnut, but may be bay, grey, or dun

The Døle Gudbrandsdal, or Døle Horse, is a native of Norway. These horses have ancient origins but it was only as recently as 1967 that a breed society – the National Døle Horse Association – and a state breeding programme was established. This was done in an effort to revive and maintain interest in these horses.

BLACK　BROWN　CHESTNUT　DUN　GREY　BAY

ORIGINS AND CHARACTERISTICS

The breed comes from, and is named after, the Gudbrandsdal valley, which runs between the North Sea coast and the region of Oslo, the Norwegian capital.

Due to the similarities between the two breeds, it is likely that he descended from the Friesian Horse (*see* p 216), which has been known of since Roman times. Other Dutch breeds may well have been used as the breed evolved.

There are two types of Døle horse: the heavy draught, which is known as the Gudbrandsdal, and the Døle Trotter, a lighter more refined animal. In recent times the two have been interbred and there is little to differentiate them today.

Since the inception of the breed society, stallions have to be tested and graded before being given a breeding licence. The draught horse is tested for his pulling power and his trotting ability. The lower limbs are x-rayed and if any defects show up the horse is not allowed to be used for breeding. The horses were traditionally used as pack animals and for farm work. Although one of the smallest draught breeds, the Gudbrandsdal is renowned for its great pulling power and stamina.

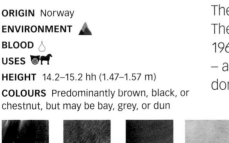

HANDSOME HORSE They have short, strong legs, with dense bone, and some feathering. The mane and tail are full and luxuriant.

Dutch Draught

ORIGIN Holland
ENVIRONMENT
BLOOD ⬦
USES 🐴
HEIGHT 16.0–16.3 hh (1.63–1.70 m)
COLOURS Usually chestnut, grey, or bay, but sometimes black or roan

The Dutch Draught was only established as a breed in 1914 with the formation of the Royal Dutch Draught Society. It is the largest and heaviest of the Dutch breeds and is popular at agricultural shows. To be entered in the breed's stud book each horse is tested and assessed for conformation, fertility, action, and type.

| BLACK | CHESTNUT | GREY | BAY | ROAN |

ORIGINS
The breed developed from crosses between the Brabant Draught Horse (*see* pp 134–35) and native horses, as well as occasional outcrosses to the Ardennais (*see* pp 128–29). They were bred for heavy agricultural work and their strength, stamina, and docility made them popular with the farmers of the Zeeland and North Brabant regions, where the arable farms are based on heavy marine clay.

CHARACTERISTICS
The horse is of quite massive build, with a short, thick body and wide, prominent neck. The loins and hindquarters are heavily muscled, and slope quite steeply from the croup down to the tail. He has quite a small, straight head and lightly feathered legs. Despite his size he has an active walk and easy trot.

The breed matures early and is long-lived and a good-doer, making him a good investment as a workhorse for farmers.

DOCKED TAIL The tail of the Dutch Draught was traditionally docked, a controversial practice that is now widely banned.

Freiberger

ORIGIN Switzerland
ENVIRONMENT 🏔
BLOOD 🜄
USES 🐎 🐎 🐎
HEIGHT 14.3–15.2 hh (1.50–1.57 m)
COLOURS Black, brown, chestnut, or bay

The Freiberger is a relatively light-framed draught horse. His smaller frame and more athletic ability has made him an adaptable animal who finds himself put to a variety of uses. Bred originally for farm work in mountainous regions, he is tough, agile, and surefooted.

BLACK   BROWN   CHESTNUT   BAY

ORIGINS

The Freiberger is named after an area of mountains in the Jura region of Switzerland. He was developed in the 19th century to suit the agricultural and transport needs of the farmers in this mountainous region. He developed from crossing a variety of breeds: the native cold bloods refined by French, English, Belgian, and Arab blood. Today, there is a controlled breeding programme run by the Swiss National Stud at Avenches – the care and breeding of the horses being sponsored by the Swiss government. The breed is performance-tested for a variety of traits from driving and riding attributes, to general behaviour. The requirement is for a docile but active and reliable horse.

CHARACTERISTICS

The mixture of blood in the Freiberger's pedigree means there is some variation in the appearance of the breed but generally he should appear compact, well muscled, and stocky. The head should be neat and have a slightly concave profile. The hindquarters are thick, cobby, and well developed. The legs are relatively short with good joints, plenty of bone, and tough hooves. The legs carry very little feather.

RIDING HORSE The Freiberger is a calm and versatile horse, with well-balanced paces and a steady character, which makes him popular for riding.

VERSATILE HORSE The Freiberger is an active, agile, surefooted horse, well suited to light draught work. He is often used by the Swiss army for patrol work and as an artillery horse.

Irish Draught

ORIGIN Ireland
ENVIRONMENT
BLOOD 💧
USES 🐎 🏇 🐴
HEIGHT 15.2–16.3 hh (1.57–1.70 m)
COLOURS All solid colours

| BLACK | BROWN | CHESTNUT | GREY | BAY |

Irish men, women, and their horses are renowned for being great 'crossers of the country'; Irish horses, and the Irish Draught crosses in particular, being among the most sought-after hunters anywhere in the world. The influence of the Irish Draught has been hugely beneficial in the development of sports horses.

ORIGINS

The ancestors of the Irish Draught breed were brought to Ireland by the Normans as war horses during the Anglo-Norman invasion of 1172. These were probably French and Flemish draught horses that were then bred with the smaller native stock. Some refinement was added in the 16th century with the introduction of Andalucian and, possibly, Arab blood. The early Irish Draught was smaller on average than the horse we know today, and heavier in stature. He had to be a multi-purpose beast, able to work on the farm, either ploughing or carting, and able to be ridden when necessary, which to an Irishman, meant hunting.

The horse became renowned for his common sense and 'sixth leg' when crossing the country, making him a comfortable and safe mount.

THOROUGHBRED

The Great Famine of 1845–49, followed by a general agricultural recession, saw thousands of these horses slaughtered. In the 1900s, when agriculture had begun to thrive again in Ireland, Clydesdales and

BRUSH WITH EXTINCTION The pure Irish Draught was in danger of dying out by the middle of the 20th century. The Irish Draught Horse Society was formed in 1976 to preserve and promote the breed.

SHOW HORSES The Irish Draught horse was improved by the introduction of plenty of Thoroughbred blood in the late 18th century, and again in the early 20th century.

STRONG FEATURES The head is generous in size and outlook, the eyes set well apart with a bold expression. A Roman nose is acceptable but there should be no other signs of coarseness.

Shires were imported from Great Britain to meet the demand for farm horses. Some of these were bred to the remaining Irish Draughts, which led to a trend towards a heavier animal again. The swift intervention of Thoroughbred blood improved the breed again. The Government supported the breeding of the Irish Draught horse with subsidies and, in 1917, a stud book was opened. The need for horses on the land was by now waning and the Irish Draught was used to great effect as a crossbreed to produce sports horses of international ability. The Irish Draught Horse Society was formed in 1976, and there are now breed associations and stud books in many other countries.

CHARACTERISTICS

The Irish Draught should present a picture of strength refined by quality. Despite their tremendous power they must be free-moving and agile. The Irish Draught has plenty of strong, clean bone; large knees and hocks; short strong cannon bones; and the feet of a hunter and not a carthorse!

Italian Heavy Draught

ORIGIN Italy
ENVIRONMENT 🌱
BLOOD 💧
USES 🐂
HEIGHT 15.0–16.0 hh (1.52–1.63 m)
COLOURS Predominantly chestnut, but also grey, bay, and roan

CHESTNUT   GREY   BAY   ROAN

The Italian Heavy Draught, also known as the Italian Agricultural Horse, has seen various changes to type during his development as farming needs and practices have changed. The breed standard we recognize today began to evolve during the early to mid-20th century, and a stud book was opened as recently as 1961.

ORIGINS

The Italian Heavy Draught originated in Ferrara, in North Italy, during the mid- to late 19th century. Hackney and Arab blood was mixed with local stock to produce a lightweight, active farm horse. When the need arose for a heavier horse for farm and artillery work, Percheron and Boulonnais bloodlines were used. But the result still didn't quite suit the purposes of Italian farmers who valued agility as well as strength. In the 1920s strong outcrossing to the lighter Breton Postier produced today's type. The brand mark on the quarters of registered Italian Heavy Draught horses shows a ladder within a shield.

CHARACTERISTICS

Many of the traits of the Breton (*see* pp 136–37) are still evident in the Italian Heavy Draught. The head features a broad forehead, large eyes and nostrils, but tapers to a refined nose. The ears are small but mobile. The neck is thick, short, and cresty, which, along with the high-set tail, creates a jaunty look. There is depth through the girth; the back is short and strong.

MIXED BAG Despite quite a mixed bag of breeding, the end result is an attractive package of a compact, well-balanced stamp of horse. The common colouring of chestnut with a flaxen mane and tail is illustrated here.

GENTLE NATURE The breed is well known for its kind, docile temperament. It is cheap to keep, which contributes to its popularity.

Japanese Draught Horse

ORIGIN Japan
ENVIRONMENT
BLOOD ◊
USES 🐴
HEIGHT 14.2 hh (1.47 m)
COLOURS Usually chestnut, but also brown

Domesticated horses were present in Japan from as early as the 4th century AD, imported from Mongolia. Originally used as war horses, they were later employed to work the land and for transport in the late 19th century, pulling carriages and street cars. Heavy-horse racing is still popular in some rural areas.

BROWN   CHESTNUT

ORIGINS AND CHARACTERISTICS

The first Japanese horses were very small and were used in warfare and for transport. Oxen worked the land until the Meiji Era (1868–1912), when the government encouraged the breeding of larger horses and ran training classes for farmers. Belgium and Breton draught horses were among those imported to use in the development of the Japanese Draught horse. Although it is less important in agriculture now, it still has a place in Japan. For example, in the colourful Chagu Chagu Umakko Festival nearly 100 decorated draught horses are ridden by children, from the village of Takizawa to the city of Morioka in northern Honshu.

MARE AND FOAL The development of modern agricultural horse breeds was largely based on the island of Hokkaido, where progress was initially hampered by indigenous wolves, wild dogs, and bears that preyed on the foals.

Jutland

ORIGIN Denmark

ENVIRONMENT

BLOOD

USES

HEIGHT 15.0–16.0 hh (1.52–1.63 m)

COLOURS Generally chestnut with flaxen mane and tail

BLACK	CHESTNUT	BAY	ROAN

The sturdy Jutland horse has been bred on the Jutland Peninsula, in Denmark, for over a thousand years. He proved an ideal mount for the heavily armoured knights of the Middle Ages. The Vikings brought similar-looking horses to Britain during their raids in the 9th and 10th centuries.

ORIGINS AND CHARACTERISTICS

The main influence in the development of the Jutland was the Suffolk Punch (*see* pp 166–67). In 1860, the Suffolk Punch stallion Oppenheim LXII was imported to Denmark and used on the existing mares. This strong influence shows in the powerful but 'roly-poly' body and in the common dark-chestnut colouring.

The Jutland has short, strong legs and a quick, free action. He is heavily feathered – a feature that breeders strive to reduce to avoid the risk of mud fever. The shoulders are heavily muscled and the chest is very broad. He is a tireless worker with an exceptionally tractable nature and is still used for city draught work.

CITY HORSE Today there is limited use for the horse on the land but they are still paraded at shows and are ideal for draught work in a variety of situations.

Muraközi

ORIGIN Hungary
ENVIRONMENT
BLOOD ○
USES 🐎🐴
HEIGHT 16.0 hh (1.63 m)
COLOURS Commonly chestnut or grey, but also occasionally bay

CHESTNUT	GREY	BAY

This medium-sized draught horse takes its name from its home town of Muraköz in South Hungary. The breed was developed to be used on the farms along the Mura river. A small breeding colony is maintained by the Farmers' Association of Valicka Valley.

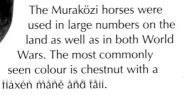

ORIGINS AND CHARACTERISTICS

A relatively new breed, which was developed in the late 19th/early 20th century. Native Hungarian mares (*Mur-Insulan*) were bred to Ardennais, Percheron, and Noriker stallions, as well as some light, half-bred Hungarian stallions. The result was a strong, but swift-moving workhorse with a kind and willing temperament.

The Muraközi horses were used in large numbers on the land as well as in both World Wars. The most commonly seen colour is chestnut with a flaxen mane and tail.

DEEP BODIED A short but deep-bodied horse with clean legs. the Muraközi has a broad head with generous, intelligent eyes, and large ears.

Murgese

ORIGIN Italy
ENVIRONMENT
BLOOD ○
USES 🐎🐴🏇
HEIGHT 14.2–16.3 hh (1.50–1.67 m)
COLOURS Usually black, but also occasionally grey

BLACK	GREY

The Murgese is a light draught and riding horse from the Murge area of Italy. Usually black but also grey, it originated from Oriental horses crossed with local horses. A herd book was set up in 1926, in a government-backed effort to save this rare breed.

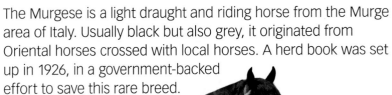

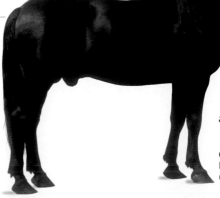

ORIGINS AND CHARACTERISTICS

This striking horse has a mixed ancestry dating back to the 15th century. It has a reputation for being an easily managed farm horse; and it was highly valued for its rustic nature, which was necessary for its survival in its harsh local environment. The modern Murgese is as comfortable under saddle as it is in harness. It has a robust build. The chest is broad and the limbs are solid. The forehead is wide and is often fully covered by the characteristic flowing forelocks. The eyes are kind and expressive.

GOOD QUALITY The Murgese is solidly built but well proportioned with a good degree of quality about him. The limbs are free of feather.

MURAKÖZI These powerful horses formed the backbone of the Hungarian farming industry during the 20th century, prized for their quickness and versatility. They are still used for agricultural purposes today in some regions.

Noriker

ORIGIN Austria
ENVIRONMENT
BLOOD 🜄
USES 🐴 🐎 🐎
HEIGHT 15.3–17.0 hh (1.60–1.73 m)
COLOURS Usually dark liver chestnut with flaxen mane and tail

Also known as the Noric, this ancient breed takes its name from the Roman province of Noricum, which covered the area that is now Austria. The Noriker is an attractive light draught horse, renowned for his surefootedness – a result of the mountainous environment he evolved and worked in.

| BLACK | BROWN | CHESTNUT | GREY | ROAN |

RIDDEN NORIKERS, GERMANY The modern Noriker is a particularly good-tempered horse used for riding, farm, and carriage work. He has a reputation for toughness and willingness to work hard. His mountain environment has ensured that he is a good mover with a particularly active trot.

ORIGINS

It was thought that the forefather of the Noriker was the heavy war horse of Thessalonica, in Macedonia, and that these horses were taken to Noricum by the Romans. Another theory is that a small band of wild horses existing in the Alps migrated along the Apennines into Italy, where they were crossed with Oriental horses to produce the Italian war horse.

During the 1500s the breeding of the Noriker was managed by the wealthy Salzberg monasteries, which had their own stud farms. They introduced Italian and Spanish bloodlines, although many other breeders resisted these outcrossings – a policy that allowed the Pinzgauer Noriker to retain the purest bloodlines. This strain of the breed (there were four strains at one time) came from the remote valleys of Pinzgau, Pangau, and Lungau and was chosen to form the foundation of the modern Noriker breed. In 1803, the state had taken over the breeding programme for the Noriker but, once again, traditional breeders evaded the introduction of Clydesdale, Holsteiner, and Norman bloodlines. As the demand for a faster-maturing, more manageable horse grew, however, they finally relented and used Belgium blood to achieve these aims.

CHARACTERISTICS

Although relatively small, the Noriker is very strong and exceptionally surefooted, having adapted to mountainous regions. He has good sloping shoulders; a short, strong back; and, for a draught breed, relatively long but strong limbs. His legs are lightly feathered. He has a calm nature and is renowned for his bravery. He has a relatively small head with a distinctive long, curly mane.

CHESTNUT COLOUR A common coat colour is this striking dark liver chestnut with a flaxen – and always curly – mane and tail. Too much white on the head or limbs is not considered desirable.

HIGH STANDARDS The breeding of the Noriker is now carefully monitored. To be accepted the horses are performance tested for the ability to haul weight and for the quality of their walk and trot. There are also minimum measurements for bone, height, and chest size that must be met.

Norman Cob

ORIGIN France
ENVIRONMENT
BLOOD
USES
HEIGHT 15.3–16.3 hh (1.60–1.70 m)
COLOURS Generally chestnut, bay, or brown, but may be grey or roan

Normandy in France is a famous breeding area for horses and is home to two particularly famous studs, Le Pin and Saint Lô. Both studs continue to breed the popular Norman Cob who, although used for draught work, is not really in the same heavyweight class as the other draught breeds.

| BROWN | CHESTNUT | GREY | BAY | ROAN |

ORIGINS AND CHARACTERISTICS

The Norman Cob has ancient origins, descending from hardy little horses, called Bidets, which were brought from Asia by the Celts, through Russia and into France. During Roman times the Bidet was crossed with the heavy pack mares that were used by the Roman legions and the result was a middle-sized, powerful work horse that was the forefather of the Norman Cob. The horse was widely employed as a war horse.

During the 16th and 17th centuries, the horse was refined using first Barb and Arabian horses and, a century later, Norfolk Roadster and Thoroughbred blood. The result was a mixture of types of horse, some suitable as cavalry mounts and others more suited to light draught work. In the early 20th century the two were distinguished by docking the tails of the draught types. They were given the name Cob as they looked similar to the dual-purpose English Cob. They have a powerful, squarish build with a thick neck and a kindly, expressive head. They are equally comfortable under saddle or in harness.

STOCKY FRAME The Norman Cob has a powerful stocky frame. His tail is high-set, and his legs are short and thickly muscled on the second thigh. There is light feathering on the heels.

GOOD PACES A characteristic of the breed is his particularly good paces, his trot being free and active. He is still popular as a carriage horse and is still used to work the land in the La Manche region of Normandy.

North Swedish Horse

ORIGIN Sweden

ENVIRONMENT

BLOOD

USES

HEIGHT 15.0–15.2 hh (1.52–1.57 m)

COLOURS Commonly black or brown, but may also be chestnut or dun

BLACK	BROWN	CHESTNUT	DUN

The North Swedish Horse is a hardy light draught horse, suited to the forestry work in which they are often employed. Quick to mature, they start work at three years old. The breed originated from a mixture of Scandinavian breeds, with Døle Gudbrandsdals (*see* p 141) from Norway being a particular influence.

ORIGINS
The breed's main purpose was – and still is – in forestry so a strong but agile, and not overly large, horse was sought. During the 19th century outcrosses produced a light stamp of horse. Towards the end of the 19th century, the availability of heavier machinery fuelled a move towards a heavier horse. Heavy draught breeds such as Clydesdales were used. To avoid the risk of the breed dying out a stud book was started in 1909, followed by the formation of the North Swedish Association in 1924, with its strict selection criteria.

CHARACTERISTICS
The head is wedge-shaped and the neck is muscular. The back is long but muscular and the shoulders are well placed. The legs are well proportioned, with broad joints and strong tendons. Movement is energetic and rhythmic.

ENERGETIC ACTION Despite not being massive, the North Swedish Horse has immense strength in his neck and shoulders. His legs are short and thick, with some feathering, and his feet – an indicator of soundness – are broad and strong.

Percheron

ORIGIN France

ENVIRONMENT 🌾

BLOOD 💧

USES 🐎 🐎🐎 🐎🐎

HEIGHT 15.2–17.0 hh (1.57–1.73 m)

COLOURS Predominantly dapple grey or black, but occasionally chestnut, bay, or roan

| BLACK | CHESTNUT | GREY | BAY | ROAN |

The Percheron, despite his massive size, was greatly influenced as a breed by the delicate – by comparison – Arab horse (*see* pp 184–87). Similarly, Arab influence was important in the development of the Boulonnais (*see* pp 132–33) and both these breeds reflect a combination of size, strength, and quality.

ORIGINS

The breed developed in Le Perche in the south of Normandy. It is thought that he descends from the heavy war horse that carried the knights of Charles Martel who defeated the Muslims at Poitiers in 732AD. Whether or not this was the case, this defeat of the Muslims delivered into the hands of the French a large number of Barb and Arab horses. These were bred to the heavy horses and a further influx of Arab blood followed the First Crusade in 1099. Normandy itself has long been an important horse-breeding region

and, during the 18th century, Arab stallions were again made available to local breeders by the stud at Le Pin. Two particularly influential Arab sires were Godolphin and Gallipoly, the latter siring one of the most important foundation Percheron stallions, Jean le Blanc, around 1830.

CHARACTERISTICS

The Arab gave to the Percheron great soundness and stamina, as well as the attractive refined head, good action, and clean legs. These qualities, combined with his size and strength, made him a popular draught horse, not only in his native France but also around the world, with America and Canada proving to be a huge market for the breed. They were used for farm work, riding, and carriage work. Sadly, Percherons served in their thousands in World War I.

The Percheron has a particularly beautiful head for such a massive horse. He has a broad forehead; large, dark, expressive eyes; large but fine ears; and large, open nostrils. The neck is long and

POLICE HORSE Not an obvious choice for a riding horse perhaps, but it is easy to see the temptation: his good conformation, particularly through the withers, shoulder and neck, allow him to carry a rider well. He makes a formidable police mount.

gracefully arched and set well onto large, sloping shoulders.

The back is short and strong, there is great depth through the girth and his ribs are well sprung. His hindquarters are well sloped and have good length. So many attributes contribute to his open, free paces, which help make him such an elegant horse. He is sometimes crossed with the Thoroughbred to produce a quality heavyweight hunter.

REFINED POWER The Percheron presents a picture of refined power. He has none of the obvious coarseness about him that is seen in some of the other draught breeds. His amenable temperament and adaptability to different climates made him a hugely popular export.

BIG IN AMERICA Although the breed is predominantly grey, the black Percheron found great favour in North America, where the large, heavier stamp of horse was preferred.

ADAPTABLE GIANT The adaptable powerhouse that is the Percheron has found work in many spheres. He has served in war, both in ancient and modern times, and is used as a riding horse, as well as a farm and carriage horse.

Poitevin

ORIGIN France
ENVIRONMENT
BLOOD
USES
HEIGHT 15.2–16.2 hh (1.57–1.67 m)
COLOURS Usually dun

BLACK   DUN   GREY

The poor old Poitevin breed seems to have very little going for it in its own right in these modern times. A coarse-looking horse with slow reactions, it has found a niche – albeit a small one – in mule breeding! Crossed with the Baudet de Poitou Jackass, the result is the Poitevin Mule.

ORIGINS

The Poitevin has its origins in the heavy draught breeds that were brought to the Poitou region in the 17th century to drain this marshland region. The original mix was mainly Dutch, Danish, and Norwegian draught breeds bred to the native marshland mares. In his homeland he is rather more favourably described than by the casual observer. The romantic description of the French is that the Poitevin is a reflection of his birth place: a marshland based on a heavy, mineral-rich, marine clay, which dries to bone hard in the summer and is a saturated swamp in the winter. They say this makes him 'the son of the sea wind, the land, and water'.

CHARACTERISTICS

A realistic description of the horse is a lot less subtle, although it is only a question of not having the most refined physical attributes. As a work horse on the marshes he obviously served his masters well. He has a long, heavy head with a thickset jaw, topped by big long ears. The neck and back are long, but he has the wide chest of a workhorse. He has thick, strong legs with large joints

WINDSWEPT LOOK The head of the Poitevin cannot really be described as beautiful, but it is testimony to his character (albeit ponderous) that he has been put to the hardest work in the past and served man well.

which can be a bit fleshy. He has very big, flat feet – no bad thing for the inhabitant of a marsh. The mane and tail are long and thick and often curly. The coat hair itself is also thick and coarse, and in the winter grows very long. The legs carry a lot of hair, which is often curly around the knees and fetlocks. To top it all, his action and reactions are slow and ponderous.

MULE BREEDING

The Poitevin seemed to be heading towards extinction (and is still very much endangered) but he found a role in the production of mules. Poitevin mares are bred to the large

RUNNING OUT OF OPTIONS The options of this foal when it matures are sadly limited. The mares still have a job of work in the breeding of mules, but for most others their destiny will now be the meat market.

Baudet de Poitou Jackass donkeys to produced the Poitevin mule. These mules are renowned for their strength and versatility, having the strength to carry out the work of draught horses over terrain that a typical draught horse would not be able to handle.

Poitevin Mules were used in large numbers across Europe and America, some even being exported to Russia. Up until, and during, World War I, the American army took large numbers of the Poitevin mules. After the war demand dropped away but there has been a small revival in recent years. Sadly, the only other market for the Poitevin himself is for meat.

BAD HAIR DAY The dun and grey colouring is commonly found in the Poitevin. The mares clearly illustrate the general 'hairiness' of the breed.

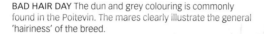

Polish Draught

ORIGIN Poland
ENVIRONMENT
BLOOD
USES
HEIGHT 15.0–15.3 hh (1.52–1.60 m)
COLOURS Usually chestnut; sometimes bay or brown

BROWN   CHESTNUT   BAY

Also known as the Sokolsky, the Polish Draught was developed through crossings between the Brabant (*see* pp 134–35), the Ardennais (*see* pp 128–29), the Døle Gudbrandsdal (*see* p 141), and Anglo-Norman stock. The result was a versatile draught and farm animal of great strength but without excessive heaviness.

ORIGINS AND CHARACTERISTICS

This is quite a new breed, having been established for about one hundred years. The relatively large head has a straight profile; large, kind eyes; and alert ears. The neck is powerful, and quite long. The shoulders are well put together with a reasonable slope, which accounts for the breed's free, energetic action. The girth is deep, and the back is short and straight. He has strong legs with short cannon bones and little or no feathering.

CARRIAGE HORSES
Polish Draught Horses are tough, with great stamina, and an excellent forward-going gait – characteristics that have ensured their popularity as carriage horses.

Russian Heavy Draught

ORIGIN Russia
ENVIRONMENT
BLOOD
USES
HEIGHT 15.0 hh (1.52 m)
COLOURS Predominantly chestnut, but also brown and bay

BROWN   CHESTNUT   BAY

Russia had some well-organized breeding-programmes in the late 1800s with the aims of producing a relatively small and fast draught horse as well as the more typical large draught types. The result was the cheap-to-keep and easy-to-manage Russian Heavy Draught. Ardennais (*see* pp 128–29) bloodlines had a major influence.

ORIGINS AND CHARACTERISTICS

The foundations of the Russian Heavy Draught were native Ukrainian breeds, the Ardennais, and, to a lesser degree, the Brabançon and the Orlov Trotter. The breed was nearly lost in World War I, but breeding stock was isolated and moved to various studs where it was revitalized. Now widespread through Russia, the Russian Heavy Draught is attractive with a refined head and a powerful neck, and an amenable personality.

COMPACT BUILD
The Russian Heavy Draught is commonly chestnut with a flaxen mane and tail. He is compact but immensely strong.

Schleswig Heavy Draught

ORIGIN Germany
ENVIRONMENT
BLOOD ⬦
USES 🐎 🐎
HEIGHT 15.2–16.0 hh (1.57–1.63 m)
COLOURS Usually chestnut, but also bay and grey

| CHESTNUT | GREY | BAY |

The horse originates from Schleswig-Holstein in north Germany, a region bordering on Denmark. The Jutland Horse (*see* p 148), from Denmark, provided the foundation stock for the Schleswig Heavy Draught, which was bred to meet demand for a medium-size draught horse to be used in forestry and for pulling carriages and trams.

ORIGINS

In the early 19th century, this horse's development was based mainly on the Jutland and crossbreeding to the Thoroughbred (*see* pp 284–87) and the Yorkshire Coach Horse. More selective breeding continued using Jutland bloodlines, particularly the Munkadel line, and it was officially recognized as a new breed in 1888.

In 1891 the Society of Schleswig Horse Breeding Clubs was founded. The horse was used in large numbers pulling buses and trams as well as for forestry work. World War I greatly reduced the breed's numbers and quality but from the 1940s onwards, efforts were made to improve it, using Boulonnais (*see* pp 132–33), Breton (*see* pp 136–37), and Suffolk Punch (*see* pp 166–69) blood.

CHESTNUT COAT The Schleswig is very similar to his forefather the Jutland, especially in the chestnut coat colouring with flaxen mane and tail, and in the feathering on the legs.

Although still used for forestry work, the city roles have been lost and numbers have fallen accordingly. Today, the German government helps support the breed.

CHARACTERISTICS

The head is well proportioned but slightly plain, with sharp alert ears and a small but kind eye. The body can be a little long but has great strength through the neck and shoulders, and a good depth of girth.

Shire Horse

ORIGIN United Kingdom
ENVIRONMENT 🌾
BLOOD 💧
USES 🐴
HEIGHT 16.2–18.0+ hh (1.67–1.83+ m)
COLOURS Commonly black, but also brown, grey, and bay

BLACK   BROWN   GREY   BAY

The Shire Horse is the largest of the heavy horses in the UK. With his massive size and weight he is truly a gentle giant, much loved for his docile, generous nature. His name derives from the fact that he was bred in the middle 'shires' of England: Lincolnshire, Leicestershire, Staffordshire, and Derbyshire.

ORIGINS

Picture an armoured knight upon his charger, and you will find yourself looking at the forefather of the Shire. The Medieval Great Horse came to England with William the Conqueror in 1066. He was bred to be strong enough to carry an armoured knight complete with heavy weapons, and yet have the agility to move out of danger or 'in for the kill' during the confusion of battle.

The introduction of firearms saw the end of his use as a war horse and his strength was put to use in heavy draught work, ploughing the land or pulling carts and wagons. During the 17th century, Flemish blood was added to the mix as a result of Dutch workers bringing their own draught horses to the east of England. As time went on another import, the Friesian, was crossbred to give the emerging 'Black Horse', as he was known, better movement. In the Midlands of England, more selective breeding led by Robert Bakewell resulted in the Shire Horse that we recognize today.

STILL POPULAR

Today, Shire Horses are still used for beer and bread deliveries, and even for street cleaning and rubbish collecting. Recently, the Shire Horse Society has been encouraged by the promising results of a feasibility study to reintroduce the pulling power of

FARM WORK Shire Horses are still used on some farms and are given the chance to show off their working skills at ploughing matches. The horse brasses seen decorating the harness were once believed to ward off evil.

FOAL A Shire foal can grow up to over 18 hh, and will weigh approximately 1,000 kg (2,205 lb) when fully mature. A resurgence of interest in the use of genuine horse power means he may well grow up to have a serious job to do.

MAMMOTH Shires are famed for their massive build. The tallest horse ever recorded was a Shire called Sampson. He was born in 1846 in Bedfordshire, England, and grew to stand at 21.2 hh (2.18 m), weighing 1,524 kg (1½ tons). As he grew he was renamed Mammoth!

the Shire for both commercial and leisure barges on canals. Also, the Shire's strength and size make him a popular cross with Thoroughbred mares to produce an impressive weight-carrying riding horse or hunter.

CHARACTERISTICS

The Shire's average height is 17.2 hh (1.8 m) and his girth measurement can vary from 1.8 m (6 ft) to 2.4 m (8 ft). The head is long and lean, with a slightly Roman nose and large, kind eyes. He has a good length of neck, set into deep shoulders that must be wide enough to carry a harness collar. His back is short, strong, and muscular, especially over the loins. The hindquarters are long and sweeping, and very well muscled. Although he should be broad across the chest and hindquarters, his hocks must be carried quite close together. His lower legs should display the characteristic feathers, which should be fine, straight, and silky. As with any workhorse his feet should be, and generally are, very strong, wide, and well shaped.

Suffolk Punch

ORIGIN United Kingdom
ENVIRONMENT 🌾
BLOOD ⬡
USES 🐴 🐎
HEIGHT 16.0–16.3 hh (1.63–1.70 m)
COLOURS Only chestnut, seven shades of which are recognized by the breed society

The Suffolk Punch is Britain's oldest heavy-horse breed and his 'roly-poly' shape makes him an easily recognized and very endearing horse. All Suffolk Punch horses are 'chesnut' in colour, the word being spelt without the first 't' in all Suffolk breed records.

ORIGINS

The Suffolk Punch originated in East Anglia, in England. A unique feature of the breed is the fact that every Suffolk Punch can trace its lineage back to a single stallion: Thomas Crisp's horse of Ufford, which was foaled in the 1760s. The exact origins of this particular stallion are not known but it is highly likely that the Flanders Horse, brought to East Anglia by Dutch workers in the 17th century to help to drain the fenlands, was instrumental in its development. Also likely to have had some influence on the development of the breed is the Norfolk Roadster, a popular trotting horse that was bred at the time.

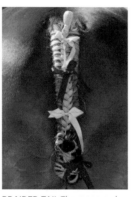

BRAIDED TAIL The mane and tail of the Suffolk Punch are traditionally braided. The tail, as with most draught breeds, is plaited or tied up to keep it out of the way of the mud and machinery.

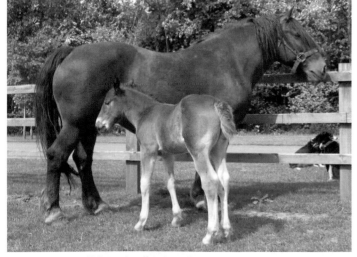

RARE BREED The Suffolk Punch suffered greatly as a result of the mechanization of farming. In 1966 only nine foals were born. Great efforts have been made to restore its numbers with the establishment of several breeding programmes, but it remains rare.

CHARACTERISTICS

The horse was bred to work the heavy clay soils of East Anglia, so a strong, but clean-legged animal was needed. The breed is instantly recognizable by its colour (any one of seven shades of chesnut) and its shape. It has an adorably big, round body set on relatively short legs. The head is large, with small ears. The renowned pulling power of the horse starts with the deep neck set well onto long, low, muscular shoulders. The low set of the shoulders is a characteristic that has been carefully retained by breeders. The quarters have great width and strength but the hind legs must be close set so that the horse can walk between rows of crops without causing excessive damage.

INTELLIGENT HEAD Suffolks have intelligent-looking heads with active ears, and powerful necks that are clean-cut at the throat. The mane is decorated for show purposes.

HOT TO TROT The Suffolk Punch is also a good trotter, making him a popular choice for carriage as well as draught work; testimony to the Norfolk Roadster and Flanders blood in his pedigree.

CHESNUT TEAM A well-matched team of three Suffolk Punches, all exhibiting the reddish-brown coat colouring that is the most common of the accepted seven shades of 'chesnut'.

Trait du Nord (French Heavy)

ORIGIN France
ENVIRONMENT
BLOOD ○
USES
HEIGHT 15.2–17.0 hh (1.57–1.73 m)
COLOURS Mainly bay or roan

The Trait du Nord was developed from the Ardennais breed and Belgian Heavy Draught Horses, and, although now declining in numbers, he is still bred in the areas around Lille, the Somme, and the Pas-de-Calais. He is taller and larger framed than the Ardennais but some regard the Trait as a strain of that breed.

| BLACK | CHESTNUT | GREY | BAY | ROAN |

ORIGINS

Despite the controversy over his pedigree, the Trait du Nord was recognized as a breed in his own right at the beginning of the 20th century and a stud book was opened in 1903. There was also some use of Boulonnais blood, which has contributed to the energy and activeness of the breed's paces.

CHARACTERISTICS

The horse has immense strength and stamina and a particularly good trot. His head is relatively small with a straight profile and is set on a short,

ALL ROUNDER His easy-going, gentle nature has made him a versatile horse, used for farm and harness work, timber hauling, and also for leisure, carriage driving, and even riding.

slightly arching, muscular neck. It has an abundant main and tail. The body is compact, and the flat withers and a relatively short, flat back lead to very muscular and powerful hindquarters. The shoulders are long and sloping and the chest is broad and deep. The legs are massive and there is substantial feathering on the lower limbs.

Vladimir Heavy Draught

ORIGIN Russia

ENVIRONMENT

BLOOD ⬦

USES 🐴 🐎

HEIGHT 15.3–16.1 hh (1.60–1.65 m)

COLOURS Usually bay but also black and chestnut

BLACK	CHESTNUT	BAY

The Vladimir is a draught horse from the provinces of Vladimir and Ivanovo, which are to the northeast of Moscow, in Russia. The breed is early maturing, being strong enough to work or to use at stud as a three-year-old. The horse has a particularly kind and gentle disposition. He has a characteristic marking on his head: a star or blaze.

ORIGINS

The breed was developed early in the 20th century. Draught stallions from Britain and France were imported to cross with the native mares. A big horse was wanted for very heavy draught work and the most influential bloodline proved to be that of the Clydesdale. There was some use of Shire, Suffolk, Cleveland Bay, Ardennais, and Pecheron but the Clydesdale (*see* pp 138–39) was used in the main. From the Clydesdale he inherited his active paces, making him popular for pulling Russian Troikas.

CHARACTERISTICS

The Vladimir is the largest of the Russian heavy horses and, as well as being early maturing, the stallions are also renowned for their good fertility rates. The breed was named and officially recognized in 1946. The head is large and long with a notably convex profile. The withers are pronounced and the neck long and arched. The back and croup are long but broad, while the chest is broad but not deep. The legs are relatively long, giving him an elegant look despite his weight and strength. The legs carry some feather and the mane and tail are luxuriant and wavy.

CLYDESDALE ANCESTRY The Vladimir is renowned for his kind and gentle temperament. He has proved to have the strength for heavy draught work without being a cumbersome beast – his active paces are a hallmark of his Clydesdale ancestry.

LIGHT HORSES

The category of light horse contains the greatest number of breeds. It is any breed, other than a heavy (draught) horse or pony, that is suitable for riding. The earliest light-horse breeds, such as the Arab and the North African Barb, provided the foundation blood for Spanish horses and the Thoroughbred. These light-boned, agile breeds were, over time, bred with native heavy horses and ponies, to produce lighter-framed horses required for riding and also carriage driving. Historically, light horses provided cavalry mounts, but by the early 20th century, mechanization of armed forces led to breeders concentrating on the sport and leisure industries.

HOT BLOOD The Arab (*see* pp 184–87) is the oldest and purest of all the horse breeds. He is one of only a handful of 'hotblood' breeds in the world. The Arab breed has had the greatest influence worldwide on the development and refinement of other breeds, including the famous Thoroughbred (*see* pp 284–87).

Akhal-Teke

ORIGIN Turkmenistan

ENVIRONMENT

BLOOD 🌢

USES 🏇 🏇 🏇

HEIGHT 14.3–16.0 hh (1.50–1.63 m)

COLOURS Commonly chestnut, but also black, dun, grey, bay, and palomino

| BLACK | CHESTNUT | DUN | GREY | BAY | PALOMINO |

The Akhal-Teke is a distinctive horse in terms of shape and colour. His coat, whatever the colour, has a truly metallic sheen to it. The horse is a picture of athleticism, although his long back and rather tubular body would be considered poor conformation by some. Like the Arab (*see* pp 184–87), he has remarkable powers of endurance.

ORIGINS

The true origins of the breed are not exactly known. Some argue that he is an older breed than the Arab, others that the Arab is the forefather of the Akhal-Teke. He closely resembles what we call Horse Type 3: one of the four sub-species of horses and ponies that had developed around the time that horses were first being domesticated.

LEGENDARY ENDURANCE In 1935, a group of Akhal-Teke horses were ridden from Ashkabad in Turkmenistan to Moscow in Russia. A distance of over 4,000 km (2,500 miles) was covered in just 84 days.

TOUGH HORSE Courage, endurance, and toughness are breed characteristics. Although the Akhal-Teke is said to have a tricky temperament, the Turkmen people obviously understood the breed well, as the horses were renowned for being devoted to their owners.

Horse Type 3 inhabited Central Asia. He stood about 14.3 hh (1.50 m), had a long, narrow body, and was well suited to the hot, arid climate of his environment. What we do know is that the Turkmen people have ridden and raced the Akhal-Teke for over 3,000 years. These horses were greatly prized and received exceptionally good care. They were wrapped in heavy blankets to protect them from the cold desert nights, and were fed a low-bulk/high-protein diet including eggs and mutton fat mixed with barley.

CHARACTERISTICS

The Akhal-Teke should represent a picture of elegance and agility. He has a fine head, with large expressive eyes and long, beautifully shaped ears. His neck is long, elegant, and high set. The back is long and the body can be tubular looking. The legs are long, slender and quite close set, but the breed is renowned for his toughness and stamina. The mane and tail are fine and silky, often with no forelock, and the coat colour carries a striking metallic sheen. This effect is due to the structure of the hairs, which have a very thin outer layer. This allows the core of the hair to act like a light-tube that dramatically reflects the light, so affording some protection from the searing desert heat. Today, the Akhal-Teke is used as a racing horse, both for speed and endurance, and also competes in jumping and dressage.

RACING BREED Akhal-Tekes were traditionally used for racing, and the sport still flourishes. However, they are also popular as riding and sports horses, particularly for dressage and showjumping.

Alter-Real

ORIGIN Portugal
ENVIRONMENT 🌾
BLOOD 🜄
USES 🐎 🐴
HEIGHT 15.0–16.0 hh (1.52–1.63 m)
COLOURS Commonly brown or bay, sometimes black

BLACK	BROWN	BAY

The Alter-Real was bred in Portugal to provide horses for High-School (dressage) work and for carriage driving. They are a strain of the Lusitano (*see* p 244), and were fortunate to survive the devastation of the Peninsular War (1808–14). Successful efforts were made in the 1940s to resurrect the Alter-Real, which retains much of its original 'noble' character.

ORIGINS

The Alter-Real takes its name from the place where it was originally bred: the royal Vila de Portel Stud in Alter do Chão, in Portugal. *Real* is Portuguese for 'royal'. The purpose of the stud was to breed an impressive horse suitable for both classical equitation and carriage driving. Starting in 1748, the horses were bred from the existing Lusitano breed but by selectively breeding for a particular stamp of horse, the Alter-Real became recognizably distinct and much in demand across the region.

The stud was devastated during the Peninsular War and its aftermath, and the Alter-Real line suffered further blows with the fall of the Portuguese monarchy in the early 20th century, which was swiftly followed by the outbreak of the two World Wars.

CHARACTERISTICS

Now bred by the state at the original Alter stud, this horse is renowned for its courage and versatility. Its elevated, extravagant paces make it well suited to High-School work. It has a small, 'noble' head and a luxuriant mane and tail, that add to the 'star' quality.

PACES The paces of the Alter-Real are typically showy with a relatively short stride but high knee action. They have a naturally high, arched neck.

BACK FROM THE BRINK The efforts of the d'Andrade family saved the breed from extinction – in the 1940s, they began a breeding programme based on a few stallions and mares that they had rescued.

American Crème

ORIGIN United States
ENVIRONMENT 🌾
BLOOD 💧
USES 🏇 🏇 🐴 🐎 🏇
HEIGHT 14.2–16.3 hh (1.47–1.70 m)
COLOURS 'Cream'

The American Crème breaks all the rules of breed and even type, as it is simply a breed defined by its colour. Ponies, light, and heavy horses can all qualify to be registered as 'Crèmes' provided they meet the colour specification. Despite the variation in animals that qualify as 'Cremes', they are generally trainable and showy.

ORIGINS AND CHARACTERISTICS

The American Crème is an offshoot of the American Albino Horse, a phenomenon started by the birth of an albino horse called Old King, in 1908. He was 15.2 hh (1.57 m), had white hair, pink skin, and dark brown eyes. He was trainable and versatile and, in 1917, was chosen by the Thompson brothers of Nebraska to be the foundation stallion for a new breed. Old King was selectively bred to Morgan mares and was successful in passing on his colour trait. By the 1970s, a register had been formed for American Albinos, now known as the American White Horse, with a division for cream horses: the American Crème Horse. There was also a French Crème Horse stud book, which closed in 2002 to allow the breed to be purely defined by colour, (now Crème Horses) rather than country. The Crème Horse must have pink-through to 'pumpkin-' (tan-) coloured skin.

CREAMY COAT COLOUR Coat hair can vary from pale ivory through to rich cream; mane- and tail-hair colour varies from white to cinnamon. Eye colour may be pale blue, pale amber, or brown.

American Saddlebred

ORIGIN United States
ENVIRONMENT 🌾
BLOOD 💧
USES 🏇 🏇 🐎 🏇
HEIGHT 15.0–16.0 hh (1.52–1.63 m)
COLOURS Black, chestnut, grey, bay, palomino, and roan

BLACK	CHESTNUT	GREY	BAY	PALOMINO	ROAN

Left in his natural state, the American Saddlebred horse is a fine riding and harness horse. He was originally bred to be a good all-purpose animal, but refinements made for the show ring, such as an unnatural tail carriage and unusually long hooves, have led to him being looked upon by some as rather artificial.

ORIGINS

In the early 19th century, settlers in the southern states of America set about breeding a horse that would be elegant but practical. He had to carry a man for many hours over rough terrain to inspect crops, he had to be smart enough to pull a carriage, and he had to be tough enough to work cattle. His main bloodlines include two pacer breeds: the now-extinct Narrangansett Pacer and the Canadian Pacer, as well as the Thoroughbred (*see* pp 284–87).

CHARACTERISTICS

He has unique paces and is trained to be either a three- or five-gait horse. Three-gait Saddlebreds work in walk, trot, and canter, with all three paces being slow, collected, and elevated. The five-gait horse also shows a high-stepping slow gait and the 'rack' – a fast, flashy four-beat gait. The hooves are grown very long and shod with heavy shoes to exaggerate the gaits.

QUALITY HEAD The head carries many of the same qualities of a Thoroughbred: cleanly defined lines, alertly pricked ears, and a proud, bold, and intelligent expression.

OUTLINE The Saddlebred's distinctive outline features a high-set, long, arched neck; a short, strong back; and a level croup. The artificially-induced tail carriage is clearly illustrated here, as are the long hooves and big, heavy shoes.

Andalucian

ORIGIN Spain
ENVIRONMENT
BLOOD
USES
HEIGHT 15.0–15.2 hh (1.52–1.57 m)
COLOURS Grey or bay

GREY   BAY

The Andalucian was, for centuries, known as the Spanish Horse. He was a much admired and coveted animal, taken as a spoil of war and used in many countries to improve the native stock. Spanish Horses were the foundation stock of many American breeds, having been taken to the Americas by the Spanish *conquistadores* in the 16th century.

ORIGINS

The Andalucian originated in southern Spain and most likely evolved through crossing North African Barbs (*see* pp 190–91) with native pony stock (possibly Sorraia Ponies, *see* p 357). Before the last Ice Age, there was a land bridge (now the Straits of Gibraltar) between North Africa and Spain, which would have made this possible. During many turbulent periods of war, the Andalucian owed its survival to the monasteries. The Carthusian monks of Jerez were particularly conscientious about maintaining the best bloodlines.

CHARACTERISTICS

The Andalucian is a handsome, proud breed, which, although not overly tall, is compact and muscular. They have great spirit and courage, but are also gentle and exceptionally trainable. The big, lofty paces and the powerful hindquarters with particularly flexible hocks make the breed adept at High-School work. They are also used for bullfighting.

GREY COLORATION Grey is the predominant colour of the breed, and the horses always have a particularly luxuriant, and often wavy, mane and tail.

Anglo-Arab

ORIGIN United Kingdom
ENVIRONMENT
BLOOD
USES
HEIGHT 15.3–16.3 hh (1.60–1.70 m)
COLOURS Brown, chestnut, or bay

BROWN   CHESTNUT   BAY

The Anglo-Arab is simply a cross between an Arab (*see* pp 184–87) and a Thoroughbred (*see* pp 284–87) with the aim of combining the best qualities of these two outstanding breeds. The Anglo-Arab bred in Britain has only these two breeds in its pedigree. The longer-established French Anglo-Arab, in its early evolvement, included other bloodlines.

ORIGINS

The breed origins of the Arab and the Thoroughbred are well reported and, given the qualities of these two famous breeds, it was only a matter of time before someone thought to cross the two together. The first 'Anglo-Arabs' were registered simply as part Arabs, although the breed is now recognized separately.

CHARACTERISTICS

The many permutations afforded by crossing and recrossing between the Thoroughbred and Arab mean that

SUCCESSFUL SPORTS HORSE The Anglo-Arab has proved to be particularly successful in the sport of three-day eventing as well as dressage.

the size and stamp of the breed varies. But generally its appearance favours that of the Thoroughbred, the profile of the head being straight as opposed to concave, with a strong body and good limbs.

The ideal Anglo-Arab should combine the Thoroughbred's greater speed and scope, with the soundness and stamina of the Arab. Having hotblood parentage on both sides, the Anglo-Arab joins the elite group of hotblood horses.

Appaloosa

ORIGIN United States
ENVIRONMENT 🌾
BLOOD 🌢
USES 🏇 🐎
HEIGHT 14.2–16.0 hh (1.47–1.63 m)
COLOURS Coloured

Spotted coat colouring has been found in horses for thousands of years; cave drawings from 20,000 years ago depicted horses with these coats. In the United States, the word 'Appaloosa' refers to a breed of spotted horses, but the word can also refer simply to the coat colour.

ORIGINS

Spotted coat coloration featured on many of the horses reintroduced to the Americas by the *conquistadores* in the 16th century, and the Appaloosa breed was developed in the 18th century by the Nez-Perce Indians. This tribe lived in Palouse country, the area that is now north Idaho and Oregon – a fertile stretch of country that includes the Palouse river. They selectively bred their horses to promote the spotted coat colouring that they so prized. The horses became known as Palouse Horses which, over time, changed to Appaloosa Horse. The defeat of the Indians by the US army in the late 19th century very nearly led to the loss of this type of horse. Many were killed in the fierce fighting; those that survived escaped to run wild. In the

INTELLIGENT BREED The Appaloosa often has a thin mane and tail, white sclera around the eye, and mottled skin, particularly around the eyes, muzzle, and genitalia. They are usually intelligent and co-operative, despite the white eye suggesting otherwise.

VARIED BREED As a breed, Appaloosas are usually strong, compact horses, although because the breed is defined by colour rather than bloodlines, they can vary tremendously both in size and shape. They are popular for Western and endurance riding as well as for general competition classes.

1920s, the breed was revived by enthusiasts breeding from the descendants of the Indian ponies.

SPOT THE DIFFERENCE

Whilst all Appaloosas have spots, there are five officially recognized coat patterns: Blanket, with a spot-free area of white over the hips; Frost, with white specks in a dark coat colour; Leopard, with a predominantly white area over the loins and hips featuring large dark spots within the white; Marble, with a mottled pattern all over the body; and Snowflake,

with a white body covered all over in dark spots, but the spots being particularly prevalent over the hips.

CHARACTERISTICS

The Appaloosa has a generally sparse tail and mane, which was encouraged to avoid snagging on thorn bushes in its native environment. White sclera around the eyes and mottling on the muzzle is also characteristic. (Too much white around the eye is considered a poor character trait by many horse people, but in the Appaloosa it is a breed requirement.) The limbs are notably strong, and the hooves are good and hard, often with distinctive vertical stripes. The Nez-Perce Indians never shod their horses.

HORSE CLUB
The Appaloosa Horse Club was formed in 1938 in Oregon, US. Their aim was to preserve and improve the Appaloosa breed as well as to act as a register for Appaloosa horses.

BLANKET SPOT There are five different Appaloosa coat patterns. This foal would be classed as a Blanket spot if this white area over his hips remains spot-free. His coat may change as he matures and, if spots appear on the white, he would be classed as a Leopard spot.

Arab

ORIGIN Middle East
ENVIRONMENT
BLOOD
USES
HEIGHT 14.2–15.0 hh (1.47–1.52 m)
COLOURS All solid colours

The Arab is the oldest and purest of all horse breeds, and also one of the most beautiful and distinctive. Believed by many to be a gift from God, 'fashioned from the desert wind', a horse that 'could fly without wings', the Arab is also the forefather of the Thoroughbred (*see* pp 284–87).

BLACK   BROWN   CHESTNUT   DUN   GREY   BAY

ORIGINS

The exact origins of the breed are unknown, but the Bedouin tribe who religiously guarded the breeding of their 'desert horse' trace him back as far as 3000BC to a mare called Baz, said to be have been captured in Yemen by Bax, 'the great-great-grandson of Noah'.

The Bedouin people put great value on their Arab mares, breeding only from the very best and passing down from generation to generation the pedigrees and dam lines that they prized the most. The Arab Horse was introduced to other parts of the world – the rest of the Middle East, North Africa, China, and Europe – as a result of the Muslim conquests, started in 600AD. By the 1700s, the Arab Horse had found his way into Asia and North America. Everywhere he went, his blood was used to refine and improve that of the native breeds.

MARENGO

A grey Arab called Marengo was the favourite charger of Napoleon Bonaparte. Marengo was captured by the British after the Battle of Waterloo in 1815. When he died, his skeleton was displayed in the National Army Museum.

CHARACTERISTICS

Arabs are generally around 15 hh (1.52 m) and are well proportioned, elegant, and athletic. Stamina and soundness were attributes valued by the nomads who nurtured this breed, and this has given them a natural edge, allowing them to excel in endurance riding. A unique skeleton defines the distinctive shape: it has 17 ribs, 5 lumbar, and 16 tail vertebrae. Others breeds have an 18–6–18 bone arrangement. The neck is arched and the head is set at an angle that allows great mobility. A unique feature of the head is the jibbah, a shield-shaped bulge between the eyes.

DISHED PROFILE The Arab's head is very distinctive. It has a broad forehead and a slightly dished profile. The nostrils are large and the eyes are set low and wide. The ears are small and may curve inwards.

ELEGANT SHAPE The Arab's back is short and concave, the loins are strong, and the croup long and level. The tail is high set and carried high and arched.

ARABS IN THE SNOW The beauty, spirit, and stamina of the Arab Horse has long been prized. As humans made their early conquests around the world, the Arab Horse made its own impact in the countries it was introduced to – always refining and improving the native stock.

Australian Stock Horse

ORIGIN Australia
ENVIRONMENT
BLOOD
USES
HEIGHT 15.0–16.3 hh (1.52–1.70 m)
COLOURS Commonly bay, but also black, brown, chestnut, dun, and grey

BLACK   BROWN   CHESTNUT   DUN   GREY   BAY

There were no horses in Australia until they were taken there by early settlers in the late 18th century. The early horses were probably Barbs (*see* pp 190–91) and Arabs (*see* pp 184–87). Until 1971, the Australian Stock Horse was known as the Waler, after the horse that had been developed in New South Wales.

ORIGINS
Once more regular contact was made with Europe, cargo ships would have brought more horses, often Thoroughbreds (*see* pp 284–87). Horse racing became popular very early in Australia, so increasingly Thoroughbreds were imported. In more recent years, outcrossing to Quarter Horses (*see* pp 267–69),

QUARTER HORSE INFLUENCE The modern-day Australian Stock Horse still carries plenty of Thoroughbred qualities, but also often shows the additional power, particularly in the hindquarters, of the American Quarter Horse.

ponies, and heavy draught horses such as the Percheron (*see* pp 156–59) and the Clydesdale (*see* pp 138–39) have been made in order to develop the breed's strength.

CHARACTERISTICS
The mixed bloodlines of this breed means there is no standardized type, but typically the Australian Stock Horse will show quality combined with strength, and should always have particularly good limbs and hooves, and powerful hindquarters.

STOCK HORSE AT WORK The Waler had been developed mainly as a tough ranch horse, but those same qualities of strength and reliability saw large numbers used as cavalry horses.

Azteca

ORIGIN Mexico
ENVIRONMENT
BLOOD
USES
HEIGHT 14.2–16.0 hh (1.47–1.63 m)
COLOURS All colours, including black, brown, chestnut, dun, grey, palomino, bay, and roan

The Azteca is a very new breed. Its development started in 1972 and it was officially recognized in 1982. It was the fulfilment of a dream for Mexico to have its own national horse breed. The Azteca is said to combine the best equine bloodlines of the Old and the New World, and is suitable for many equestrian uses.

BLACK   BROWN   CHESTNUT   DUN   GREY   BAY   PALOMINO   ROAN

ORIGINS

The Azteca was the result of the Mexican cowboys' need for a horse with agility, speed, and, importantly, 'cow-sense' to work their big cattle ranches. It was a careful crossing of Andalucian (*see* p 180), Quarter Horse, (*see* pp 267–69) and Criollo (*see* p 207) bloodlines that produced the horse that rapidly earned the title 'the National Horse of Mexico'. The balance of these three bloodlines is strictly controlled within the breed. An Azteca may have between three- and five-eighths Andalucian or Quarter Horse blood, and no more than a quarter Criollo blood.

CHARACTERISTICS

Azteca enthusiasts pride themselves on aiming to produce the best of the Andalucian and Quarter Horse qualities in the breed. They should possess the elevated and powerful movement of the Andalucian, combined with the agility and 'cow-sense' of the Quarter Horse. Another characteristic is a kind, co-operative, and trainable temperament.

QUALITY BREED The Azteca has a broad, slightly concave head, with large expressive eyes. The neck is gracefully arched and the mane and tail luxuriant. The back is short and strong and the hindquarters big and powerful.

Barb

ORIGIN North Africa
ENVIRONMENT
BLOOD ●
USES 🐎
HEIGHT 14.2–15.2 hh (1.47–1.57 m)
COLOURS Solid colours; commonly black, brown, grey, and bay

BLACK	BROWN	GREY	BAY

The Barb is little used outside his native North Africa, and yet he has had almost as great an influence as a foundation bloodline as the Arab (*see* pp 184–87). He played a major role in the development of both the Andalucian (*see* p 180) and the Thoroughbred (*see* pp 284–87). He has the qualities of the Arab, but not its refined looks.

ORIGINS

It is possible that the Barb was one of a small group of horses that survived the Ice Age. This would make the breed older than the Arab. Certainly, his primitive head lends credence to him being an ancient breed.

The coastal region of Morocco, Algeria, and Tunisia known as the Barbary coast was home to the Barb horse. The spread of Islam, and hence the arrival of a Muslim army in Europe in the early 8th century, saw the spread of the Barb Horse

STRAIGHT PROFILE Unlike the Arab, the Barb has a straight or even convex profile.

also. He was the mount of the Berbers, who led the early Muslim conquests, invading Spain in 711AD. In modern times, the most famous use of Barb horses was in the Algerian and Tunisian cavalry regiments of the French Army.

CHARACTERISTICS

The Barb is remarkably quick and agile. Although the head has a straight profile, unlike that of the Arab, the neck is distinctly arched. The legs are slender and very hard, and the hooves are extremely tough.

SPRINTING HORSE The Barb Horse can show tremendous speed over short distances, and this is dramatically exhibited during the wild, rifle-firing charges that feature in many North African festivals.

HANDSOME IS AS HANDSOME DOES Whilst not classically beautiful in the same way as the Arab and Thoroughbred, there is a lot to like about the tough, knowing look of the Barb; perhaps telling us that he has been around longer than we think!

Bavarian Warmblood

ORIGIN Germany
ENVIRONMENT
BLOOD
USES
HEIGHT 16.0–16.2 hh (1.63–1.67 m)
COLOURS Usually chestnut, but may be any solid colour

BLACK	BROWN	CHESTNUT	DUN	GREY	BAY

The Bavarian Warmblood is one of the heavier of the warmblood breeds. He evolved from an older breed of horse, the Rottaler, from a region of southern Germany. The continuation of regional breeds such as this one is supported and encouraged by the German government.

ORIGINS
Bavaria is one of the oldest horse-breeding regions in Germany. The Bavarian Warmblood was based on the local Rottal (or Rottaler) horse from the Rott Valley, which was used as a battle charger. Since World War II, the breed has been refined using Thoroughbred (see pp 284–87) and Trakehner (see pp 288–89) bloodlines. The Bavarian Warmblood was first registered as a separate breed in 1963, and is used as a good all-round sports horse.

CHARACTERISTICS
The Bavarian is a large, elegant horse, similar to the Hanoverian (see p 224), with a strong, well-set neck; a powerful chest; long, sloping shoulders, and high withers. He has a well-muscled, long back, and strong legs with massive hocks. He is renowned for his strength and good character.

POWERFUL SPORTS HORSE This powerful animal has a heavy chest, well-muscled back, strong legs and hocks, but with a well-set neck and long, sloping shoulders. He lacks speed but is well suited to dressage and showjumping.

Belgian Warmblood

ORIGIN Belgium
ENVIRONMENT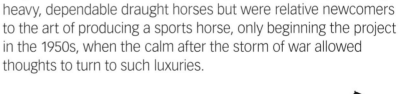
BLOOD 🜄
USES 🐎 🤺
HEIGHT 16.0–16.2 hh (1.63–1.67 m)
COLOURS Black, brown, chestnut, grey, and bay

| BLACK | BROWN | CHESTNUT | GREY | BAY |

Belgian horse breeders had made a great success of producing heavy, dependable draught horses but were relative newcomers to the art of producing a sports horse, only beginning the project in the 1950s, when the calm after the storm of war allowed thoughts to turn to such luxuries.

ORIGINS
In the 1950s, a heavyweight riding horse had been developed by crossing some of the light Belgian farm horses to the Gelderlander (*see* p 220). The result was nothing much more than a reliable weight-carrying riding horse. There was then a period of outcrossing to a number of breeds, including the Thoroughbred (see pp 284–87), Arab (*see* pp 184–87), and the neighbouring Dutch Warmblood (*see* p 210). The result was a horse with sufficient speed, scope, and stamina to meet the demands of equestrian sports, but with a good, calm temperament.

CHARACTERISTICS
The breed has retained the soundness and strength of its heavy draught forefathers and has good paces, with a degree of elevation but not the spectacular movement of some of the other warmblood breeds.

CAREFUL MIX Strong hindquarters and loins, sound limbs, and good overall proportions are the result of the careful mix of breeding that has produced the Belgian Warmblood.

STRONG JUMPER The breed has been able to put its power to good use in showjumping, his trainable temperament also being an asset in a sport that demands an accurate technique.

Boerperd

ORIGIN South Africa
ENVIRONMENT 🌱 🌾
BLOOD 💧
USES 🏇 🐎 🏇
HEIGHT 14.2–16.2 hh (1.47–1.67 m)
COLOURS All solid colours but commonly bay and grey. Albino is not acceptable

BLACK   BROWN   CHESTNUT   DUN   GREY   BAY

The history and development of the Boerperd is intrinsically linked with that of the white settlers in South Africa. The horse played an important role in the ability of the Boers to fight off the might of the British Army for as long as they did during the Second Anglo-Boer War (1899–1902).

ORIGINS

In 1652, Jan van Riebeeck landed in Table Bay, charged with establishing a colony that could serve the ships of the Dutch East India Company. A number of ponies of Berber-Arabian breeding were initially imported from Java. These were bred and sold to other white settlers. A stroke of good fortune for the breed occurred when a ship carrying 14 of the Shah of Persia's best Arab Horses (*see* pp 184–87) became stranded; the

horses swam ashore and were captured and bred to the existing ponies. A century later, with some input from Andalucians (*see* p 180) that had also

been imported, the basis of the breed was set.

During the late 1800s, a greater variety of breeds were imported into South Africa and these all played a part in the development of the Boerperd; Thoroughbred (*see* pp 284–87), Flemish, Hackney (*see* p 223), Norfolk Trotters, and Cleveland Bays (*see* p 205) were all used to some degree or other. Two dreadful outbreaks of African Horse Sickness, in 1719 and 1763, killed great swathes of the horse population, but possibly served to enhance the hardiness of the horses that survived.

THE SACRIFICES OF WAR

The horse that developed from this mix found fame as the tough, agile war horse used by the Boer people during the Anglo-Boer War. Thousands of these brave little horses were lost during the fighting.

After the war, a concerted effort was made to conserve and encourage the breeding of the Boerperd. A stud-book register was formed in 1905. The Boerperd was formally recognized as a breed in 1996.

QUALITY BLOOD The quality of the foundation bloodlines, featuring Arabs and Andalucians, shows in the refined head and features of this Boerperd foal. The ancient pony and draught blood accounts for its hardiness.

CHARACTERISTICS

The South African Boerperd has a broad forehead between prominent eyes. The sharp ears are of medium length. The profile is straight or slightly concave with a deep, well-defined jaw. Cheeks must be well muscled but not fleshy. The well-formed neck is of average length, and the shoulders are sloping with prominent withers. The back is broad and well muscled, with well-developed loins and powerful hindquarters. The chest is deep and powerful. The well-muscled legs have good, hard hooves.

SOUND TEMPERAMENT Intimately linked with the development of white settlements in South Africa, the Boerperd breed is renowned for its qualities of bravery, intelligence, hardiness, surefootedness, and sound temperament.

VERSATILE, INTELLIGENT BREED The Boerperd Horse is popular for a wide range of activities; they are used for many horse sports, for police and patrol work, and for ranch work, as well as for hunting, endurance riding, and pleasure riding. They are renowned for being trustworthy and alert.

Brandenburger

ORIGIN Germany
ENVIRONMENT
BLOOD
USES
HEIGHT 16.2–17.0 hh (1.67–1.73 m)
COLOURS Mainly bay, but also black, brown, and chestnut

BLACK   BROWN   CHESTNUT   BAY

The development of the Brandenburger breed was greatly influenced by the National Stud at Neustadt, founded by King Frederick Wilhelm II in 1788. As horses' work changed over the years, so did the breed, which was altered to meet the needs of the sporting industry rather than agriculture and transportation.

ORIGINS

The aim in breeding the original Brandenburger was to produce a large, strong horse that could carry out all manner of agricultural tasks, but was also smart and light enough to be used as a carriage horse. By the mid-20th century, the need for such a strong horse was diminishing, and breeders turned their attention to refining the breed for the sports-horse market. Trakehner (*see* pp 288–89), Hanoverian (*see* p 224), and Thoroughbred (*see* pp 284–87) blood all aided in this process. A further injection of quality was introduced in the 1990s using Holsteiner (*see* p 226) and Selle Français (*see* p 273) bloodlines.

CHARACTERISTICS

The Brandenburger is still one of the stronger, larger warmblood breeds. He has a well-set neck; great strength in his back, loins, and limbs; and a lively but co-operative temperament. The National Stud remains the main breeding centre.

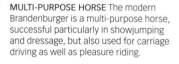

MULTI-PURPOSE HORSE The modern Brandenburger is a multi-purpose horse, successful particularly in showjumping and dressage, but also used for carriage driving as well as pleasure riding.

REFINING THE BREED After reunification with East Germany, Hanoverian bloodlines were introduced. In more recent years, the famous 'Ladykiller' Holsteiner line as well as the 'Cor de la Bryère' Selle Français line has done much to refine the Brandenburger breed.

British Warmblood

ORIGIN United Kingdom
ENVIRONMENT
BLOOD
USES
HEIGHT 15.2–17.0 hh (1.57–1.73 m)
COLOURS All colours

The British Warmblood is a gathering of types of British-bred sports horses rather than an actual breed. There are strict selection criteria to be met, but the bloodlines of the various horses classed as British Warmbloods cover a multitude of breeds. The aim is for the horses to have the potential to be successful international sports horses.

| BLACK | BROWN | CHESTNUT | DUN | GREY | BAY | PALOMINO | COLOURED |

ORIGINS

Britain has long relied on the success of the Thoroughbred (*see* pp 284–87) and various crosses with it as a source of competition horses. But as the demand for competition horses grew, many British riders started to look to Europe and the well-established warmblood breeds for top-class prospects. And in 1977, the British Warmblood Society was formed with the aim of producing a British equivalent that would allow British riders to buy a British rather than a European sports horse. Horses have to pass a grading process to be accepted as breeding stock, and an annual show is held where the progeny of graded parents are promoted.

CHARACTERISTICS

The aim of the Breed Society is to produce sound and athletic horses with excellent movement and trainable temperaments, so making them suitable for all disciplines. The graded stallions must meet all the grading criteria and have at least 50% warmblood in their pedigree. To achieve Group-One status, the stallion must be graded and entered in the British Warmblood stud book, be performance tested, or be the sire of an advanced dressage or event horse, or be a grade-A showjumper.

BRITISH BRED The aim of the British Warmblood Society is to have British team riders mounted on British Warmblood horses.

Brumby

ORIGIN Australia
ENVIRONMENT ▲ Ⱳ
BLOOD ◍
USES 🏇 🏇 🏇
HEIGHT 15.0–16.1 hh (1.52–1.63 m)
COLOURS All solid colours

Brumbies are the feral horses of Australia, with numbers in their thousands. Those who love them see them as a symbol of the wilderness and freedom of Australia; others see them as a pest causing damage to the environment and eating up resources that are needed for cattle and sheep.

BLACK	BROWN	CHESTNUT	DUN	GREY	BAY

ORIGINS

The Brumbies that roam free today are the descendants of horses that were either lost by, or escaped from, the early European settlers. The first horses imported into the country were Cape Horses from South Africa. Later, there were shipments of Chilean horses as well as ponies and draught horses from Britain. The occasional Thoroughbred (*see* pp 284–87) or Arab (*see* pp 184–87) also joined the 'mob' or 'band', as a herd of Brumbies is known. From this diverse early mix of bloodlines, the harsh and unforgiving environment and landscape of Australia – through natural selection – created the tough, cunning, wiry little horse that is the Brumby.

HARD TIMES

Today, Brumbies are found mainly in Queensland and the Northern Territory. Their successful survival has led to conflict with farmers and conservationists and since the 1960s, they have been culled, although this has been banned in some states after a gruesome cull when hundreds were shot from helicopters, causing mass panic and injuries as well as death.

SANCTUARY After the controversy raised by culling methods, some were offered sanctuary by sympathetic landowners and others are captured and offered for 'adoption'.

Budenny

ORIGIN Russia
ENVIRONMENT
BLOOD
USES
HEIGHT 16.0–16.1 hh (1.63–1.65 m)
COLOURS Predominantly chestnut, often showing a striking golden gleam

BLACK   BROWN   CHESTNUT   BAY

During the 1920s, Russia went through a phase of creating new horse breeds. They used complex crossbreeding systems to meet a demand for tough cavalry horses. The Budenny was one result of these breeding policies, and he was a horse of sufficient quality that he soon evolved into a popular competition horse.

ORIGINS

The Budenny resulted from the crossing of Don (*see* p 209) and Chernomor mares with Anglo-Don stallions. Dons were the famous mounts of the Don Cossacks; the Chernomor was a smaller, lighter version of the Don. The breeding programme for the Budenny was based at a military stud in the Rostov region, and used the best mares and stallions as the foundation stock.

REFINED The head of the Budenny should be well proportioned, full of quality, and set on a long, fairly straight neck. The eyes are bright and intelligent, and the ears are sharp and alert.

CHARACTERISTICS

The overall conformation is one of lean athleticism, but the shoulders are not as long and sloping as the Thoroughbred and the hind legs can be relatively straight and weak looking.

RACEHORSE The Budenny was recognized as a breed in 1949. Today he is in demand as a competition horse and racehorse.

NOWHERE TO GO Even a continent as huge as Australia doesn't seem to be big enough to allow herds of wild horses to roam free. Those that have the right temperament are broken in and re-homed as riding horses; many are culled.

Campolina

ORIGIN Brazil
ENVIRONMENT 🌾
BLOOD 🌢
USES 🐎 🐎 🐎
HEIGHT 14.1–15.3 hh (57–63 in)
COLORS Usually dun, but can be any color

Cassiano Campolina began a breeding program in 1857 on his ranch in Minas Gerais, Brazil. He wanted to produce horses with great presence yet with calm temperaments and comfortable paces. The Campolina is gaited—as well as the usual paces it has an additional four-beat diagonal and four-beat lateral gait.

BLACK   BROWN   CHESTNUT   DUN   GRAY   BAY   PALOMINO   COLORED

ORIGINS

In 1870, the Brazilian horse breeder Cassiano Campolina was given a black mare of Barb (*see* pp. 190–91) breeding that he bred to a pure Andalucian (*see* p. 180) stallion. The resultant dark gray colt foal, named "Monarca," is considered to be the Campolina's foundation sire. He served as a stallion on the ranch for 25 years, being bred mainly to Criollo mares. Sr. Campolina also used a mix of other stallions to achieve his aims, including Anglo-Norman, Holsteiner (*see* p. 226), American Saddlebred (*see* p. 179), a part-Clydesdale (*see* pp. 138–39) and, to futher refine the breed, the Mangalarga Machador (*see* p. 244). In 1934, the studbook was closed and a Breed Association and breed standard was created in 1951.

CHARACTERISTICS

The Campolina has presence and substance. He has an attractive head with quite big ears and kind, dark eyes, set on a strong, arched neck. He has a full, silky mane, indicative of the Andalucian blood. The croup is slightly sloped, and the hindquarters round with a lowset tail.

THE DUN THING Campolina horses can be any color, but a great many exhibit the attractive dun coloring, evidence of Criollo blood. A dorsal stripe and zebra markings on the legs are also common.

Canadian Cutting Horse

ORIGIN Canada
ENVIRONMENT
BLOOD
USES
HEIGHT 15.2–16.1 hh (1.57–1.65 m)
COLOURS All solid colours but generally brown, chestnut, grey, or bay

Cattle ranching is big business in Canada, and large numbers of horses are still used for ranch work. Canada does not have any indigenous horse breeds, but it does have a thriving horse-breeding industry. The Canadian Cutting Horse has evolved from this industry, to meet the needs of the ranch owners.

BLACK   BROWN   CHESTNUT   DUN   GREY   BAY   PALOMINO

ORIGINS
The main aim of the Canadian Cutting Horse Association is to promote the sport of cutting cattle – separating a specified animal from a herd. The Association does not have a closed stud book, so the bloodlines of the horse are not specified. It is left to the horse to prove he has the necessary attributes to cut cattle.

CHARACTERISTICS
Most Canadian Cutting Horses carry a high percentage of Quarter Horse blood (*see* pp 267–69). In turn, the Quarter Horse evolved from the Spanish Horse, from which both these breeds inherit their 'cow-sense'.

In cutting competitions, once the selected cow is split from the herd, the rider drops the reins and leaves the horse to 'mark' the cow and prevent it rejoining the herd. The horse's agility, stamina, and intelligence enable it to outmanoeuvre the cow.

CONFORMATION The well-proportioned head is set on a gently arched neck. The shoulders are sloping and powerful, the chest broad and deep, and the hindquarters immensely powerful.

Carthusian

ORIGIN Spain
ENVIRONMENT
BLOOD
USES
HEIGHT 15.0 hh (1.52 m)
COLOURS Predominantly grey but also black and chestnut

BLACK	CHESTNUT	GREY

The Carthusian is considered to be the purest strain of the Andalucian (*see* p 180) and is also known as the Carthusian Andalucian and the Carthujano. One of Spain's oldest breeds, it owes its purity to the work of Carthusian Monks. Today, it is bred at state-owned studs in Cordoba, Jerez, and Badajoz.

ORIGINS

The foundation Carthusian stallion was bred by the two Zamoras brothers who had a herd of Spanish mares and purchased an old stallion called El Soldada (it is said that one of the brothers recognized him as his old cavalry horse). The first colt they produced was the dark grey Esclavo. He had many offspring and, in 1736, a group of his mares were given to the Carthusian Monks as settlement for a debt. The monks, determined to protect their horses' purity, even defied royal orders to introduce outside blood. The line they preserved became known as the Zomoranos. In 1854, Don Vincent bought as many of the Zomorano line as he could find and continued to improve the breed still without using outside blood.

GOOD CONFORMATION The breed is renowned for its conformation – from its fine head, set on a muscular neck, to its round, muscular quarters. Its shoulders are sloping, its chest is deep, and its back short and broad.

UNIQUE FEATURE The head is noble and elegant and the mane luxuriantly abundant. A unique feature sometimes displayed in this breed is two small, horny growths, either on the temple or by the ears.

Cleveland Bay

ORIGIN United Kingdom
ENVIRONMENT
BLOOD
USES
HEIGHT 16.0–16.2 hh (1.63–1.67 m)
COLOURS Bay

The Cleveland Bay is a very attractive bay horse. Popularly used for carriage driving, he also makes a good hunter, and crosses with the Thoroughbred (*see* pp 284–87) result in a good stamp of sports horse, particularly for showjumping. The Cleveland Bay is always bright bay, which sets off the black 'points' of his legs and the mane and tail.

CARRIAGE HORSE The 18th century was the golden age of carriage driving. The Cleveland Bay was crossed with the Thoroughbred to produce the faster Yorkshire Coach Horse. These exceptional carriage horses were exported all over the world.

ORIGINS

The Cleveland Bay is believed to be Britain's oldest breed, descended from a particular stamp of bay pack horses that were bred in the monasteries of northern England during the Middle Ages. The bay horse they bred was used by travelling tradesmen, known as chapmen, and the horse became known as the Chapman Horse.

BOLD AND HONEST An active, elegant but very powerful horse, the Cleveland Bay is bold and honest, but he has a strong character, which can make him difficult if mishandled.

CHARACTERISTICS

In the 17th century, it was crossed with Barb (*see* pp 190–91) and, in some cases, Andalucian (*see* p 180) horses. The result, which became known as the Cleveland Bay, was a strong but elegant horse with a level, free, long-striding action, which could be used for riding, carriage, and light draught work.

Cob

ORIGIN United Kingdom
ENVIRONMENT 🌾
BLOOD 💧
USES 🐎 🏇 🐎
HEIGHT 14.2–15.1 hh (1.47–1.55 m)
COLOURS All colours

A Cob is another anomaly that is a type rather than a set breed despite the fact that it has easily recognized characteristics in much the same way as true breeds do. The difference is that an infinite variety of crossbreeds can be used to produce the stamp of horse that is recognized as a Cob.

BLACK   BROWN   CHESTNUT   DUN   GREY   BAY   PALOMINO   COLOURED

ORIGINS
Irish Draught (*see* pp 144–45), Hunter (*see* pp 228–31), and sometimes even Shire Horses (*see* pp 164–65), crossed with Thoroughbreds (*see* pp 284–87) can result in a good stamp of Cob. The point of breeding a Cob was to produce a strong, sound, active, sensible, and not overly large horse that would be cheap and easy to keep whilst being adaptable enough to ride as a hack or hunter, or to drive.

CHARACTERISTICS
Cobs are stockily built with a big body set on short, powerful legs. They vary quite considerably within their recognized type: some are quite plain and perhaps a little too 'roly-poly' in shape; others are really smart, with quality heads and powerful but active paces. For showing purposes, a Cob should have bone and substance but also quality, and should be capable of carrying a substantial weight. The head may be Roman nosed, but should be set on a crested neck.

THE BEST TYPE A good Cob should be a very smart little horse with a jaunty, jolly character; good, low paces; and a powerful jump. They make very popular hunters despite not possessing great speed. They are comfortable, tough, easy to manage, and can usually take on a hedge with the best of them!

Colorado Ranger

ORIGIN United States

ENVIRONMENT 🌾

BLOOD 💧

USES 🐴 🐴

HEIGHT 14.2–16.0 hh (1.47–1.63 m)

COLOURS Predominantly Appaloosa, but all colours accepted

The Colorado Ranger is a relatively new breed; the result of a breeding programme aimed at producing a good cowhorse. Most Rangers have Appaloosa colourings, but whilst many are double registered with Appaloosa breed societies, the Colorado Ranger is not a type of Appaloosa.

BLACK	BROWN	DUN	GREY	BAY	PALOMINO

ORIGINS AND CHARACTERISTICS

In 1878, two stallions were given to General Grant by the Sultan of Turkey: an Arab called 'Leopard' and a Barb called 'Linden Tree'. Two descendants of these stallions, 'Patches' and 'Max', became the foundation stock of the Colorado Ranger. They were bred to working mares on the ranges of Colorado, and their offspring were popular for their often striking spotted colours, agility, and intelligence. Registered horses are all directly descended from either Patches or Max.

OFFICIAL BREED The Colorado Ranger Horse Association was formed in 1935, and keeps meticulous handwritten records of the pedigree and coat pattern of each horse.

Criollo

ORIGIN Argentina

ENVIRONMENT 🌵 🌾

BLOOD 💧

USES 🐴 🐴

HEIGHT 14.0–15.0 hh (1.42–1.52 m)

COLOURS Predominantly dun, but also chestnut

The Criollo is a famously tough, hardy little horse, shaped by the harsh environment of the pampas of Argentina. The extremes of climate – hot, arid summers and severe winters – ensured the survival of only the soundest and fittest.

CHESTNUT	DUN

VERSATILE Originally used as a riding and pack horse, the Criollo is also the chosen mount of the gauchos for herding cattle. Crossed with the Thoroughbred, it produces a superb Polo Pony.

ORIGINS AND CHARACTERISTICS

The Criollo descends from Spanish horses taken to South America by the *conquistadores*, which were mainly Andalucian Horses (*see* p 180). Many of these early imported horses ran wild and formed feral herds. A very tough horse emerged. Dun is the most common colour and provides effective camouflage.

Danish Warmblood

ORIGIN Denmark

ENVIRONMENT 🌾

BLOOD 💧

USES 🏇 🏇

HEIGHT 15.3–16.2 hh (1.60–1.67 m)

COLOURS All solid colours

The Danish Warmblood is a relative newcomer to the band of purpose-bred breeds developed across Europe to meet demand from the sports-horse industry. The Danes have a long horse-breeding history, but their native breeds, the Frederiksborg (*see* p 211) and the Knabstrup (*see* p 241), are not sports horses.

BLACK　　BROWN　　CHESTNUT　　GREY　　BAY　　PALOMINO

ORIGINS AND CHARACTERISTICS

A breeding programme with the aim of developing a sports horse was started in 1962. Local mares were bred to a selection of Swedish, Trakehner (*see* pp 288–89), Holsteiner (*see* p 226), and Polish stallions to start the process. Strict grading procedures were then introduced to ensure that only the best mares and stallions were entered in the stud book. The end result is a good-looking, courageous horse with excellent paces – a successful competition horse that excels particularly in dressage.

BRANDED All Danish Warmbloods are branded with a crown and an identification number on their hindquarters once they are accepted for registration in the breed's stud book.

DRESSAGE Like all warmbloods, the Danish Warmbloods are bred to produce an all-round performer. Warmbloods are popular for dressage due to their extravagant action.

Don

ORIGIN Russia

ENVIRONMENT

BLOOD

USES

HEIGHT 15.2–16.2 hh (1.57–1.67 m)

COLOURS Predominantly chestnut with a golden sheen

| BROWN | CHESTNUT | BAY |

The Don is associated with the Don Cossacks who helped to repel Napoleon from Russia between 1812 and 1814. It evolved in the 18th and 19th centuries, primarily as a cavalry and artillery horse.

ORIGINS AND CHARACTERISTICS

The Cossacks rode horses descended from those domesticated by the early Nomadic tribes of the Russian steppes. These horses would have been kept in herds, left to fend for themselves in the harsh environment of the steppes. The result was a hardy, sound horse with great stamina. During the 19th century, Thoroughbred (*see* pp 284–87) and Orlov (*see* p 259) blood was introduced to improve the Don, but since the beginning of the 20th century, no further outside blood has been used.

NO GREAT MOVER
The Don has an attractive head, but conformational deficiencies in the poll, shoulders, and limbs mean that, although he is tough and sound, his paces are pretty ordinary.

Dutch Warmblood

ORIGIN Holland
ENVIRONMENT
BLOOD
USES
HEIGHT 16.0–17.0 hh (1.63–1.73 m)
COLOURS All solid colours but mainly bay and brown

BLACK	BROWN	CHESTNUT	GREY	BAY

The Dutch have proved adept at producing horses to meet market demands, and the Dutch Warmblood has probably been the most successfully marketed of all the warmblood breeds. The product has lived up to its reputation with some excellent competition horses, particularly in dressage and showjumping.

ORIGINS
The Dutch already had a smart carriage horse in the form of the Gelderlander (*see* p 220), and the heavier Groningen (*see* p 221), and these two breeds were the starting point for the Dutch Warmblood. Thoroughbred (*see* pp 284–87) blood was used to correct an overly long back and also greatly influenced the head and neck. Trakehner (*see* pp 288–89) stallions were also used as well as Holsteiner (*see* p 226) mares crossed to the Gelderlander and Groningen stallions. As the basic type was formulated, further warmblood breeds were used to add the final touches.

CHARACTERISTICS
A strict selection process is used to grade and accept Dutch Warmbloods. The main aim, of course, is to continue to produce horses of good conformation and movement but, just as importantly, the breed society aims to retain good temperament and trainability. The Thoroughbred influence shows in the elegant head and neck. The Gelderlander helps to produce the good shoulder and active paces, and the Groningen ensures strength, particularly in the hindquarters, and soundness.

VERSATILE While the carriage-horse past makes this a good competition driving horse, the breed is better known for its huge successes in showjumping – 'Marius' and his son famous 'Milton' – and in dressage – 'Dutch Courage'.

Einsiedler

ORIGIN Switzerland
ENVIRONMENT ▲
BLOOD 💧
USES 🏇 🐎
HEIGHT 16.0–16.3 hh (1.63–1.70 m)
COLOURS All solid colours

The Einsiedler, also known as the Swiss Warmblood, can be traced back over 1,000 years to the Benedictine monastery at Einsiedeln. The horse is used as an army mount as well as a sports horse and is carefully performance tested as a three-year-old and a five-year-old.

| BLACK | BROWN | CHESTNUT | GREY | BAY |

ORIGINS AND CHARACTERISTICS

The Einsiedler was first bred in the 10th century from native Schwyer horses. A stud book was opened in 1784 and, in the 19th century, the breed was refined by the importation of a number of different breeds. Further changes were made in the 20th century, with the introduction of Swedish and Irish blood.

VERSATILITY The modern breed is an adaptable animal, used in all equestrian disciplines as well as for driving. It is also particularly well suited as a cavalry horse.

Frederiksborg

ORIGIN Denmark
ENVIRONMENT 🌾
BLOOD 💧
USES 🏇 🐎 🐎
HEIGHT 15.3–16.0 hh (1.60–1.63 m)
COLOURS Chestnut

In the 19th century, the Frederiksborg was one of the most sought-after horses in Europe and very nearly a victim of his own success. So many were exported that the homeland's stock was much depleted.

ORIGINS AND CHARACTERISTICS

The Frederiksborg stud was founded in the middle of the 16th century by King Frederick II. The foundation stock were Spanish horses that were then bred to the closely related Neopolitan horse. Eastern, as well as British half-bred, stock were used to further develop the breed.

Although once very popular for dressage and as a cavalry charger, by modern standards, the conformation of the Frederiksborg, with his long back, relatively short neck, and upright shoulders, is better suited to carriage rather than ridden work. His head has a straight or convex profile with expressive eyes, and pointed ears.

LIGHT HARNESS HORSE Bred mainly as a light harness horse, the Frederiksborg has recently lost out in popularity to the newer Danish Warmblood horse.

French Anglo-Arab

ORIGIN France
ENVIRONMENT
BLOOD ●
USES 🏇 🤺
HEIGHT 15.3–16.2 hh (1.60–1.67 m)
COLOURS All solid colours

The French Anglo-Arab was developed with the aim of combining the scope and speed of the Thoroughbred (*see* pp 284–87) with the endurance and good nature of the Arab (*see* pp 184–87). Anglo-Arabs are widely bred, but were particularly popular in France where they were once widely used in the military and for sport.

BLACK   BROWN   CHESTNUT   GREY   BAY

ORIGINS

The breeding programme began during the 19th century at the state stud at Pompadour by crossing the English Thoroughbred with French-bred Arabs. The offspring were bred back to the Thoroughbred, and this three-quarter cross was then crossed again with the Arab. Having established a successful type, further experiments were carried out in other state studs using varying percentages of Thoroughbred and Arab blood. For inclusion in the French Anglo-Arab stud book, there must be a minimum of 25 per cent Arab blood.

CHARACTERISTICS

The Anglo-Arab usually shows more of the Thoroughbred in his head and neck, but has a shorter back than the full Thoroughbred. They are not such good gallopers as the Thoroughbred, but they have better overall paces in terms of activity and elevation.

EVENT HORSE The Anglo-Arab place in the sports market has been displaced by the Selle Français, but he remains a popular choice for three-day eventing.

French Thoroughbred

ORIGIN France
ENVIRONMENT
BLOOD
USES
HEIGHT 16.0–17.0 hh (1.63–1.73 m)
COLOURS All solid colours

The Thoroughbred (*see* pp 284–87) was developed in Britain during the 17th and 18th centuries and a huge international racing and breeding industry has developed around him. The Thoroughbred was quickly adopted by other countries, particularly France and America which, in turn, created their own particular 'thoroughbred'.

BLACK   BROWN   CHESTNUT   GREY   BAY

ORIGINS AND CHARACTERISTICS

All Thoroughbred Horses descend from three foundation sires: the Byerley Turk, the Darley Arabian, and the Godolphin Arabian. The Thoroughbred was exported to Europe and America soon after it had been developed in Britain. The particular bloodlines taken by these countries formed the foundation pool from which they bred their own stock. The French breeding industry was almost destroyed during World War I, but was helped on its way again by good stallions such as 'Bruleur', who was foaled in 1910 and retired to stud in 1914. Traditionally, the French Thoroughbred has been a heavier, slightly plainer stamp than his English counterpart, but the influence of imported American, Irish, and English Thoroughbred blood is starting to change this.

FRENCH BRED To be considered French-bred, a horse has to have been foaled in France and not left the country before June 1st of the year following foaling (apart from temporary leave of less than one month).

French Trotter

ORIGIN France
ENVIRONMENT 🌿
BLOOD 💧
USES 🐎 🐎🐎
HEIGHT 16.1–16.3 hh (1.65–1.70 m)
COLOURS All solid colours, although grey is rare

| BLACK | BROWN | CHESTNUT | GREY | BAY |

The first French trotting competitions were ridden races as opposed to harness races. The French Trotter was bred to meet the growing enthusiasm for this sport. Now only about ten per cent of French trotting events are ridden; ridden trotters tend to be the taller, more heavily-built members of the breed.

ORIGINS

Trotting developed as a sport in France in the early 19th century. The first ridden trotting race was held in 1806, and the first purpose-made trotting circuit was built at Cherbourg in 1836. A governing body for the sport was formed in 1861, and the French proceeded to develop their own breed of trotting horse by crossing Thoroughbreds (*see* pp 284–87), half-breds, and Norfolk Roadsters to Norman mares. Five influential bloodlines developed from these early crosses: 'Fuschia', 'Lavater', 'Conquerant', 'Normand', and 'Phaeton'. Lavater and Normand were both sired by the English half-

ALL-TERRAIN Trotters are used for conventional carriage driving as well as harness racing. They are also required to race on snow surfaces, either in the sport of 'skijoring', with the horse towing a man on skis, or harness racing conventionally but with specially designed skis replacing the wheels of the sulky.

Thoroughbred 'Young Rattler', and Lavater was sired by a Norfolk Roadster. The French Trotter was recognized as a breed in 1922 and, after some importation of American Standardbred (*see* pp 276–79) blood, the stud book was closed to non-French horses in 1937. However, it is sometimes re-opened to allow the inclusion of some Standardbred bloodlines.

CHARACTERISTICS

The French Trotter has evolved as a tough harness-racer, internationally recognized for his success in the sport. Overall the horse resembles a strongly built Thoroughbred – the immensely powerful, sloping hindquarters enable the horse to trot at speeds not much below that of a galloping Thoroughbred. The decision to continue with ridden trotting races, which require a stronger, taller stamp of horse, has helped maintain the overall strength and quality of the breed. However, the biggest single factor to improve performance on the track was the development, in the 1970s, of the modern racing rig – the sulky.

SPEED MACHINE Standardbred bloodlines were introduced to inject additional speed into the French Trotter. The early Trotters had relatively steep shoulders but this conformational aspect has been improved and the modern breed has good shoulders and more quality overall.

HANDSOME HEAD The head of the French Trotter is not quite as refined as that of the Thoroughbred, but its overall impression is one of quality, spirit, and sharpness. Chestnut, along with bay and brown, is the predominant colour.

Friesian

ORIGIN Holland
ENVIRONMENT ▲
BLOOD 🜄
USES 🐎 🏇 🛷
HEIGHT 15.0–16.0 hh (1.52–1.63 m)
COLOURS Black

The Friesian is a striking little horse: strongly built, jet black, with an abundant wavy mane and tail. Originally he was used for light farm work, but today he is more likely to be employed as a carriage and riding horse, particularly for dressage. He is sometimes called a funeral horse as he is a popular choice for horse-drawn hearses.

ORIGINS

The Friesian descended from an ancient cold-blooded heavy horse that inhabited Friesland in northern Holland. The breed was noted and used by the Romans and was improved with the introduction of Arab (*see* pp 184–87) blood at the time of the crusades and Andalucian (*see* p 180) blood from the Spanish occupation of the Netherlands during the Eighty Year War. During the 19th century, some crosses were also made with Trotting breeds, the result being a slightly lighter-framed horse. In turn, the Friesian has influenced other breeds, such as the Fell Pony (*see* p 324) and the Oldenburg (*see* p 258). After World War I, the breed went into decline, but fuel shortages

HIGH STEPPER The active, high-stepping trot of the Friesian makes him a popular carriage horse. Here he is shown drawing a traditional gig. He is still used to some degree to work the land but is increasingly popular for leisure activities.

during World War II saw a resurgence of interest in the breed as he was brought back to work the land and provide transportation.

CHARACTERISTICS

The Friesian has a long but attractive head and an arched neck. The back is short and broad, and the shoulders and hindquarters are powerful. The limbs are short, with plenty of bone and some feathering. The hooves are blue horn. The full mane and tail come from his Andalucian ancestors.

BLACK BEAUTY The jet-black colouring of the Friesian – combined with his striking mane and tail, and kind, easy nature – makes him a popular choice for a number of disciplines. The breed has great presence, which adds to his appeal as a carriage horse in particular.

Furioso

ORIGIN Hungary
ENVIRONMENT
BLOOD
USES
HEIGHT 16.0–16.1 hh (1.63–1.65 m)
COLOURS Any solid colour, but usually black, dark brown, or dark bay

| BLACK | BROWN | CHESTNUT | GREY | BAY |

The Furioso was developed during the huge horse-breeding operations run by Hungary in the 18th century. One of the most famous studs was at Mezohegyes where both the Furioso and the Nonius (*see* p 257) were bred. There were originally two types of Furioso: a carriage horse and a heavyweight riding horse.

ORIGINS

In the mid-1800s, two stallions were imported into Hungary from England as foundation sires for what was to become the Furioso breed. One was the English Thoroughbred 'Furioso', and the other was 'Northern Star' – a Thoroughbred with a touch of Norfolk Roadster in his ancestry. The two stallions were bred to Nonius mares and, to begin with, produced two separate lines of offspring. Northern Star produced a good number of successful harness-racehorses. More Thoroughbred blood was added and, by the end of the 19th century, the two lines had been interbred. However, Furioso proved the more dominant bloodline and the breed acquired his name.

CHARACTERISTICS

The Furioso has developed into a kind and amenable breed that is also adaptable. They are used as riding and carriage horses, as well as for harness racing and steeplechasing. The Furioso has a Thoroughbred-like head but with a square muzzle and large nostrils. He is a clean-limbed horse with large, well-defined joints.

WELL MADE The pronounced Thoroughbred influence on the breed is clearly visible. The two foundation sires proved to be hugely successful choices in terms of their stud achievements.

HISTORIC HORSEMEN The Hungarian studs still run their horses in large herds, overseen by the traditional Csikos horsemen. Hungary boasts a long history of skilled horsemen; its Hussars were among the best light cavalrymen in the world.

WELL MATCHED Friesians are unusual in always breeding black, so this foal will grow up to be a perfect colour match for its mother. This quality has led to them being in demand for matched teams of carriage horses.

Gelderlander

ORIGIN Holland

ENVIRONMENT 🌾

BLOOD 💧

USES 🐎 🏇 🐎

HEIGHT 15.3–16.2 hh (1.60–1.67 m)

COLOURS Predominantly chestnut, but also grey and bay

CHESTNUT	GREY	BAY

The Gelderlander was developed by the breeders of the Gelder province in central Holland. Their aim had been to produce an upstanding carriage horse that was strong enough to undertake light draught work too, but which retained a docile temperament.

ORIGINS AND CHARACTERISTICS
Gelderlanders were developed in the 19th century using various European stallions on Dutch mares. The result has been a successful carriage horse popularly used for four-in-hand driving trials. The horse also excels as a showjumper and was a major influence in the development of the Dutch Warmblood (*see* p 210).

SENSIBLE HORSE The Gelderlander has a plain but kind and sensible head, a strong neck, and very good shoulders. The hindquarters are powerful with a high-set tail.

Gidran Arab

ORIGIN Hungary

ENVIRONMENT 🌾

BLOOD 💧

USES 🐎 🏇 🐎

HEIGHT 16.0–16.2 hh (1.63–1.67 m)

COLOURS Nearly always chestnut

BROWN	CHESTNUT	BAY

The Gidran Arab is also known as the Hungarian Anglo-Arab and was another breed to be developed at the famous Mezohegyes stud. The breed was developed during the 19th century and produced two lines: a light draught horse and a faster riding horse.

ORIGINS AND CHARACTERISTICS
The chestnut Siglavy Arab stallion 'Gidran', imported into Hungary in 1816, was bred to a Spanish mare, producing 'Gidran II' – the breed's foundation sire. Local and Spanish mares were used initially and then, increasingly, only Arab (*see* pp 184–87) and Thoroughbred (*see* pp 284–87), both of which have left their mark.

TRICKY The original stallion Gidran was notorious for his 'tempestuous' temperament. This trait has been passed to his offspring in varying degrees.

Groningen

ORIGIN Holland

ENVIRONMENT 🌾

BLOOD 🜄

USES 🏇 🐎 🐎

HEIGHT 15.2–16.1 hh (1.57–1.65 m)

COLOURS Any solid colour, but primarily black, brown, or bay

| BLACK | BROWN | CHESTNUT | GREY | BAY |

Named after the northwestern province of Groningen in the Netherlands, this breed was developed to meet the demand for a powerful, but not massive, draught horse to work on the region's heavy clay soils. He also performed well as an impressive coach horse, and as a heavyweight riding horse.

ORIGINS

The Groningen was developed by crossing native mares with Oldenburg (*see* p 258) and Friesian (*see* p 216) stallions. A small amount of Suffolk Punch (*see* pp 166–69) blood was also used to add size and strength. He was strong enough for farm work, smart enough for carriage driving, and could also be ridden. The demand for draught animals fell dramatically by the end of World War II. By the 1970s,

the breed was almost extinct, with only one stallion remaining. The Groningen Horse Association was formed in 1982 to ensure its survival. At the time, several other Dutch breed associations were merging into the newly formed Dutch Warmblood stud book, which meant the Groningen would have lost its distinctive identity. This initiative saw the introduction of more

Oldenburg blood to revive and improve the breed. There are now about four hundred horses registered.

CHARACTERISTICS

The Groningen is pleasant if plain, but he makes up for lack of looks in stamina and reliability. He has an honest head on a powerful, well-set neck. The back can be long, but the hindquarters are muscular, with a tail that is set and carried high. The short limbs are strong with plenty of bone.

SAVED The formation of the Groningen Horse Association in 1982 helped ensure the survival of this honest, kind horse. He is not unattractive and has plenty of good attributes.

Hack

ORIGIN United Kingdom
ENVIRONMENT
BLOOD
USES
HEIGHT 14.2–15.3 hh (1.47–1.60 m)
COLOURS Any solid colour

The Hack is a type rather than a true breed. The modern Hack is a very elegant and refined show horse, but his reason for being dates back to an age when well-to-do owners liked to spend time riding in the park. The name Hack is also used for any horse that is employed for general riding rather than competition.

BLACK   BROWN   CHESTNUT   GREY   BAY

ORIGINS

In the 19th and early 20th centuries, British gentry with the time, money, and inclination used immaculately well-mannered and turned-out 'hacks' to ride in the parklands of the big cities; the most famous of them all being Rotten Row in London's Hyde Park. The horse in question was known as the 'Park Hack' and had to be full of presence and to move with eye-catching lightness.

CHARACTERISTICS

For showing, there are two height classes for Hacks: small Hacks must be 14.2–15 hh (1.47–1.52 m) and large Hacks 15–15.3 hh (1.52–1.60 m). Most Hacks are small Thoroughbreds (*see* pp 284–87) or' mainly Thoroughbred. A Hack must have excellent conformation and, despite needing to be elegant and refined, must still have some substance: his bone measurement should be at least 20 cm (8 in). His movement must be light, active, straight, and low, with no lift to the knee.

ELEGANTLY DRESSED The elegant and refined turnout of the Hack is matched by that of his rider. This Hack is being ridden in a double bridle and is wearing a show saddle.

Hackney

ORIGIN United Kingdom
ENVIRONMENT 🌱
BLOOD 💧
USES 🐎
HEIGHT 15.0–15.3 hh (1.52–1.60 m)
COLOURS Solid dark colours

BLACK   BROWN   CHESTNUT   BAY

The high-stepping Hackney horse is instantly recognizable and, although a native of Great Britain, is prized throughout the world as an eye-catching carriage horse. Hackney-carriage turnouts are very popular in the showring, and the Hackney can be driven as a single horse or in teams of two, three, or four.

ORIGINS

The Hackney has his early origins in the 1700s as a general-purpose type used for riding, hunting, and light farm work. The horses were highly regarded and valued by the monarchy of the time; Henry VIII passed an act penalizing anyone who exported one of these horses without permission!

In 1883, the Hackney Stud Book Society was formed and a stud book was opened. During the early 20th century, Hackneys were exported in large numbers all over the world.

CHARACTERISTICS

The Hackney should express alertness and activity. The head has a straight or slightly convex profile with intelligent, wide-set eyes. The body should have good depth and well-sprung ribs. The quarters should be well muscled and the chest should have ample width.

HIGH-STEPPING ACTION The exaggerated high-stepping action is inherited from his Trotting horse ancestors. A small version of the Hackney horse, the Hackney Pony, also exists.

CLEAN LIMBS The limbs have plenty of clean, flat bone with sufficiently long pasterns to provide the characteristically light, springy step.

Hanoverian

ORIGIN Germany
ENVIRONMENT
BLOOD 🜄
USES 🏇 ♞ 🐎
HEIGHT 15.3–16.2 hh (1.60–1.67 m)
COLOURS Mainly chestnut and bay

The Hanoverian was bred to be an all-purpose horse capable of working the land, being ridden, and also suited to carriage work. More recently, the emphasis has been on refining the breed for the sports industry. The Hanoverian now suits this purpose very well and is especially popular for dressage and showjumping.

| BLACK | BROWN | CHESTNUT | GREY | BAY |

ORIGINS

The Hanoverian breed was produced at the state stud at Celle, in Germany, after 1835. Here Thoroughbred (*see* pp 284–87) stallions were crossed to mainly Holsteiner (*see* p 226) mares. The Hanoverian Breed Registry was founded in 1888, and in 1922 became the Hanoverian Horse Breeders Association. After 1945 more Thoroughbred and Trakehner (*see* pp 288–89) blood was used.

CHARACTERISTICS

Modern Hanoverians should have a quality head set on a long, elegant neck. The shoulders are large and well sloped, and the back not too long, with especially strong loins and muscular hindquarters. The limbs are strong with well-defined joints.

NOBLE BEARING
The Hanoverian's strength and noble bearing, combined with his powerfully active paces, makes him a good choice for the controlled power and athleticism required for top-level dressage.

WELL TESTED Hanoverian breeding is strictly controlled. Stallions can only be licensed after passing a veterinary examination and must then prove their ability in ridden performance tests. Great emphasis is placed on the horse's temperament, which is considered to be as important as its athletic ability.

Henson

ORIGIN France
ENVIRONMENT 🌾
BLOOD 💧
USES 🏇
HEIGHT 14.3–15.3 hh (1.50–1.60 m)
COLOURS Dun

Only created in 1975, the Henson was developed to be a calm, reliable riding horse with no greater aim in mind than to allow his rider to enjoy the spectacular scenery and wildlife of his wetland home in the Bay of Somme, France. The fixed characteristics of the breed are still being established.

OUTDOOR LIVING
The Henson is bred, reared, and kept outdoors and thrives on the waterlogged, nutritionally poor vegetation in his marshland birthplace.

ORIGINS AND CHARACTERISTICS

The Henson Horse is the result of crossing Norwegian Fjord Ponies (*see* p 342) with quality saddle horses such as Thoroughbreds (*see* pp 284–87) and Anglo-Arabs (*see* p 181). He must have between 25 and 50 per cent Fjord blood. This hardy little horse must have a dorsal stripe. Some also have 'zebra' stripes on their legs.

Hispano-Arab

ORIGIN Spain
ENVIRONMENT 🌾
BLOOD 💧
USES 🏇 🏇
HEIGHT 15.0–15.2 hh (1.52–1.57 m)
COLOURS Predominantly grey

The Hispano-Arab is a cross between two of the world's oldest and finest breeds: the Andalucian (*see* p 180) and the Arab (*see* pp 184–87). The Andalucian had already received an injection of Arab blood during the late 1800s and some breeders continued this work to produce the Hispano-Arab.

| BLACK | GREY | BAY |

ORIGINS AND CHARACTERISTICS

In 1986, the Hispano-Arab stud book opened. New entrants must be either offspring of those already documented or the offspring of a first-generation cross between a pure Arab and an Andalucian. Bred mainly for the bull ring and high-school dressage, the Hispano-Arab is similar to the old classical Andalucian.

GOOD BREEDING To be registered in the stud book, a Hispano-Arab must have between 25 and 75 per cent pure Arab or Andalucian blood in its ancestry.

Holsteiner

ORIGIN Germany
ENVIRONMENT
BLOOD 🌢
USES 🐎 🏇 🐎
HEIGHT 16.0–17.0 hh (1.63–1.73 m)
COLOURS All solid colours

The Holsteiner was one of the oldest warmblood breeds to be developed; horses of this type were established in the 16th century and were soon in demand across Europe as carriage horses and, later, cavalry mounts. German, Neapolitan, and Spanish blood shaped the original Holstein.

| BLACK | BROWN | CHESTNUT | GREY | BAY |

ORIGINS

During the 19th century, the old Holstein type was greatly influenced by the use of Yorkshire Coach Horse blood. This gave the Holsteiner its distinctive high knee action. The main breeding of the Holsteiner took place at the Travanthall Stud in Schleswig-Holstein, founded in 1867. Some Thoroughbred (*see* pp 284–87) blood was introduced as demand increased for a light, more athletic sports horse. The main breeding centre is now at Elmshorn, Germany.

CHARACTERISTICS

Temperament, paces, and soundness are important. The modern Holsteiner should have the head of a quality hunter. It owes much of its modern appearance to the Thoroughbred and has excellent limbs, sloping shoulders, and a strong back and loins.

HIGH JUMPER Holsteiners excel in the three main equestrian disciplines of showjumping, dressage, and eventing. Meteor, a bay Holstein gelding foaled in 1943, won showjumping medals at three different Olympic Games.

QUALITY The modern Holsteiner should have the overall look of a quality hunter. His coach-horse ancestry gives him strength, soundness, and a good temperament.

Hungarian Halfblood

ORIGIN Hungary
ENVIRONMENT
BLOOD
USES
HEIGHT 15.2–16.1 hh (1.57–1.65 m)
COLOURS All solid colours

The Hungarian Halfblood is also known as the Hungarian Kisber and the Kisber Felver. It is one of the less well-known warmblood breeds, and has proved itself highly adaptable. It was bred first as a cavalry horse, then used for light draught and artillery work, and later as a carriage horse. It is now a sports horse.

| BLACK | BROWN | CHESTNUT | GREY | BAY |

ORIGINS

The breed was developed at what was the Kisber Stud, founded in 1853. This was primarily a Thoroughbred (*see* pp 284–87) stud, but they also produced a half-bred horse, which became known as the Hungarian Halfblood. The World Wars took a huge toll on the breed. However, about 150 horses had been sent to America, where they were found to make good cattle horses. Another saving grace was the heroic efforts of Countess Gyurky, who fled during World War II in a bid to save sixty horses by taking them to America. Only thirteen survived the journey, but the breed itself survived and now has a registry in both Hungary and America.

IN DEMAND Prior to World War I, the Hungarian Halfblood had been in great demand across Europe. During the two World Wars, thousands of the horses were slaughtered for meat.

CHARACTERISTICS

The versatile Hungarian Halfblood was bred with performance as a prime aim, and strict selection procedures were put in place to ensure that only the very best individuals were used to generate the breed. This substantial horse should have plenty of bone; big, ground-covering paces; and an exceptional temperament. The Hungarian Halfblood is often called 'the Heavenly Horse' in recognition of the service he has given to humans with such great willingness.

Hunter

ORIGIN United Kingdom
ENVIRONMENT
BLOOD
USES
HEIGHT Over 14.2 hh (1.47 m)
COLOURS All colours

The Hunter, like the Hack, is a type not a breed, though plenty of horsemen will tell you they have the perfect recipe for breeding one. The Hunter is bred first and foremost for the sport of hunting. Even those destined only for showing have to have the attributes required of a true hunter.

| BLACK | BROWN | CHESTNUT | DUN | GREY | BAY | PALOMINO |

CHARACTERISTICS

Hunting as a sport, rather than as a means of survival, has been enjoyed for several centuries, and it is in these last few hundred years that the breeding of a good Hunter type has been established. The word 'hunter' can really apply to any horse that is ridden to hounds, and that can involve all shapes and sizes! But, in practice, the term is used to describe a horse that can easily meet the requirements of a day's hunting. He must be able to carry a weight appropriate to his size all day; he must be sound enough and surefooted enough to gallop across any type of terrain; he must have a bold, powerful jump to enable him to negotiate whatever crosses his path; and he must also have a 'fifth leg' and good sense of self-preservation to handle the often tricky obstacles and hazards that are met when following hounds.

To have sufficient speed and scope, most Hunters have a good amount of Thoroughbred (see pp 284–87) blood. Some of the best Hunters are Thoroughbred/Irish Draught (see pp 144–45) crosses. Some pony blood can also be useful in a Hunter, as long as there is sufficient speed and scope provided by other quarters. Ponies are particularly sound, tough, and surefooted, often possessing great cleverness when it comes to extricating themselves and their riders from tricky situations.

RED COATS The Hunt Masters and hunt staff traditionally wear red coats so that they are easily visible to the mounted followers. Followers are expected to allow the hunt staff space to do their job and to obey instructions from the Field Master.

Whilst boldness and courage are requisites, a Hunter should not be overly excitable and should remember his manners even in the most heady situations. A good hunter should be adept at taking his own line across country, but mannerly enough to take his turn to jump when there is only a narrow obstacle to negotiate. He should be an honest-looking horse, rather than necessarily beautiful. But the best will combine strength and size with quality.

SHOW HUNTERS

In the show ring, a Hunter is expected to show all the attributes required of him in the field: strength, stamina, soundness, a good gallop, a bold jump, and excellent manners. Classes are usually split into lightweight, middleweight, and heavyweight. In Show-Hunter competitions, the horse is judged on turnout, conformation, manners, and individual show as well as the ride he gives to the judge.

CONFORMATION A Hunter's conformation should be as correct as possible; a well-conformed horse will have more effective and comfortable paces, as well as being more likely to remain sound than one with conformational faults.

FUN FOR ALL Hunting in Europe and the United States is a very formal affair with impressively turned-out hunt staff and followers. In other countries, including New Zealand, which is shown here, it is a far more relaxed occasion that is more like a day's rough shooting than an expensive day on the grouse moors.

THE BEAUFORT HUNT One of the most famous hunts in England is the Beaufort hunt. The Dukes of Beaufort have, over several generations, acted as masters of this hunt, which has its home on the equally famed Badminton estate.

Indian Half-bred

ORIGIN India
ENVIRONMENT
BLOOD
USES
HEIGHT 15.3–16.0 hh (1.60–1.63 m)
COLOURS All solid colours

Half-bred horses have long been bred in India. The main breeding centres are owned by the Army to supply horses to the cavalry and mounted-police units. Half-breds are produced by crossing a full Thoroughbred (*see* pp 284–87) to other breeds. Its ability to adapt to the climate makes the Thoroughbred a popular cross.

BLACK BROWN CHESTNUT GREY BAY

ORIGINS

In the 19th century, great use was made of Arab (*see* pp 184–87) and part-Arab horses. By the early 20th century, a bigger, stronger horse was preferred and a number of Australian Walers were imported as they had proved themselves in many countries as exceptional cavalry mounts. With a good pool of imported horses available, the Indian Army studs began to develop the Indian Half-bred using a mixture of native mares, the Kathiawari (*see* p 238), as well as the Australian Walers, and Thoroughbred stallions. The modern Indian Half-bred is still used as a cavalry and police horse, and is finding a new role in competitive sports.

CHARACTERISTICS

The two main breeding centres are at Saharanpur and Babugarh and work hard to produce a quality equine. It can vary but is generally a medium-sized, wiry little horse. The limbs and feet are excellent as they have to withstand continually working on hard ground.

WELL RAISED At the army studs, the young horses are kept on good pastures with careful supplementary feeding. They do not start work until they are four years old, and they are broken in carefully over a nine-month initial training period.

HOME AND ABROAD The Indian Half-bred is used as a means of transport. He also finds work as a police horse, cavalry horse, and riding-club mount. He is exported in small numbers to the United Arab Emirates.

Irish Hunter

ORIGIN Ireland
ENVIRONMENT 🌱
BLOOD 🌢
USES 🐎 🏇
HEIGHT 16.0–17.0 hh (1.63–1.73 m)
COLOURS All solid colours

The Irish Hunter is a crossbred horse intended for the hunting field. Such is the reputation of Irish horses, Irish horsemen and women, particularly in the hunting field, that the Irish Hunter is considered to be one of the best horses to ride across country. He is a cross between a Thoroughbred and an Irish Draught.

BLACK   BROWN   CHESTNUT   GREY   BAY

ORIGINS

In the early 12th century, during the Anglo-Norman invasions, heavy horses, such as the Flemish Draught, were brought to Ireland and bred to native mares. This strong type was later refined using Andalucian (*see* p 180) and some Arab (*see* pp 184–87) blood, and the Irish Draught breed evolved as a versatile light draught horse with sufficient quality for ridden work. The Thoroughbred (*see* pp 284–87) blood that produces the Irish Hunter gave the horse scope and speed without losing his toughness, surefootedness, and good common sense.

CHARACTERISTICS

The Irish Hunter is bold, athletic, and scopey, whilst still being as clever as a pony at handling the hazards and obstacles of the hunting field. He has a strong, honest head with large ears and expressive eyes. The neck should be long and slightly arched. The chest and body are deep and strong with powerful hindquarters.

GOOD COUNTRY The damp climate and rich soil in Ireland produces nutritious grazing that helps produce horses with plenty of bone and substance.

Irish Sports Horse

ORIGIN Ireland
ENVIRONMENT 🌾
BLOOD 💧
USES 🏇 🏇
HEIGHT 15.0–17.0 hh (1.52–1.73 m)
COLOURS Any colour, but most commonly solid colours

The Irish Sports Horse is really a refined Irish Hunter. The attributes required of a good sports horse are fairly well met already in the Irish Hunter. However, a sports horse can afford to be lighter framed, faster, and ideally requires more impressive paces than are needed in the hunting field.

BLACK   BROWN   CHESTNUT   DUN   GREY   BAY   PALOMINO   COLOURED

ORIGINS AND CHARACTERISTICS

Despite the success of Irish breeds, Ireland has lagged some way behind the continent in terms of registering and recording breed pedigrees and in the promotion of sports horses. In 1993, the Irish Horse Board was formed with the dual roles of maintaining the Irish Horse Registry and marketing Irish Sports Horses both at home and abroad. The Registry holds both the Irish Sports Horse stud book and the Irish Draught Horse stud book. It operates schemes to improve the breeding of Irish horses and also offers training grants and sponsors competition classes. The Irish Sports Horse is generally based on a mixture of Thoroughbred (*see* pp 284–87) and Irish Draught blood (*see* pp 144–45) but additional influences include Ireland's native pony, the Connemara (*see* p 313), which is an excellent sports pony in its own right.

REFINING PROCESS In recent years, in an effort to match the often more extravagant paces of the European warmblood breeds, some of these continental breeds have also been used in the development of the Irish Sports Horse.

Kabardin

ORIGIN Russia
ENVIRONMENT ▲
BLOOD 🌢
USES 🐎 🐎🐎 🐎
HEIGHT 15.0–15.2 hh (1.52–1.57 m)
COLOURS Dark solid colours

The Kabardin takes his name from his homeland, the Karbardin-Balkar Republic in the Northern Caucasus. He has evolved to deal with the mountainous terrain and climate very well. He has an excellent sense of direction and homing instinct, making him invaluable to the mounted herdsmen working in this region.

BLACK   BROWN   CHESTNUT   BAY

ORIGINS
The Kabardin is an ancestor of the steppe horses that evolved from the Asiatic Wild Horse (*see* p 12) and the Tarpan. By the 16th century, the steppe horses had been crossed with Persian, Karabakh, and Turkmen breeds to produce the Kabardin. Originally the horse was of a fairly small, light stamp. Many were lost during the Russian revolution, but from the 1920s onwards efforts were made to improve and revive the breed. Two main studs at Malkin and Malo Karachaev were responsible for these efforts. With selective breeding and good husbandry, a larger, stronger type of horse was developed and is now used for general riding and driving, as well as for cavalry horses and to improve native stock.

CHARACTERISTICS
The Kabardin is tough and hardy, very surefooted, and possesses plenty of stamina. It has a slightly primitive head, indicative of his steppe origins, and is usually Roman nosed. His limbs are short and strong, with sufficient bone and no feather.

RIDING HORSES Both the Kabardin and the Anglo Kabardin (a Kabardin/Thoroughbred cross) make good riding horses. They have great stamina, a placid temperament, and comfortable paces.

MOUNTAIN HORSE To withstand harsh conditions, the Kabardin grows an abundant mane and tail. He has slightly heavy shoulders but a strong, short back. The forelimbs are very correct although the hind legs have a tendency to be sickle-hocked.

Karabair

ORIGIN Uzbekistan
ENVIRONMENT ▲
BLOOD 🜄
USES 🏇 🏇 🏇
HEIGHT 14.3–15.1 hh (1.50–1.55 m)
COLOURS All solid colours, and very occasionally coloured

The Karabair is one of the most ancient breeds of Central Asia. His homeland of Uzbekistan is on a network of trade routes used by numerous warriors and tribes over the centuries. Originally there were three strains: a good riding horse; a heavier, quieter riding and driving horse; and a longer-backed pack horse.

BLACK   CHESTNUT   DUN   GREY   BAY   PALOMINO   COLOURED

ORIGINS
The Karabair was a cross between local steppe mares and the more refined Oriental breeds that passed through the area with their accompanying nomadic tribes. These would have been Arab, Persian, and Turkmen breeds, which lent quality and speed to the enduring but rather primitive steppe horse. Many of the Uzbek people continue to live a nomadic existence. Their herds of Karabairs roam the pastures of the mountains and foothills of the area, resulting in a tough, very sound horse with exceptional stamina.

CHARACTERISTICS
The Karabair shares many of the Arab's attributes, but without being as refined overall. The head has a straight profile, and may be Roman nosed; the neck is a good length, but the shoulders are a little steep. This, and the fact that the forehand is more developed than the hindquarters, is often the case in mountain breeds. The coat is fine and silky and legs are clean and strong.

RAISING STANDARDS The stud farms at Dzhizal and Avangard have done much to improve the overall standard. The horses are broken in very young, in the manner of Thoroughbred flat racehorses, being performance-tested on the racecourse as two- and three-year-olds. The Karabair is crossed to the Thoroughbred to produce a horse for flat racing. The purebred Karabair is raced in a combined contest racing under saddle and in harness.

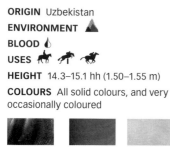

Karabakh

ORIGIN Azerbaijan

ENVIRONMENT ▲

BLOOD ◊

USES 🏇 🐎

HEIGHT 14.0–15.0 hh (1.42–1.52 m)

COLOURS Chestnut, dun, or bay, with a metallic sheen

CHESTNUT	DUN	BAY

The Karabakh is another ancient mountain breed and a near neighbour of the Kabardin. They both descended from the primitive Przewalski (*see* p 12) and Tarpan horses. Their geographical location has left them open to the influences of the horse breeds from neighbouring Iraq, Iran, Turkey, and Kurdistan.

ORIGINS

The Karabakh breed existed as far back as the 4th century, but has only had an official stud book since 1981. He is the result of crossing the native steppe horse with Arab (*see* pp 184–87) and Akhal-Teke (*see* pp 174–75) stallions. This region was in the centre of a busy network of trade routes, which is how the Eastern horses came into the area. The purebred Karabakh is rare – the Agdam stud is working to regenerate the breed.

CHARACTERISTICS

The Karabakh is lightweight but strong, sound, and hardy. The head is small and elegant; the neck is high set; and the back and loins are short, flat, and strong. The hindquarters are wide and well muscled, and the chest is deep. The legs are strong, with well-defined tendons, and small hard feet. The horse is thin-skinned with a fine, silky coat and tail hair. The influence of the Akhal-Teke shows in the metallic sheen of the coat.

HIGHLANDS Herds of Karabakh horses roam freely on the high mountain pastures in the summer before being brought down into the foothills in the winter. They are fed lucerne to supplement their grazing in the winter.

Kathiawari

ORIGIN India
ENVIRONMENT
BLOOD
USES
HEIGHT 15.0 hh (1.52 m)
COLOURS All solid colours except black

The Kathiawari breed is found mainly on India's northwestern coast, and is named after the Kathiawar Peninsula of that region; he is also found in Maharashtra, Gujerat, and southern Rajasthan. Both the Kathiawari and its near neighbour, the Marwari (*see* p 249), have unique and remarkably shaped inward curving ears.

BROWN   CHESTNUT   DUN   GREY   BAY

ORIGINS

Native horses of steppe and desert origin had roamed this region of India for centuries. Some were ancient breeds such as the Kabuli and Baluchi, from which it is thought the Kathiawari inherited the distinctive ears. From the 1500s, during the reign of the Moghul Emperors and, later, during the rule of the British Raj, Arab (*see* pp 184–87) horses were imported, as were Cape Horses from South Africa. These were bred to the native stock to produce the Kathiawari. The breed was a favourite of Indian royalty, and was bred at the royal palaces. During the 19th century, it was employed as a cavalry horse and is still used by mounted police forces in India.

CURVED EARS The most notable feature of the breed are the uniquely shaped ears; these touch each other at the tips and can rotate through nearly 360 degrees.

CHARACTERISTICS

The Kathiawari resembles the Arab in many ways. He is slightly light of bone, but is inherently sound.

Kiger Mustang

ORIGIN United States
ENVIRONMENT 🌾
BLOOD 💧
USES 🏇 🏇 🐎
HEIGHT 15.0–15.2 hh (1.52–1.57 m)
COLOURS Dun

The Kiger Mustang was discovered during a routine roundup of Mustangs in Oregon in 1977. The American Mustang descended from Spanish horses brought to the States in the 16th century, but it was thought that this Spanish blood had been diluted over the centuries. Genetic testing showed all the Kiger Mustangs retain a high percentage of Spanish horse genes.

ORIGINS AND CHARACTERISTICS

In the 16th century, many Spanish horses escaped to form feral herds, which became known as Mustangs. Over the centuries, other breeds of horses escaped to join these herds, leading to a dilution of the Spanish blood and considerable variety of type amongst the herds. During a Mustang roundup at Beatty's Butt in southeastern Oregon, in 1977, a small band of very similar horses were spotted. They were very alike, were various shades of dun, and had dorsal and zebra-stripe markings. The Bureau of Land Management, which manages the Mustang herds, decided to separate the group to preserve their distinguishing features. The group was split into two small herds and placed into two separate Herd Management Areas – the East Kiger area and an area in Riddle Mountain. Genetic testing was carried out at the University of Kentucky where it was discovered that the DNA of all the Kiger Mustangs retained a high percentage of the Spanish horse genes. The herd has been left to live and multiply naturally. Some of the horses are offered to private homes as part of the Land Bureau's 'Adopt-a-Horse' programme. These have proved to be intelligent, and keen and willing to learn.

CAPABLE Kiger Mustangs have a compact build, with strong legs and exceptionally hard feet. They possess tremendous powers of endurance and a natural 'cow-sense'. In captivity, the Kigers are proving themselves to be capable, hardworking horses.

STAR The Kiger is a very attractive horse with a head very similar to a Barb. A Kiger called 'Donner' was used as a model for the equine hero in the animated film *Spirit, the Stallion of Cimarron*.

Kladruber

ORIGIN Czech Republic
ENVIRONMENT
BLOOD 🌢
USES 🏇 🐴 🐎
HEIGHT 16.0–17.0 hh (1.63–1.73 m)
COLOURS Black or grey

BLACK   GREY

The Kladruber horse is also known as the Kladrubsky. He is long-established and, although developed from imported bloodlines, considered a Czech native. There are two strains: the white Kladruber is lighter framed and used for riding; the strongly built black Kladruber is primarily for carriage work, although both are commonly driven. The breed is now quite rare.

ORIGINS

The Kladruby stud where the breed was developed is one of the oldest studs in the world. It was founded in 1579, and bred from imported Spanish horses with the aim of producing majestic carriage horses. A mixture of bloodlines was used, including Neopolitan, Danish, Holsteiner (*see* p 226), as well as the more heavily built Oldenburger (*see* p 258).

CHARACTERISTICS

Once established, the Kladruber was further developed as two different strains. The taller, more refined, white horses were produced by outcrossing

SHOW WHITE The Kladruber is still a relatively heavy and plain horse, but his white colouring and great presence and bearing makes him a majestic, showy animal, particularly when driven in a big team.

to Lipizzaners (*see* p 242), and were developed to be used for ridden ceremonial and cavalry duties. The black Kladruber was, overall, a heavier but smaller horse with a slightly coarser head, and was bred to take its place in four- and six-in-hand ceremonial carriage teams. The black strain was almost lost in the 1930s, but the Research Institute for Horse Breeding in Slatinany re-established the breed.

Knabstrup

ORIGIN Denmark
ENVIRONMENT 🌱
BLOOD 🌢
USES 🐎 🛞
HEIGHT 15.2–16.0 hh (1.57–1.63 m)
COLOURS White with brown or black spots

The spotted Knabstrup has always been popular as a circus horse. The old Knabstrup was bred mainly for carriage work and was not as refined as the modern version, which has better overall conformation and is similar to the Appaloosa (*see* pp 182–83).

MANE Like the Appaloosa, the Knabstrup has a sparse mane.

ORIGINS AND CHARACTERISTICS

At the time of the Napoleonic Wars, a spotted Spanish mare called Flaebehoppen was bred to a Frederiksborg stallion by her owner, Judge Lunn. He named the breed after his estate. The horses were easy to train, but their conformation deteriorated when they were bred only for their spots. This has been rectified in the modern Knabstrup.

Latvian Riding Horse

ORIGIN Latvia
ENVIRONMENT 🌱
BLOOD 🌢
USES 🐎 🏇
HEIGHT 16.0–17.0 hh (1.63–1.73 m)
COLOURS All solid colours

The Latvian Riding Horse was developed by refining the original Latvian Draught Horse to produce a horse suitable for riding and equestrian sports. Until the 1980s, all Latvian horses were kept in state-owned studs.

| BLACK | BROWN | CHESTNUT | GREY | BAY |

ORIGINS AND CHARACTERISTICS

The Latvian Draught Horse was a cross between local mares and imported Oldenburger (*see* p 258), Holsteiner (*see* p 226), and Hanoverian (*see* p 224) stallions. In 1925, the state stud at Svetciems opened, and this had many mares that had been army competition horses, as well as using Trakehner (*see* pp 288–89), Arab (*see* pp 184–87), and Thoroughbred (*see* pp 284–87) bloodlines. The first stud book was also opened in 1925. The breed has had success in dressage and showjumping.

WARM NATURED Despite it being a warmblood, the Latvians have not followed the continental trend and called their horse a Latvian Warmblood.

Lipizzaner

ORIGIN Slovenia
ENVIRONMENT 🌿
BLOOD 💧
USES 🐎 🐎 🐎🐎
HEIGHT 15.1–16.2 hh (1.55–1.67 m)
COLOURS Generally grey, but also black and bay

BLACK	GREY	BAY

The Lipizzaner is known to most people through the classical riding demonstrations of 'Haute École' given by the Spanish Riding School of Vienna. But it also makes an excellent driving horse. It is bred in several countries that were once part of the Austro-Hungarian empire.

ORIGINS AND CHARACTERISTICS

During the late 16th century, some excellent horses were bred in Spain by crossing the best Arab (*see* pp 184–87) bloodlines to the athletic and elegant Spanish horses. Some of these horses were taken to Austria and used at the newly formed Kladrub stud. A second stud was formed at Lipizza in Slovenia, with the aim of producing riding horses. The Kladrub stallions 'Maestoso' and 'Favory' became two of the foundation sires of the Lipizzaner. During the 18th and 19th centuries a mixture of Spanish, Italian, and Arab blood was used. The resultant breed is distinguished by his powerful hindquarters, which enable him to perform the demanding high-school movements.

HIGH CARRIAGE Lipizzaner horses also make excellent carriage horses. A larger, free-moving stamp of Lipizzaner is bred in Hungary, and this is particularly well suited to driving work.

Lokai

ORIGIN Tajikistan
ENVIRONMENT
BLOOD
USES
HEIGHT 14.1–14.3 hh (1.45–1.50 m)
COLOURS Chestnut, grey, or bay

CHESTNUT	GREY	BAY

The Lokai is a mountain horse breed produced by the Lokai tribes people. His homeland is Tajikistan and he was bred from a base stock of primitive steppe horses crossed with the more refined breeds of Central Asia. The Lokai is the smallest of the many Central Asian horse breeds. There is some variation of type, but he is primarily a tough wiry little horse.

ORIGINS

The breed was first developed in the 12th century by the nomadic tribe from which it took its name. The base stock of native steppe horses crossed with a mixture of Asian breeds were further improved by the Lokai people using Akhal-Teke (*see* pp 174–75), Karabair (*see* p 236), and Arab (*see* pp 184–87) blood. The Lokai horse is a riding horse and pack animal, coping easily with the difficult terrain and high altitudes in the highlands. He is also used as a sports horse as he is raced and used in the local game of Kokpar, which involves a team of riders fighting for possession of a goat carcass.

CHARACTERISTICS

Despite some variation of type, he is a tough, surefooted little horse that is quite late to mature. The hocks and forefeet may have conformational faults – sickle hocks being common. The head is quite short and the neck can be lean and low set. The chest is deep and broad and the croup is long and sloped but well muscled.

RIDING HORSE The surefooted Lokai has proved his worth working in the mountainous terrain of his local habitat. A larger, better conformed horse is now being bred in Tajikistan by crossing the Lokai horse to Arab and Thoroughbred stallions.

Lusitano

ORIGIN Portugal
ENVIRONMENT ▲
BLOOD ◗
USES 🐎 🐎🐎 🐎🚗
HEIGHT 15.0–16.0 hh (1.52–1.63 m)
COLOURS Predominantly grey and bay

The Lusitano takes its name from the word 'Lusitania', which is the Latin name for Portugal. It is very like the Andalucian (*see* p 180) of neighbouring Spain and shares a similar history. Classified as the Iberian Horse, both are believed to have evolved from the Sorraia Pony (see p 357) and the Barb (*see* pp 190–91).

BLACK BROWN CHESTNUT DUN GREY BAY PALOMINO

ORIGINS AND CHARACTERISTICS

It is believed that selective breeding from the 18th century onwards created the difference between the two breeds. The greatest influence is said to have been the introduction of bullfighting on foot in Spain, whereas in Portugal, the bullfighters continued on horseback.

The Lusitano is an exceptionally courageous and agile horse, traits born of the talents required to outmanoeuvre an enraged bull. His head is long and noble, often with a convex profile. He looks 'leggier' than the Andalucian, mainly due to overly long cannon bones.

CONFORMATION The Lusitano is a well-conformed horse, as would be expected of an animal required to show the elevation and collection required for dressage work, as well as the overall agility needed in the bullring. He carries an abundant and wavy mane and tail.

SPANISH WALK The Lusitano horse is also used for the competitive discipline of dressage as well as for classical High-School work. This horse is demonstrating the Spanish Walk, an exaggerated and extended walking gait.

Mangalarga

ORIGIN Brazil
ENVIRONMENT
BLOOD
USES
HEIGHT 14.2–15.2 hh (1.47–1.57 m)
COLOURS Chestnut, grey, bay, or roan

CHESTNUT	GREY	BAY	ROAN

The Mangalarga has two strains: the Mangalarga and the Mangalarga Marchador. Both exhibit a number of gaited paces. Although closely related, they now have individual stud books and breed associations. The breed has its foundation in the Spanish Alter-Real (*see* pp 176–77). Some of these royal stallions were brought to Brazil in the early 1800s.

ORIGINS

In the mid-19th century, the Baron of Alfenas decided to breed a dual-purpose horse for pleasure riding and ranch work. He bred some of his Alter-Real stallions to local mares, which were a mix of mainly Barb (*see* pp 190–91) and Dutch horses. Arab (*see* pp 184–87), Thoroughbred (*see* pp 284–87) and American Saddlebred (*see* p 179) blood was also used, to produce a horse with a particular gait; the 'Marcha Trottada' or 'walking trot'.

CHARACTERISTICS

The horse has a look of quality about him, with a slightly long head but alert eyes and ears. He has a long, muscular neck; prominent withers; a short, strong back; well-muscled hindquarters; and a high-set tail. The Mangalarga horse exhibits both the *picada* (lateral four-beat gait) and the *batida* (diagonal four-beat gait).

VERSATILE HORSE The Mangalarga is very versatile, being used for ranch work, pleasure riding, and equestrian sports.

GAITED As the breed's popularity spread, breeders concentrated on developing different gaits within the breed and introduced Hackney, Trotter, and a whole mix of European blood.

LUSITANO STALLION Since opening their own stud book for the Lusitano, the Portuguese have greatly improved the breed by monitoring the various bloodlines to allow for more selective breeding.

Maremmana

ORIGIN Italy
ENVIRONMENT
BLOOD
USES
HEIGHT 15.2–15.3 hh (1.57–1.60 m)
COLOURS All solid colours

BLACK   BROWN   CHESTNUT   GREY   BAY

The Maremmana was bred in Tuscany. The Maremmana area is coastal and was once a marshland before being drained and reclaimed as pasture. There were no indigenous horse breeds in Italy but nonetheless, using imported stock from Spain and Italy, it was an important horse-breeding area during the 17th century.

ORIGINS

The Maremmana has his origins in the ancient Neapolitan, which was derived from a mixture of Barb (*see* pp 190–91), Spanish, and Arab (*see* pp 184–87) blood and became renowned in the Neapolitan Riding Academy in the 16th century.

To meet the needs of the Italian farmers, there was some outcrossing to other European breeds, notably the Norfolk Roadster, resulting in a strong riding horse with an equable temperament, capable of ranch work as well as light draught. The Maremmana is used as a troop horse and in the mounted police.

CHARACTERISTICS

The mixed blood can result in great variation, with some horses displaying quality and fineness but the majority being slightly plain and coarse. The general stamp is strong and workmanlike. They do not have the best shoulders, but nonetheless have evolved as a tough, sound horse that is easy to look after. The breed has great endurance and a calm and tractable temperament, making him a popular choice of the *buttero* – the Italian cowboy.

IMPROVING The original Maremmana Horse was relatively plain, but selective breeding, using better stallions, has brought much improvement to the overall quality and conformation.

Marwari

ORIGIN India
ENVIRONMENT
BLOOD
USES
HEIGHT 14.2–15.2 hh (1.47–1.57 m)
COLOURS All solid and part colours

The exact origins of the Marwari are not known, but he was developed as a distinct breed in India. His ancestors may have come from areas to the northwest of India, such as Uzbekistan and Turkmenistan. He is a wiry but elegant horse, and his most distinctive feature is his fascinating, inward-curving ears.

BLACK   BROWN   CHESTNUT   DUN   GREY   BAY   PALOMINO   COLOURED

ORIGINS AND CHARACTERISTICS

Selective breeding to develop the Marwari Horse began as early as the 12th century. Some of the finest stallions were kept by the Rathores, who ruled the region of Marwar at the time. The breed is most likely to have been influenced by Turkmen and Arab blood (*see* pp 184–87) and is also similar to the neighbouring Kathiawari (*see* p 238). He has found many uses: as the mount of warriors; and as a sports horse, being used to play polo and 'pig-sticking'.

The Marwari often displays a natural pacing gait called the *revaal* and is adept at High-School movements. The head, with its scimitar-shaped ears, is full of quality. The neck is long, arched, and proud, and is high set. The chest is well developed and the limbs are long and slender.

WARRIOR HORSE The Marwari has long been prized and nurtured as a breed by the royal families of India. He was a courageous, agile, and tough little war horse, who found plenty of employment in his native India.

Missouri Foxtrotter

ORIGIN United States
ENVIRONMENT ▲
BLOOD 🌢
USES 🏇 🏇 🏇
HEIGHT 14.0–16.0 hh (1.42–1.63 m)
COLOURS All colours, but predominantly chestnut

The Missouri Foxtrotter was developed out of a need for settlers in Missouri to have a horse that could comfortably travel for many miles over the rugged terrain of the Ozark Hills. Although named and most famous for its 'foxtrot', the Foxtrotter has two other distinctive gaits: the flat-foot walk and a 'rocking-horse' canter.

BLACK   BROWN   CHESTNUT   DUN   GREY   BAY

ORIGINS

Early settlers crossed the Mississippi River and began to make their homes in Missouri in the early 1800s. They came mainly from Tennessee, Virginia, and Kentucky, and brought with them various saddle horses such as Morgans (*see* p 252), Thoroughbreds (*see* pp 284–87), and Spanish horses. These were interbred to produce a horse best suited to the rugged terrain of this area. Some use of the American Saddlebred (*see* p 179) as well as the Tennessee Walker (*see* p 282) helped produce the Missouri Foxtrotter. His defining gait is best described as walking with the front legs and trotting with the hind legs. Any jarring or concussion is eliminated in the way that the horse places his hind feet; they touch the ground and slide forwards to follow the tracks of the front feet. Moving in this way, the horse can maintain a speed of up to 13 kph (8 mph) over considerable distances.

The early breeders were able to develop a horse with this natural gait without losing the equally important traits of soundness, stamina, and a gentle and kind temperament. The Missouri Foxtrotting Horse Breed Association was founded in

THE FOXTROT The gait after which the horse is named is comfortable and efficient, allowing horse and rider to travel over difficult terrain with minimum exertion. The horse walks with the front legs and trots with the hind legs, sliding them forwards as the feet touch the ground to follow in the tracks of the front feet.

1948. A fire destroyed the original stud book and records, and the association was reformed in 1958. There are well over 40,000 registered Missouri Foxtrotters in Canada and America.

CHARACTERISTICS

The breed has developed into a muscular, compact horse that is particularly versatile. In comparison to the Tennessee Walker and American Saddlebred that influenced its development, the

COMPACT The Foxtrotter is not as showy as the Tennessee Walker or the American Saddlebred. He looks more of a workhorse with his powerful, compact body, and his relatively low outline. He is renowned for his stamina and overall soundness.

Missouri Foxtrotter has a relatively low outline and lower action. The head can be a little plain, although it is neat and clean and tapers to a narrow muzzle. The expression is alert and intelligent. The chest is wide and deep and the shoulders sloped and powerful – the movement coming from the shoulders rather than from any exaggerated knee action. The hindquarters, too, are powerful and muscular with a low-set tail.

PLEASURE RIDING The kind, gentle temperament and the comfortable gait of the Missouri Foxtrotter makes him a popular choice for pleasure and trail riding. There are also specialist showing classes for the breed. His size and temperament make him a suitable mount for both adults and children.

Morab

ORIGIN United States
ENVIRONMENT
BLOOD ⬧
USES
HEIGHT 14.2–15.3 hh (1.47–1.60 m)
COLOURS All solid colours

BLACK   BROWN   CHESTNUT   GREY   BAY   PALOMINO

The Morab is a cross of an Arab (*see* pp 184–87) with a Morgan (*see* below). It is accepted as a breed (rather than half-breed) because of its ability to transmit its distinguishing characteristics consistently to its offspring.

ORIGINS AND CHARACTERISTICS
Early breeding of Morabs – in nature if not in name – was reported and recommended by Mr Lindsley, a Morgan Horse historian. In the 1920s, the name was coined by William Randolph Hearst. He bred two Arab stallions to Morgan mares, and found the Morab ideal for ranch work. The breed register was founded in 1999.

BLOODLINES
Foundation stock or first generation Morabs are half Arab and half Morgan, making them eligible for registration with all three breed societies.

Morgan

ORIGIN United States
ENVIRONMENT
BLOOD ⬧
USES
HEIGHT 14.1–15.3 hh (1.45–1.60 m)
COLOURS All dark colours, no white leg markings permitted above the knee or hock

BLACK   BROWN   CHESTNUT   BAY

The foundation sire of the Morgan Horse breed is a legend. Of unknown breeding, he found fame for his courage, strength, speed, and indomitable spirit despite his tiny stature. Originally called Figure, his name was changed to that of his owner, Justin Morgan.

ORIGINS AND CHARACTERISTICS
Justin Morgan was foaled in 1789 and may have been a mixture of Dutch, Thoroughbred (*see* pp 284–87) and Arab (*see* pp 184–87) blood. Only 14 hh (1.42 m), he was lightweight and full of quality. He worked hard for thirty years, ploughing, hauling, and even racing. An exceptional sire, he passed his qualities to his offspring.

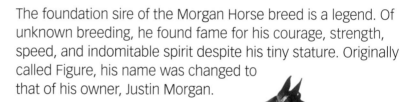

FINE BREEDING Morgans have a fine, expressive face; an arched neck; strong, sloping shoulders; and well-defined withers. His long pasterns aid his light springy step.

Mustang

ORIGIN United States
ENVIRONMENT ▲ 🌾
BLOOD 💧
USES 🏇 🏇 🏇
HEIGHT 14.0–15.0 hh (1.42–1.52 m)
COLOURS All colours

The Mustang is the feral horse of the Americas. Of Spanish descent, it mixed with other breeds that escaped or lost their homes over the years. In the early 19th century, numbers were estimated at over two million. Widespread culling took place until the horses were protected under an act passed in 1971.

BLACK   BROWN   CHESTNUT   DUN   GREY   BAY   PALOMINO   COLOURED

ORIGINS AND CHARACTERISTICS

There had been horses in North America in prehistoric times but, about 12,000 years ago, they disappeared. In the 16th century horses from Spain were introduced by the *conquistadores*. These would have been of Andalucian (*see* p 180), Arab (*see* pp 184–87), and Barb (*see* pp 190–91) blood. Many of them escaped to run wild. They soon captured the imagination of the native American Indians who kept them in large numbers.

Over time, horses of any number of breeds joined the herds, creating much variation in type. However, they all shared traits necessary for survival: soundness, hardiness, and cunning. Many have been used as riding horses and army mounts. The Bureau of Land Management is now responsible for their management and numbers are approximately 25,000. More than half are found in Nevada, with other significant herds in Montana and Oregon.

TOUGH The Mustang is found in a variety of types and all colours. They are a tough horse, and are very trainable. The Bureau of Land Management offers captured Mustangs for re-homing but there are usually more horses than homes.

BREED SOCIETY The Morgan Horse Club was founded in 1909 to promote the breed. Modern Morgan Horses are used for riding and driving, and are unlikely to ever have to work as hard as their foundation sire, Justin Morgan.

Namibian Warmblood

ORIGIN Namibia
ENVIRONMENT
BLOOD 🔆
USES 🏇 🐎
HEIGHT 16.0–17.0 hh (1.63–1.73 m)
COLOURS All solid colours

The Namibian Warmblood developed in the early 1900s with the importation of European warmblood breeds. The Warmblood Horse Society looks for a horse that is a 'noble, big-framed, correct and performance-orientated warmblood, with elastic and balanced movement and a strong aptitude for jumping'.

BLACK	BROWN	CHESTNUT	GREY	BAY

ORIGINS AND CHARACTERISTICS

In 1936 the Voigtland Stud imported a Trakehner (*see* pp 288–89) stallion called 'Ermanerich', who was used on local mares, which started a breeding programme for warmblood performance horses. In 1952, the same stud imported a Shagya Arab (*see* p 274) stallion and sometime later, a Hanoverian (*see* p 224) called 'Alba'. At this time, a second stud, the Onduno stud, imported a Westphalian (*see* p 291) stallion, 'Raban'. This mix of foundation warmblood sires was balanced by the continual importation and use of Thoroughbred (*see* pp 284–87) stallions, as the breeders of the Namibian Warmblood recognized the importance of the Thoroughbred.

As implied in the breed guidelines, breeders of the Namibian warmblood are free to choose from any number of bloodlines to create their ideal sports horse. The Society was founded in 1994 and insists that all stallions and broodmares are licensed and graded.

PERFORMANCE BRED The Namibian Warmblood is a strong sports horse and should be full of quality. They are graded on conformation, movement, type, and jump. Both mares and stallions are assessed by loose jumping.

Nonius

ORIGIN Hungary
ENVIRONMENT 🌾
BLOOD 💧
USES 🏇 🐎
HEIGHT 15.3–16.2 hh (1.60–1.67 m)
COLOURS Predominantly bay

Hungary had a huge breeding industry during the 19th century, having an estimated horse population of over 2 million. The country was a large-scale provider of cavalry horses throughout Europe. The Nonius was one of a number of enduring breeds developed at the Mezohegyes stud, which was founded in 1784.

BLACK   BROWN   CHESTNUT   BAY

ORIGINS

The foundation stallion 'Nonius Senior' was foaled in Normandy in 1810. He is thought to have been of Anglo-Norman breeding. He was captured by Hungarian cavalrymen at the defeat of Napoleon in 1813 and placed at the Mezohegyes stud. Despite not being very attractive, he turned out to be an outstanding sire. He was bred mainly to Arab (*see* pp 184–87), Hungarian, Lipizzaner (*see* p 242), and Spanish horses, and then the best of his offspring were bred back to him, which is how the distinctive type of the Nonius was developed. In the 1860s, Thoroughbred (*see* pp 284–87) blood was introduced, a move that allowed two types of Nonius to be produced. One was a smaller, more refined horse suited to riding, while the original heavier stamp was used mainly for carriage driving and light draught work.

CHARACTERISTICS

Today's Nonius is a strongly built attractive horse. His neck is well proportioned, strong, and powerful; the withers are well defined; and the shoulders are well sloped. The back and loins are particularly strong and the hindquarters are well muscled. The limbs are clean and strong.

HONEST LOOKS The Nonius has a strong, plain head, but it is nonetheless attractive in its look of gentle honesty. The breed has a good nature and a willing attitude. It is interesting how a perfectly acceptable stamp of horse can be bred from a sire who was reportedly not an inspiring-looking individual.

ACTIVE The strength and power of the Nonius lends itself to carriage work – the larger, heavier type generally being used for this purpose. The horse has paces that are free and active, which helps make him a good riding horse as well.

Oldenburger

ORIGIN Germany
ENVIRONMENT
BLOOD 🜄
USES 🐎 🐎 🐎
HEIGHT 16.0–17.2 hh (1.63–1.78 m)
COLOURS All solid colours, but usually black, brown, or grey

BLACK	BROWN	CHESTNUT	GREY	BAY

Bred since the 1600s, the Oldenburger is the heaviest of the German warmbloods. The birthplace of the Oldenburger was an area near what is now Lower Saxony, near the city of Oldenburg. The horse was developed from a mixture of breeds but was heavily influenced by the Friesian (*see* p 216) in particular.

ORIGINS

Count Johann XVI von Oldenburg set up several stud farms in the late 16th century using a good mix of stallions, mainly to produce carriage horses. His successor also used a variety of stallions of Polish, Barb (*see* pp 190–91), and English blood. In 1861 the Oldenburg stud book and branding was introduced. The breed society followed in 1897. With the arrival of mechanization, breeders refined the Oldenburger to obtain a performance horse, using Thoroughbreds (*see* pp 284–87) among others.

POWERHOUSE The Oldenburger is the largest and heaviest of Germany's warmblood breeds. But he is very well made and certainly not a cumbersome animal.

CHARACTERISTICS

The head is relatively plain, but the expression is kind. The hind limbs and quarters are strong – this is the powerhouse that is such as asset for dressage and showjumping.

Orlov Trotter

ORIGIN Russia

ENVIRONMENT

BLOOD 🜄

USES 🐎 🐎

HEIGHT 15.3–16.0 hh (1.60–1.63 m)

COLOURS All solid colours, but predominantly grey

| BLACK | BROWN | CHESTNUT | GREY | BAY |

The Orlov Trotter is one of Russia's oldest breeds, and is one of the three most successful trotting breeds in the world, the others being the American Standardbred (*see* pp 276–79) and the French Trotter (*see* pp 214–15). The Orlov is now not so well known outside his homeland, but is important in Russian harness racing.

ORIGINS AND CHARACTERISTICS

The Orlov Trotter takes its name from Count Alexis Orlov. During the late 1700s, he imported a grey Arab stallion called 'Smetanka'. One of his offspring was another grey stallion called 'Polkan I' who was bred to a Danish mare to produce 'Bars I', foaled in 1784. Bars I was a successful sire and the foundation stallion of the Orlov Trotter. The head of the Orlov Trotter is small with a broad forehead and alert, pricked ears. His neck is high set, and swan-like, giving him an elegant bearing. The back is long but strong, with muscular loins.

FOUNDATION SIRE Because of the close inbreeding programme that was used to produce the definitive stamp that characterizes the Orlov Trotter, the pedigrees of purebred Orlovs all trace back to the foundation sire, Bars I.

THE TROIKA A popular harness set-up in Russia is the Troika. The centre horse maintains a trot while the outrunners canter to keep pace. Each outrunner is made to carry its head and neck to the outside.

Palomino

ORIGIN United States
ENVIRONMENT 🌾
BLOOD 🌢
USES 🐎 🏇
HEIGHT 14.0–17.0 hh (1.42–1.73 m)
COLOURS Light, medium, or dark gold

The word 'palomino' properly describes a coat colour rather than a breed. Many different breeds can produce palomino horses, but in America, the 'colour' has become virtually accepted as a breed through the Palomino Horse Association and the Palomino Horse Breeders Association.

ORIGINS

The Palomino coat colour has been depicted in the ancient art of Europe and Asia, as well as featuring in Japanese and Chinese artefacts since 200BC. These horses were ridden by the Arabs and the Moors and, during the crusades, a 'splendid Golden Palomino warhorse' was presented to Richard *Coeur-de-Lion* by the Emir Saladin. Queen Ysabella de Bourbon of Spain was an enthusiastic breeder of Palominos, and it is reported that she sent a Palomino stallion and five brood mares out to New Spain (as newly discovered Mexico was known) so that the 'breed' could be developed in the New World. The idea of registering Palominos as a type began in 1935 when Dick Halliday registered his Palomino stallion 'El Rey de los Reyes'. He was a 'golden-

ALL SORTS The Palomino Horse Association now accepts cream-coloured horses with blue eyes as they produce palomino offspring.

horse' enthusiast, and his subsequent articles inspired breeders to specialize in producing horses with this coat colour. The original register was incorporated into the newly formed Palomino Horse Association in 1936.

CHARACTERISITICS

The Palomino Horse Association accepts any breed provided it meets their conformational and colour requirements. The ideal palomino colouring is described as being that of a newly minted gold coin, with shades varying from light, medium, to dark palomino. The mane and tail should be white, silver, or ivory, with no more than 15 per cent dark hairs.

STRIKING GOLD There is no denying that the palomino colouring is striking. The origins of the name are not known, but it may derive from a certain Don Juan De Palomino who was given a 'golden horse' by the *conquistador* Hernán Cortés.

Paso Fino

ORIGIN Puerta Rico and Columbia
ENVIRONMENT ▲
BLOOD ◊
USES 🏇 🏇 🏇
HEIGHT 13.2–15.2 hh (1.37–1.57 m)
COLOURS All colours

The Paso Fino is a naturally gaited horse developed from the Spanish Jennet, the Barb (*see* pp 190–91), and the Andalucian (*see* p 180). *Paso* means 'step' and *fino* means 'fine', providing a good description of the breed's defining features. It is said that speeds of up to 26 kph (16 mph) can be achieved with the rider in total comfort.

BLACK   BROWN   CHESTNUT   DUN   GREY   BAY   PALOMINO   COLOURED

WELL BALANCED The Paso Fino has developed as a well-balanced horse in every sense of the word. Conformationally, he is well proportioned, handsome, and full of quality.

ORIGINS AND CHARACTERISTICS

The foundation stock of this breed were taken from Spain to what is now the Dominican Republic and, as Spanish settlers continued to explore the New World, on into Puerto Rico, Columbia, Cuba, and Mexico. The Paso Fino exhibits three natural gaits. The *classic fino* is the slowest of the gaits and is usually only seen in show horses. The *paso corto* is a working trot with good, ground-covering strides. The *paso largo* is an extended trot, which can achieve the same speed as a canter.

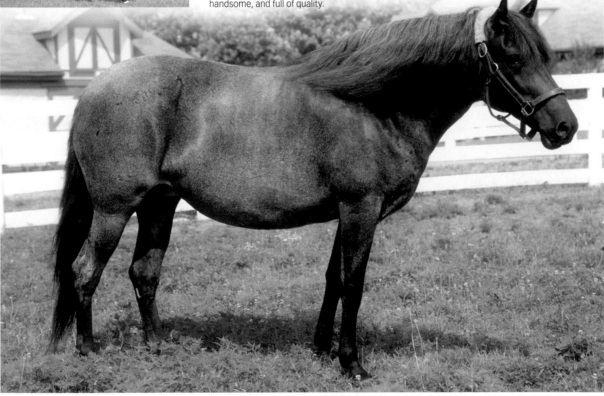

Peruvian Paso

ORIGIN Peru
ENVIRONMENT ▲
BLOOD 💧
USES 🏇 🐎
HEIGHT 14.1–15.2 hh (1.45–1.57 m)
COLOURS All solid colours including dun, palomino and roan

Horses were brought to Peru by the Spanish *conquistadores*, and it was a mixture of Spanish Jennet, Barb (*see* pp 190–91) and Andalucian (*see* p 180) blood that gave rise to the Peruvian Paso – the 'National Horse of Peru'. Its origins are similar to those of the Paso Fino (*see* p 261), but it is quite distinct.

| BLACK | BROWN | CHESTNUT | DUN | GREY | BAY | PALOMINO | ROAN |

ORIGINS AND CHARACTERISTICS

Three of the breeds imported from Spain in 1532 produced the Peruvian Paso. The smooth, ambling gait came from the Spanish Jennet; the strength and stamina from the Barb; and the conformation, beauty, and action from the Andalucian. It differs from the Paso Fino in having the *termino* action (similar to the arms of a human swimmer in crawl) and greater extension. It is guaranteed to transmit its gaits to its offsping.

FAST Now mainly employed for pleasure riding and showing, in the past the Peruvian Paso's extended paces allowed him to carry his rider over mountainous terrain at speed.

INHERITED TRAITS The Spanish Jennet has passed on its high-stepping gaits to the Peruvian Paso, a horse that is valued for giving a comfortable ride over rough ground.

Pinto

ORIGIN United States
ENVIRONMENT
BLOOD
USES
HEIGHT 14.2–16.2 hh (1.47–1.67 m)
COLOURS Broken pattern of white and any other coat colour

The Pinto horse covers a multitude of actual breeds because the word 'pinto' refers to the broken coat colouring of the animal. In all other countries, pinto is used simply to describe the coat colour but, in the United States, the Pinto Horse is accepted as a breed.

ORIGINS AND CHARACTERISTICS

Pinto Horses descend from the Spanish horses that were introduced to the Americas with the arrival of the *conquistadores* in the 16th century. Although any breed, provided it has the required coat pattern, can register as a Pinto, the stamp of horse is generally that of a stock horse. There are two coat patterns: Overo has a solid coat colour as a base with large splashes of white; Tobiano has a white coat colour with large splashes of a solid colour. The Pinto Horse Association of America was formed in 1956 and the breed was recognized in 1963. Additionally, Pinto Horses are registered as one of four different types: stock, hunter, pleasure, and saddle type.

SKEWBALD In many European countries, the Pinto would be described as piebald if it was a mixture of black and white, or skewbald if it was any other colour mixed with white.

TOBIANO A white coat with splashes of colour denotes a Tobiano. The genes responsible for these colourings are complex and different crosses may produce a variety of results.

Plantation Horse

ORIGIN United States
ENVIRONMENT
BLOOD 🜄
USES 🏇 🏇 🏇
HEIGHT 14.2–16.0 hh (1.47–1.63 m)
COLOURS All solid colours, but predominantly grey

In the late 1800s, a family called McCurdy ran a large plantation in central Alabama. In 1905, they bred a fine grey stallion called 'McCurdy's Dr McLain'. He was bred to a number of gaited mares, and the breed line, popular with other plantation owners, became known as 'the McCurdy'.

BLACK	BROWN	CHESTNUT	GREY	BAY

ORIGINS AND CHARACTERISTICS

All the McCurdy's Plantation Horses were registered as foundation stock for the Tennessee Walking Horse Association in 1930. In 1993 the McCurdy Plantation Horse Association was formed. The breed has a smooth gait, rounded hips, a broad chest, short back, and good bone. It has a thick mane and tail.

MCCURDY LICK The four-beat lateral gait of the Plantation Horse is called the McCurdy Lick.

Pleasure Horse

ORIGIN United States
ENVIRONMENT 🔺
BLOOD 🜄
USES 🏇 🏇 🏇
HEIGHT Over 14.0 hh (1.42 m)
COLOURS All colours

The Pleasure Horse is, in most instances, a type rather than a breed. Western Pleasure Horse classes are held at many shows and are open to any light-horse breed. They judge the paces, balance, obedience, conformation, and temperament of the horse. Some 'pleasure' classes are open to all breeds.

BLACK	BROWN	CHESTNUT	DUN	GREY	BAY	PALOMINO	COLOURED

ORIGINS AND CHARACTERISTICS

The Mountain Pleasure Horse was bred in Kentucky to provide a fast, efficient, and comfortable means of transport over rugged and steep terrain. Like the American Saddlebred (*see* p 179), and the Tennessee Walker (*see* p 286), the Pleasure Horse was bred from the mid-1800s from early gaited breeds. The defining gait of the Pleasure Horse is described as an 'evenly spaced, four-beat lateral gait with moderate forward speed and extension but without exaggerated knee and hock action'.

GAITED The Mountain Pleasure Horse is a breed rather than a type, and he is a gaited breed. But there are Pleasure Horse showing classes for both gaited and non-gaited horses.

Polish Warmblood

ORIGIN Poland
ENVIRONMENT
BLOOD
USES
HEIGHT 16.0–17.0 hh (1.63–1.73 m)
COLOURS All colours

The Polish were renowned as great horsemen, their cavalry in particular gaining worldwide fame. Prior to World War II, the Poles had the fifth largest horse population in the world (four million), but there were significant losses during the war. Since then, Poland has turned its attention to sports-horse breeding.

BLACK   BROWN   CHESTNUT   DUN   GREY   BAY

ORIGINS AND CHARACTERISTICS

Polish Warmbloods are bred from a number of successful bloodlines, including Arab (*see* pp 184–87), Anglo-Arab (*see* p 181), Thoroughbred (*see* pp 284–87) and Trakehner (*see* pp 288–89) stallions. All stallions have to undergo a 100-day performance-testing procedure and, since 1992, there has been a Polish Championship of Young Horses, where the best of the Warmbloods can be assessed and promoted. They are used for all equestrian disciplines, including carriage driving, and have competed at international level, at the Olympics and other key events.

CLASS Polish Warmbloods are carefully bred for quality and performance.

Polo Pony

ORIGIN Worldwide
ENVIRONMENT
BLOOD
USES
HEIGHT 14.2–16.0 hh (1.47–1.63 m)
COLOURS All colours

Polo originated in Persia over two-and-a-half-thousand years ago. Polo Ponies can be produced from any mix of light horse and pony breeds, so are a type rather than a breed, but in Argentina, a very set stamp of Polo Pony has been bred by crossing Criollo (*see* p 207) mares to Thoroughbred (*see* pp 284–87) stallions.

| BLACK | BROWN | CHESTNUT | DUN | GREY | BAY | PALOMINO | COLOURED |

ORIGINS

The first polo ponies would have been light, Oriental-type horses, the standard mounts of army officers in India and other eastern countries. In the early 20th century the sport was established in Argentina, which quickly achieved dominance due to the players' natural affinity for the game, as well as the quality of the ponies they bred. Up until 1914 there was a 14.1 hh (1.45 m) height limit, which obviously limited the bloodlines that could be used to produce a Polo Pony. In Britain native ponies were bred to small Thoroughbreds, and, in Argentina, their native Criollos were bred to imported Welsh ponies (*see* pp 362–65). Once the height limit was abolished, the Argentines quickly changed tack and bred their Criollos to Thoroughbred stallions and then refined the result further by crossing the resultant half-bred back to a Thoroughbred again.

CONFORMATION A Polo Pony generally displays a long, lean neck and a strong and deep body with well-defined withers and good sloping shoulders. The back is short and strong and the hindquarters muscular without being too bulky.

ARGENTINE PONY The Argentine Polo Pony has became the most sought after in the world. It is based on the Criollo, which is famed for its hardiness, soundness, and stamina.

Quarter Horse

ORIGIN United States
ENVIRONMENT 🌾
BLOOD 🔥
USES
HEIGHT 14.3–16.0 hh (1.50–1.63 m)
COLOURS All colours

The Quarter Horse was the first established American breed after horses were re-introduced to the Americas by the *conquistadores*. The breed was primarily a workhorse but the English settlers brought with them their love of racing, and used it for entertainment in quarter-mile racing – hence the name.

| BLACK | BROWN | CHESTNUT | DUN | GREY | BAY |

ORIGINS

The origins of the breed lie with the ranchers of 17th-century Virginia, who bred a versatile cowpony using imported English native breeds and local Spanish-type horses. In the mid 1700s, Thoroughbreds (*see* pp 284–87) were bred to the cowpony, eventually developing the Quarter-Mile Horse, refined to show explosive acceleration over this distance. As the early pioneers headed west onto the great plains during the 1800s, they took Quarter-Mile Horses. Some crossbreeding with the feral Mustangs (*see* p 253) and Indian ponies enhanced the breed's toughness and cow-sense. Further inputs of Thoroughbred blood, plus some Morgan (*see* p 252), Arab (*see* pp 184–87) and Standardbred (*see* pp 276–79) followed.

CHARACTERISTICS

The Quarter Horse has a long neck which he carries quite low. He has a broad, deep chest and powerful, well-sloped shoulders, then wide and powerful hindquarters, extending down into well-muscled limbs.

AMERICAN DREAM The American Quarter Horse Association was formed in 1940 by ranchers keen to preserve the dual qualities of cowpony and racehorse. The breed's hugely powerful hindquarters allow it to reach speeds of 72.5 kph (45 mph) over short distances.

QUARTER HORSE The versatile Quarter Horse remains one of the United States' most popular breeds. Its adaptability has allowed it to continue to find popular employment, particularly in Western and trail-riding competitions.

Rhinelander

ORIGIN Germany
ENVIRONMENT
BLOOD ◊
USES
HEIGHT 16.2 hh (1.67 m)
COLOURS Black, brown, chestnut, grey, bay, or palomino

A relatively modern breed of warmblood, the Rhinelander has developed from the heavier Rhinish Draught Horse in just over fifty years. The Rhinelander competes successfully at the highest level, particularly in showjumping, and is becoming increasingly popular in the United Kingdom and United States.

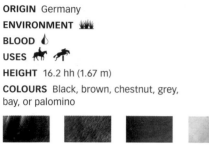

| BLACK | BROWN | CHESTNUT | GREY | BAY | PALOMINO |

ORIGINS AND CHARACTERISTICS

The development of the breed began in the 1950s to meet demand for a leisure and competition horse. Mares by Trakehners (*see* pp 288–89), Hanoverians (*see* p 224), and Thoroughbreds (*see* pp 284–87) out of dams with Rhinish blood were crossed with Hanoverian and Westphalian (*see* p 291) stallions. The breeders concentrated on conformation, temperament, and action. Some of the early horses lacked bone, which is still often evident, although overall the horse has a look of substance about him.

SUBSTANTIAL HORSE The head is plain but still has quality and is proudly set on a neck that tends to be heavy and short.

Rocky Mountain Horse

ORIGIN United States
ENVIRONMENT ▲
BLOOD ⬥
USES 🏇 🚶
HEIGHT 14.2–16.2 hh (1.47–1.67 m)
COLOURS Brown or chestnut

The breed registry of the Rocky Mountain Horse was established in 1986. The breed originates from one gaited colt – the 'Rocky Mountain Stallion' – brought from the Rocky Mountain area to the foothills of the Appalachian Mountains in the late 1800s. He was chocolate coloured with a flaxen mane and tail.

BROWN   CHESTNUT

DISTINCTIVE The breed has a fine, elegant head with a bold eye, and some unusual colouring.

ORIGINS AND CHARACTERISTICS

It is said that the Rocky Mountain Stallion was crossed with local mares and the line continued eventually becoming the modern Rocky Mountain Horse. Sam Tuttle kept the breed going during World War II, primarily using one stallion called 'Old Tobe', who appears in the pedigree of many of these horses.

Russian Trotter

ORIGIN Russia
ENVIRONMENT 🌿
BLOOD ⬥
USES 🏇
HEIGHT 15.3–16.0 hh (1.60–1.63 m)
COLOURS Black, brown, chestnut, grey, or bay

The Russian Trotter is the successor of the Orlov Trotter (*see* p 259), which could not compete with the dominant American Standardbred (*see* pp 276–79). It was developed by crossing the Orlov to the Standardbred.

BLACK   BROWN   CHESTNUT   GREY   BAY

ORIGINS AND CHARACTERISTICS

Selective breeding continued during the late 1800s and early 1900s. In 1950, the breed characteristics were set and continue to improve. The Russian Trotter has a plain straight head on a long, muscular neck. The shoulders are long and sloping, which gives the stride great reach. The legs are strong with well-defined tendons. The common defect of knock-knee and sickle-hocks allows them to lengthen more easily, an advantage for any racehorse.

SPEEDY TROTTER
Because of the influence of the Standardbred, the Russian Trotter is larger and heavier than the Orlov Trotter. They are quiet and easy to train, but have energy when it is needed.

Salerno

ORIGIN Italy
ENVIRONMENT 🌾
BLOOD 🩸
USES 🐎 🏇
HEIGHT 16.0–17.0 hh (1.63–1.73 m)
COLOURS Black, chestnut, or bay

BLACK	CHESTNUT	BAY

The Salerno was developed in the 16th century in Salerno, Italy, as a result of crossing Andalucians (*see* p 180), Neapolitans, and Oriental breeds. The breed was promoted by King Charles III, at the time King of Spain and Naples. There was no fixed breeding until 1780, when selection was started at the Persano Stud.

ORIGINS AND CHARACTERISTICS
The foundation sires of the Salerno are 'Conversano', 'Pluto', and 'Napoletano'. Hackney (*see* p 223) and Thoroughbred (*see* pp 284–87) blood was introduced in the 20th century and increased the size and refinement of the breed, which is now well proportioned, with sloping shoulders and muscular quarters.

CHAMPIONS
The most famous Salerno horses are 'Merano' and 'Posillipo'. Merano led the Italian team to victory in the 1956 World Showjumping Championships, and Posillipo took gold at the 1960 Olympics.

Sanfratellano

ORIGIN Italy
ENVIRONMENT ⛰️
BLOOD 🩸
USES 🐎 🐎 🐎
HEIGHT 16.0–17.0 hh (1.63–1.73 m)
COLOURS Black, brown, grey, or bay

BLACK	BROWN	GREY	BAY

Named after the small town of San Fratello at the foot of the Nebrodi Mountains in eastern Sicily, these horses roam in Nebrodi Park. There are only a few hundred of them in Sicily. The stud book was established in 1990, when the Italian Government Horse Breed Association took an interest in preserving this breed.

ORIGINS AND CHARACTERISTICS
The Sanfratellano has had many outside influences, including the Thoroughbred (*see* pp 284–87), Sardinian (*see* p 352), Murgese (*see* p 149), Sicilian, and Camargue (*see* pp 306–09). The foundation stock includes Arabs (*see* pp 184–87) and Norman Horses. It is a strongly built horse and attractive but lacks refinement.

TOUGH AND VERSATILE The Sanfratellano has evolved as a very hardy individual. It has had various uses, including general riding, some competition success, as well as harness and light draught work. It is also slaughtered for meat.

Selle Français

ORIGIN France
ENVIRONMENT
BLOOD
USES
HEIGHT 16.0 hh (1.63 m)
COLOURS Black, brown, chestnut, grey, or bay

BLACK   BROWN   CHESTNUT   GREY   BAY

The Selle Français was recognized as a breed in 1958 as a result of the amalgamation of French regional breeds of riding horses that were not Thoroughbred (*see* pp 284–87), Arab (*see* pp 184–87), or Anglo-Arab (*see* p 181). The regional breeds had been classed as halfbloods with pedigrees dating back many generations.

ORIGINS
The most popular of the original French regional breeds was the Anglo-Norman. Other regional breeds included the Vendéen Charollais and Angevin. Since the 19th century, the Anglo-Norman was used for crossbreeding with other regional breeds until a characteristic stamp of horse began to be produced. This became the Selle Français. The Selle Français remains an amalgamation of the regional breeds and falls into three categories: competition horses, racehorses, and non-specialist horses that are used in riding schools and for leisure riding. They are also divided into middleweight and heavyweight, according to their weight-carrying ability.

CHARACTERISTICS
A highly courageous horse, he excels in cross-country riding and is a useful driving trials horse. He has a muscular body, large hindquarters, and strong limbs with plenty of bone and well-defined joints. The sloping shoulder gives freedom and activity to his paces.

SECOND DIVISION There are several French races held for horses that are not Thoroughbreds. Horses from this division often make excellent eventers.

DISTINGUISHED The Selle Français has a distinguished head with expressive eyes, an intelligent expression, and large ears. Its paces are free and supple.

Shagya Arab

ORIGIN Hungary
ENVIRONMENT
BLOOD ◗
USES 🏇 🐎 🐎
HEIGHT 15.0 hh (1.53 m)
COLOURS Black, brown, chestnut, grey, or bay

BLACK	BROWN	CHESTNUT	GREY	BAY

This Hungarian breed, based on the Arab (*see* pp 184–87), was developed at the state-owned Hungarian Arab Stud of Babolna. Similar to the Arab, this breed is famous as the light cavalry horse of the Hungarian army. It is a larger-framed horse than the pure Arab, and has proven itself to be very versatile.

ORIGINS AND CHARACTERISTICS

The Shagya breed is named after its foundation sire, born in 1830 and taken from the Bedouins. 'Shagya' was crossed with local stock that included Arabs, Thoroughbred (*see* pp 284–87), Hungarian, and Spanish breeds to produce a stronger stamp of horse. The offspring of these crosses were bred back to Shagya until a distinctive type of horse was established. The result of 150 years of selective breeding has defined this famous cavalry and carriage horse. It is stronger and more versatile than a purebred Arab, and was exported to several countries, including Poland, Austria, and the United States.

The Shagya Arab is a hardy breed that can survive on poor food. It has a very wide forehead with large eyes dominating the typically Arabian dished head, on an elegantly curved neck. The body is well proportioned.

BUILT FOR SPEED The shoulders are sloping, and the body is compact. The legs are set clear of the body, allowing freedom of movement.

SHAGYA HERD Mares and foals are loose-housed in large barns at the Hungarian Arab Stud of Babolna. The Shagya Arab conformation is that of the Arab but with a larger frame and substantially more muscle.

South African Thoroughbred

ORIGIN South Africa
ENVIRONMENT ⚘
BLOOD ◊
USES 🏇 🏇 🏇
HEIGHT 15.3–16.3 hh (1.60–1.70 m)
COLOURS Brown, chestnut, grey, or bay

Horse racing in South Africa, and the subsequent development of the South African Thoroughbred, began when the country fell under British Rule in 1795. As they settled in their new colony, they imported Thoroughbred Horses (*see* pp 284–87) from Australia and England to upgrade the local Cape Horse.

BROWN	CHESTNUT	GREY	BAY

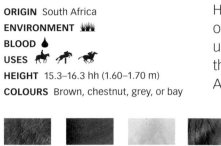

ORIGINS AND CHARACTERISTICS

In 1814 the Governor set up a state stud, which bought Thoroughbred mares and stallions to supply the growing racing industry. Another boost occurred with the discovery of gold in South Africa. By the 1960s, the South African Thoroughbred was achieving recognition on the track at home and also abroad.

RACER The first stud book was opened in 1907. Of the 98 registered stallions, 77 were English Thoroughbreds, 9 were from Australasia, 5 from South America – only 7 had been born in Africa.

South African Warmblood

ORIGIN South Africa
ENVIRONMENT ⚘
BLOOD ◊
USES 🏇 🏇 🏇
HEIGHT 15.1–16.3 hh (1.55–1.70 m)
COLOURS All colours

The South African Warmblood is a relatively new breed that is essentially a European Warmblood that has been imported and entered into the South African stud book. The horses vary in size and shape but South Africa is now home to many excellent horses that perform well in the main competition disciplines.

BLACK	BROWN	CHESTNUT	DUN	GREY	BAY	PALOMINO	COLOURED

STEADY AND TALENTED South African Warmbloods perform well, have good limbs and balance, and a markedly steady temperament.

ORIGINS AND CHARACTERISTICS

The first Warmblood, a German-bred stallion, was imported from Namibia into South Africa in the late 1960s by the breeder Theo Laros. Since then, horses have been imported from Sweden and Germany and, today, many of the world's top stallions' offspring are present in the South African arenas.

The South African Warmblood has a quality head on a well-set neck. The shoulder is sloping with a deep girth, and the legs are straight with well-muscled forearms.

Standardbred

ORIGIN United States
ENVIRONMENT 🌾
BLOOD 💧
USES 🐎
HEIGHT 14.0–16.0 hh (1.42–1.63 m)
COLOURS All solid colours

The Standardbred is the fastest trotter in the harness-racing world, capable of covering 1.6 km (1 mile) in 1 min 55 sec. The breed got its name when it was decided to set a performance standard for horses to gain entry into the Registry, which was founded in 1871.

BLACK   BROWN   CHESTNUT   GREY   BAY

ORIGINS

The Standardbred was developed mainly from Thoroughbred (*see* pp 284–87) stock – the most influential sire being 'Messenger', who was born in 1780, and who can be traced back to the Darley Arabian. Messenger was bred to race on the flat but, like many of the early Thoroughbreds, had Norfolk Roadster blood in his pedigree. Messenger was bred to many Thoroughbred mares, and it was soon found that he had the ability to produce good trotting horses. Nearly all of today's Standardbreds can be traced back to four of Messenger's sons, one of which, 'Hambletonian 10', is classed as the breed's foundation sire. He sired 1,335 offspring between 1851 and 1875. Another

DOMINANT The American Standardbred proved to be such a successful trotter that it has been exported all over the world to improve and upgrade other breeds of trotters, with the result that the breed dominates the sport. As harness racing has gained worldwide popularity, a winning Standardbred is becoming as valuable as a flat racehorse.

influential sire was the Thoroughbred 'Diomed', born in 1777. When the sport started to gain popularity, more selective breeding was employed to produce the faster harness trotter.

CHARACTERISTICS

The Standardbred has very strong legs and very hard hooves; the legs are shorter than those of the Thoroughbred. It is generally more robust in appearance with powerful quarters, and the hind legs are out behind the quarters rather than under.

Often the croup is higher than the withers, which gives thrust to the pace and is a characteristic that has come from the foundation sire Hambletonian, whose high-croup confirmation may have contributed to his success as a harness-horse sire.

EARLY STANDARD The early acceptance standards of 2 min 30 secs for trotters and 2 min 25 secs for pacers to cover a mile soon had to be reduced as the breed has became gradually faster and faster. Today, registration is based on bloodlines.

THOROUGHBRED The Standardbred has been developed mainly from the Thoroughbred, the influence of which can be seen in the quality of his head.

TROTTER There are over seventy racetracks in the United States alone, and racing often takes place in the evening under floodlights. This horse is wearing blinkers to help to prevent him being distracted by his surroundings.

Swedish Warmblood

ORIGIN Sweden
ENVIRONMENT
BLOOD
USES
HEIGHT 15.2–16.3 hh (1.57–1.70 m)
COLOURS All solid colours, including dun and palomino

The stud book was started in 1874 and the standard, including action, veterinary, and conformation tests, were laid down. Stallions have to go through extensive trials in dressage, jumping, harness, and cross country, which has helped produce a horse with a good reputation for competitive performance.

BLACK   BROWN   CHESTNUT   DUN   GREY   BAY   PALOMINO

ORIGINS
During the 19th century, native horses were crossed with carefully selected Thoroughbreds (*see* pp 284–87), Trakehners (*see* pp 288–89), and Hanoverians (*see* p 224) to produce a suitable mount for the Swedish Cavalry. The Swedish government actively support the breeding of their Warmblood, and run the National Stud at Flyinge.

CHARACTERISTICS
The Swedish Warmblood has a refined head with an intelligent, bold eye.

The neck is long and slightly crested. The big, sloping shoulders are set on a muscular body with well-developed hindquarters. The limbs are strong, and the action is free, springy, and athletic.

COMPETITION HORSE The ideal competition horse, with sound conformation and sensible temperament, the Swedish Warmblood has become an exceptional dressage horse but is also sought-after for carriage driving, harness racing, and showjumping.

BJORSELLS BRIAR Ridden by Jan Brink, the Swedish Warmblood 'Bjorsells Briar' is currently the world's highest-ranked dressage stallion.

Swiss Warmblood

ORIGIN Switzerland
ENVIRONMENT
BLOOD
USES
HEIGHT 15.3–16.0 hh (1.60–1.63 m)
COLOURS All colours

The National Stud at Avenches, owned by the Swiss government, is dedicated to producing riding, work, and army horses. This has led to the development of the relatively new but successful breed of the Swiss Warmblood. The Einsiedler (*see* p 211) played a defining role in the development of this successful breed.

| BLACK | BROWN | CHESTNUT | DUN | GREY | BAY | PALOMINO | COLOURED |

ORIGINS

This post-World War II breed has its foundation stock in local Swiss mares, many of which can be traced to Holsteiner (*see* p 226) and Anglo-Norman breeds. The foundation stallions were imported, but now the breed is established, Swiss Warmblood stallions stand at the National Stud.

The aim of the National Stud was to produce a versatile competition horse. Stallions undergo two performance tests: one at 3½ years old and another at 5½ years. Mares undergo a progeny test.

CHARACTERISTICS

The Swiss Warmblood is a strong, athletic horse with a calm and trainable temperament. He is courageous with a strong muscular body, large hindquarters, with powerful limbs. The joints are well defined and the limbs have plenty of bone. The shoulder is sloping, giving freedom and activity to the paces.

GOOD JUMPER Beat Mandli and 'Indigo IX' are a successful showjumping partnership having been placed at many international competitions.

Tennessee Walker

ORIGIN United States
ENVIRONMENT
BLOOD
USES
HEIGHT 15.0–16.0 hh (1.52–1.63 m)
COLOURS All solid colours

Tennessee plantation owners who wanted a horse to ride around their plantation developed this gaited horse in the 19th century. The horse is renowned for its agility, comfortable paces, and swiftness. It is also called the Plantation Walker and the Turn-Row, referring to its ability to turn within the plantation rows.

BLACK   BROWN   CHESTNUT   DUN   GREY   BAY

THE RUNNING WALK This is the horse's most famous gait. It is a four-beat pace with each foot hitting the ground at regular intervals. The head nods in time and the teeth also click! He can reach speeds of up to 24 kph (15 mph) in the running walk.

ORIGINS
The main foundation stock was the Narragansett Pacer and the Canadian Pacer, both lateral-gaited horses from the colonies. The Standardbred (*see* pp 276–79) stallion 'Black Allen', born in 1886, became one of the most influential sires of this breed. The Tennessee Walking Horse Breeders' and Exhibitors' Association founded the breed registry in 1935, and has successfully promoted the breed with more than 430,000 registered horses throughout the world.

CHARACTERISTICS
The most outstanding characteristics of the breed are the comfortable but unusual gaits: the flat-foot walk, running walk, and rocking-chair canter. All are natural to the breed. Foals perform the running walk within days of birth.

LONG FEET This close-coupled horse is robust, with a short and strong back. The head is large and plain and the croup slopes. Controversially, the front hooves are usually kept long and weighted to increase the elevation and activity of the gaits.

Tersk

ORIGIN Russia
ENVIRONMENT
BLOOD ⬤
USES 🏇 🏇 🏇
HEIGHT 14.3–15.1 hh (1.50–1.55 m)
COLOURS Predominantly grey, but also black, chestnut, and bay

BLACK CHESTNUT GREY BAY

Developed at the Tersk and Stavropol studs during the 1920–40s, this athletic horse is suitable for many purposes, such as endurance and non-Thoroughbred races. It is popular with the Russian Army for riding and harness. It has upgraded other breeds including the Karabakh (*see* p 237) and Lokai (*see* p 243).

ORIGINS AND CHARACTERISTICS

Prior to the Strelet breed becoming extinct, the Tersk stud crossed them with Arabs (*see* pp 184–87), Arab-Don crossbreds, Strelet-Karbardin crossbreds, and Shagya Arabs (*see* p 274). Selective inbreeding then followed until the required stamp and characteristics became firmly established. The Tersk was officially recognized as a breed in 1948. The aim of the breeding programme had been to produce a horse with the best features of the Arab Horse, but with some of the robustness and hardiness of the native breeds.

There are three main types of Tersk – the basic, eastern, and heavy – all descending from five sire-lines and five mare-families.

CHARACTERTICS

The head is light and slightly dished, with a broad forehead, and a long poll on a high-set neck. The chest is deep and wide with long sloping shoulders. The croup is rounded and well muscled with clean legs.

NOT FRAGILE The Tersk is usually grey, often with a silvery metallic sheen. It looks fragile, with its thin coat, but survives the harsh Russian winters as an army mount.

BAY The Tersk has a kind temperament and makes a good riding horse. He is also widely used as a liberty horse in circuses.

Thoroughbred

ORIGIN United Kingdom
ENVIRONMENT 🌱
BLOOD 🌑
USES 🏇 🏇 🏇
HEIGHT 15.2–17.0 hh (1.57–1.73 m)
COLOURS All solid colours

The English Thoroughbred is the world's fastest and most valuable horse, forming the basis of the multi-billion pound horseracing industry. It is used extensively to improve and upgrade numerous other breeds. The Thoroughbred is the king of the horse breeds: fast, courageous, and spirited.

BLACK   BROWN   CHESTNUT   GREY   BAY

ORIGINS

The breed evolved with a certain amount of luck that saw the three founding sires of the breed gathering together in England during the 18th century. English breeders were given a golden opportunity to develop the Thoroughbred racehorse. The three foundation sires were the 'Byerley Turk', the 'Darley Arabian', and the 'Godolphin Arabian'. They in turn produced four main Thoroughbred lines: 'Herod', 'Eclipse', 'Matchem', and a son of Herod called 'Highflyer'.

The Darley Arabian was brought from Syria by Thomas Darley to stand at stud in Yorkshire in 1704. The Goldolphin Arabian came from Yemen and found his way into the ownership of Lord Godolphin, who stood him in England. The Byerley Turk was captured in battle by Capt Byerley who then rode him in the Battle of the Boyne in 1690, before sending him to England for stud duties. These Arabian sires were bred to native English stock, many of which were referred to as 'running horses'. The running horses would have included breeds such as the Irish Hobby, the Norfolk Roadster, and the Galloway crossed with Spanish and Italian bloodlines.

The first great British racehorse was 'Flying Childers', sired by the Darley Arabian – born in 1715, he was never beaten. He passed on his winning streak to his great-great-nephew, Eclipse, who was born in 1764, which created one of the four main Thoroughbred lines.

British breeders started to keep track of pedigrees and, as this became increasingly important, the *Introduction to a General Stud Book* was published in 1791 with Volume I of the *General Stud Book* in 1808. A horse is classed as a Thoroughbred if both its parents are entered in the *General Stud Book* or in the equivalent official Thoroughbred stud books in other countries.

The Thoroughbred was originally bred as a flat racehorse and this today remains the main reason for the breeding. The most valuable racehorses are those that show potential for being winners as 3-year-olds over 1–1¾ miles (1.6–2.8 km); these races are called 'Classics' such as the Derby or the Kentucky.

Another category is the National Hunt racehorse; these are raced over fences and hurdles and are usually the later-maturing, larger Thoroughbreds with great stamina and toughness. Thoroughbreds are now specifically bred for the different race types, although plenty of flat-bred horses go on into National Hunt racing. They are also used for other sporting disciplines such as hunting, showjumping, dressage, and eventing.

CHARACTERISTICS

The best Thoroughbreds have a refined head, with large, bold eyes. The Arab influence can sometimes be seen in the slight dishing of the face. The neck is arched and elegant leading to pronounced withers and a long sloping shoulder that helps to give the ground-covering stride. The back is short, with muscular quarters. The chest and girth are deep giving plenty of room for the heart and lungs. The legs should be clean and hard. However, defects are often found in the legs and hooves, such as lack of bone, poor horn quality, collapsed heels, and thin soles.

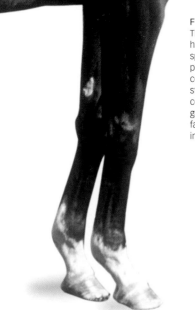

FULL OF PRESENCE
The Thoroughbred is a handsome horse: alert, spirited, and full of presence. He has endless courage and immense stamina. His ground-covering stride at the gallop makes him the fastest breed of horse in the world.

RETRAINING With over 16,000 racehorses owned in the United Kingdom alone there is a great need for the rehabilitation and retraining of horses from the track that retire either through injury or poor performance.

BIG BUSINESS Betting turnover in the United Kingdom alone is £5 billion. At Tattersalls, the United Kingdom's biggest auction house for Thoroughbreds, 4,737 horses were sold in 2005 for a total of £185,518,800.

CHELTENHAM FESTIVAL The four-day racing extravaganza at Cheltenham, England, is held in March each year. It is the pinnacle of every National Hunt trainer's year, with some of the industry's biggest prizes.

Trakehner

ORIGIN Poland
ENVIRONMENT 🌾
BLOOD 💧
USES 🐎 🏇 🐎🐎
HEIGHT 16.0–16.2 hh (1.63–1.67 m)
COLOURS Any solid colour

The Trakehner is one of the oldest warmbloods and is also the most refined and closest to the Thoroughbred (*see* pp 284–87) in quality and stamp. As well as being a successful performance horse in its own right, it has been used to a great extent to upgrade and refine many other European sports-horse breeds.

BLACK   BROWN   CHESTNUT   GREY   BAY

ORIGINS

The area that is now part of Poland but which used to be East Prussia was colonized by the Order of Teutonic Knights. They established the Trakehnen stud and used native ponies as a base. These were the tough, hardy Schweiken Ponies, descendants of Poland's Konik Pony (*see* p 334), which itself is descended from the Tarpan. In 1732, the Royal Trakehner Stud Administration was founded by King Frederick William I of Prussia. Using Danish, Turkish, and Thoroughbred stallions on the native mares, a quality coach horse was developed. From the early

ABDULLAH One of the most successful Trakehners was 'Abdullah'. This stallion competed for the United States, winning team gold and individual silver Olympics medals in 1984. The following year he won showjumping's World Cup.

1800s, to meet the need for a more refined cavalry horse for the Prussian army, a number of Arab (*see* pp 184–87) and Thoroughbred stallions were imported to upgrade the breed now known as the East Prussian or Trakehner. The Trakehner stud book was established in 1878. Of all the Thoroughbred blood used to develop the breed, the greatest influence was that of 'Perfectionist' – an English Thoroughbred by 'Persimmon', winner of the Derby and St Ledger in 1896. A son of Perfectionist was 'Tempelhüter' who produced a particularly good line of horses that is recognized as the foundation stock of the modern Trakehner breed. His influence was on the dam line as well as a direct sire. The 'Dingle' line, which was equally influential in the breed's development, was based very much on Tempelhüter's daughters. Trakehners were dominating the sports-horse scene as early as 1936, with the German team being mounted mainly on Trakehners to win every equestrian medal at the 1936 Berlin Olympics.

The Royal Trakehnen Stud had to be evacuated during World War II. As the Russians advanced during the winter of 1944, brave efforts were made to evacuate the breed to safety. Up to 25,000 horses, including mares and foals, set off on a trek of 1,450 km (900 miles) westwards to

Germany. Fewer than 2,000 reached safety, but the breed was saved by the efforts of many of the original breeders. Using the original stud book, they tracked down the survivors and re-registered them in West Germany. Breeding resumed and the Trakehner quickly regained its prominence as a successful sports horse.

CHARACTERISTICS

The head of the Trakehner is full of quality, reflecting his Thoroughbred and Arab bloodlines. He has good strong limbs, stands close to the ground, and has good, hard feet.

The shoulders are well shaped and defined, and overall the horse is well balanced and agile.

SPIRITED The Trakehner is a refined horse with excellent conformation. Whilst very successful at international level as a sports horse, the Trakehner has a spirited temperament.

SPORTS HORSE The Trakehner has excelled in all three main equestrian disciplines. Many of the other warmblood breeds have traditionally lacked the speed required for the sport of three-day eventing, but the Trakehner has plenty of speed and scope, as well as great freedom of movement.

Ukrainian Warmblood

ORIGIN Ukraine
ENVIRONMENT
BLOOD
USES
HEIGHT 16.0–17.0 hh (1.63–1.73 m)
COLOURS All solid colours

BLACK   BROWN   CHESTNUT   GREY   BAY

The Ukrainian Warmblood or Riding Horse is a relatively new breed. It was developed in the second half of the 20th century when demand grew in the Ukraine for a sports horse. The first attempt at refining existing stocks took place at the Dnepropetrovsk stud.

ORIGINS AND CHARACTERISTICS

The Ukrainian was developed using a mixture of well-established breeds, notably the Trakehner (*see* pp 288–89), Hanoverian (*see* p 224), and English Thoroughbred (*see* pp 284–87). These bloodlines were bred to each other as well as crossed to existing Russian breeds. To establish a set stamp, any of the early offspring that were considered too lightweight were bred back to Hanoverians, and those that were too heavy were crossed back to Thoroughbreds.

LONG BACK
The Ukrainian Warmblood has an attractive head set on a relatively long, lean neck. They have good shoulders and a deep chest, but the back can be overly long and a little hollow.

Walkaloosa

ORIGIN United States
ENVIRONMENT
BLOOD
USES
HEIGHT 14.2–16.0 hh (1.47–1.63 m)
COLOURS Appaloosa

The Walkaloosa is a relatively new American breed and in most other countries would be considered a type because of the great variation in stamp. The defining characteristics of the Walkaloosa are that he should have the Appaloosa (*see* pp 182–83) coat pattern and should be a gaited horse.

WELL SPOTTED The Appaloosa itself is a head turner, so with the addition of a gaited action, the Walkaloosa can't fail to be noticed. The breed can carry any of the accepted Appaloosa coat patterns, but conformation and soundness must not be overlooked.

ORIGINS AND CHARACTERISTICS

The original Appaloosa horse had its own gait – the Appaloosa Shuffle. It was a low, lateral four-beat movement, probably inherited from the Spanish Jennet and Paso Fino (*see* p 261). In the pure Appaloosa breed, the gait has been lost; the aim of the Walkaloosa Horse Registry is to restore the gait to the Appaloosa breed through recognition and acceptance of the Walkaloosa.

Westphalian Warmblood

ORIGIN Germany
ENVIRONMENT
BLOOD
USES
HEIGHT 15.3–16.2 hh (1.60–1.67 m)
COLOURS All solid colours

The Westphalian Warmblood was developed in Westphalia in northwest Germany. He is primarily a strain of the Hanoverian (*see* p 224), and is defined by the area in which he was bred. The state stud at Warndorf has Thoroughbred (*see* pp 284–87) and Hanoverian stallions, as well as Westphalian Warmbloods.

BLACK   BROWN   CHESTNUT   GREY   BAY

ORIGINS AND CHARACTERISTICS

The original horses of the Westphalian region were primarily work or draught horses with an appropriately heavy build. After some experimentation to refine these horses, the greatest influence became the Hanoverian. The horse displays a quality head, a good length of neck with depth and power through the body and hindquarters. He tends to be a slightly leggier horse than the Hanoverian, and usually has a flatter croup. A rigorous selection procedure is applied to the breed.

SPORTS HORSE Stallions are tested for 'pulling power' at three-and-a-half years old, and then tested under saddle on the flat and loose jumped at four years old.

Wielkopolski

ORIGIN Poland
ENVIRONMENT
BLOOD
USES
HEIGHT 16.0–17.0 hh (1.63–1.73 m)
COLOURS All solid colours

The Wielkopolski, Poland's most important warmblood breed, is closely related to the Trakehner (*see* pp 288–89) of Germany. The country has only recently begun to find ways of promoting the breed, which was established by crossing two of Poland's already well-established breeds, the Masuren and Poznan.

BLACK   BROWN   CHESTNUT   GREY   BAY

ORIGINS

At one time, Poland had many royal studs and made use of Arabs (*see* pp 184–87) and part-Arabs, particularly to mount their famous light cavalry.

The Poznan was a dual-purpose light draught and riding horse, developed from the native Konik (*see* p 334) crossed with Arab, Thoroughbred (*see* pp 284–87), Hanoverian (*see* p 224), and Trakehner blood. The Masuren was

bred in the Masury region and was basically a Trakehner, having been founded on mainly Arab and Thoroughbred lines.

The Wielkopolski was developed in the 20th century by crossing these two breeds. Further outcrossing to Thoroughbred, Arabs, and Anglo-Arabs (*see* p 181) helped establish the stamp of horse required to meet the growing demand for a sports horse.

CHARACTERISTICS

The heavier types are suited to light draught and carriage work. However it is the lighter, more athletic type that is most commonly bred now.

WELL PROPORTIONED The Wielkopolski is a balanced, well-proportioned animal. He has good paces and an excellent jump. His attributes of courage, stamina (both physical and mental), and speed have made him well suited to the sport of three-day eventing.

Württemberger

ORIGIN Germany

ENVIRONMENT

BLOOD

USES

HEIGHT 16.0–16.2 hh (1.63–1.67 m)

COLOURS All solid colours, though rarely grey

| BLACK | BROWN | CHESTNUT | GREY | BAY |

The Württemberger is one of Germany's oldest breeds, having its origins in long-established breeds developed at the Marbach stud, founded in 1573. Spanish, Eastern, and draught horses were crossbred to produce horses for riding and harness work. Work on the Württemberger began in the 17th century.

ORIGINS AND CHARACTERISTICS

The Württemberger was evolved from a mixture of local mares crossed to Arab (*see* pp 184–87), Spanish, and Barb (*see* pp 190–91) stallions. Friesian (*see* p 216) blood was also added. Another influence was an Anglo-Norman stallion, 'Faust'.

A stud book was opened in 1895. The horse that was developed was of a relatively stocky build. In search of a dual-purpose animal, the breeders used Clydesdale (*see* pp 138–39), Cleveland Bay (*see* p 205), and Yorkshire Coach Horse blood. After 1950, emphasis changed towards producing a lighter, more athletic

SPORTING A full, or hunter, clip, such as that used on this horse, shows off the well-proportioned body.

riding and sports horse. The modern Württemberger has its foundations in the Trakehner sire, Julmond, who came to Marbach in 1960.

The modern Württemberger is medium weight, so remains a relatively strong, substantial horse, and has true, active paces. He has a sensible head, prominent withers, and strong limbs.

SENSIBLE The modern breed has a 'hunter'-type head on a muscular neck. It is long-lived, tough and hardy, with a calm, quiet temperament.

PONIES

Ponies are, theoretically, equines that measure 14.2 hh (1.47 m) or under. But ponies are much 'bigger' than any height definition. For many of us, particularly in countries such as the United Kingdom where there is a wealth of native ponies, they are our introduction to the equine world. You could say they are purpose-designed for this task – tough and hardy, and often with a singular sense of purpose. Ponies succeed in teaching us the best and worst of the horse world – there is a pony for every person and for every occasion!

ICELANDIC PONY Ponies are renowned for their hardiness, toughness, and surefootedness. They have learnt to adapt to any number of different environments and situations, and their quick reactions, determination, and 'sixth sense' often belie their outward impression of solid docility.

American Shetland

ORIGIN United States
ENVIRONMENT 🌾
BLOOD 🌢
USES 🐴🛷
HEIGHT Up to 46 in (1.17 m)
COLOURS All colours

Shetland Ponies (*see* pp 353–55) were first imported to North America from the Scottish Shetland Islands in the mid 1800s to haul coal from the mines. The American Shetland Pony Club was formed in 1888 to record all the Shetland Ponies being imported from Europe. It is the oldest horse registry in the United States.

BLACK   BROWN   CHESTNUT   DUN   GREY   BAY   PALOMINO   COLOURED

ORIGINS AND CHARACTERISTICS

The modern American Shetland bears no resemblance to Shetland Ponies from Scotland. It was produced by crossing finer Shetland Ponies with small Hackney Ponies (*see* p 328), and then introducing a small amount of Thoroughbred (*see* pp 284–87) and Arab (*see* pp 184–87) blood.

The modern American Shetland is much more like a miniature Hackney. It moves with elegance and cadence;

the influence of the Hackney is very clear in the high-stepping action. The head is refined, and some have the characteristics of the Arab. They tend to be long and narrow through the back, with long, fine, clean legs. The hooves are generally neat and hard.

The American Shetland Pony Club has two studbooks: Division A is for ponies with 12.5 per cent or less outcross blood; and Division B is open to any pony with

12.5 per cent or more outcross blood. Foundation Certificates go to ponies from four generations of Division A breeding.

SHOWING CLASS Showing classes for the American Shetland Pony are divided into height divisions: under 43", and 43" to 46". The classes include 'in-hand', and 'performance', which includes roadster, harness, and pleasure driving.

American Walking Pony

ORIGIN United States

ENVIRONMENT

BLOOD ○

USES

HEIGHT 14.0 hh (1.42 m)

COLOURS Black, brown, chestnut, dun, grey, bay, or palomino

| BLACK | BROWN | CHESTNUT | DUN | GREY | BAY | PALOMINO |

A relatively new breed, the American Walking Pony is a cross between the Tennessee Walker (*see* p 282) and the Welsh Pony (*see* pp 362–65). It has three unique gaits: the pleasure walk; the merry walk (both of these walks are four beat, but much faster than the normal walk); and the canter.

ORIGINS

The American Walking Pony Registry was first established in 1986 by Joan Hudson Brown, who bred the first American Walking Pony – a feat that took 14 years. It regulates the breed by allowing only horses that are registered with both the Walking Horse and the Welsh Pony stud books to be crossed. The first mare registered was 'Browntree's Flicker' and the first stallion was 'BT Golden Splendor'.

LOVING TEMPERAMENT In 1981, an American Walking Pony was the Junior Competitive Trail National Champion, proving its versatility. It is renowned for its 'loving' temperament.

CHARACTERISTICS

One of the larger pony breeds, the Walking Pony has a finely shaped and attractive head, and a well-arched and muscled neck. The back is short and the shoulders are well sloped to allow freedom of movement. The chest is broad and he has well-muscled hindquarters. A very versatile breed, it has a natural jump inherited from the Welsh Pony and is successful in a wide range of classes, including Western and carriage driving.

NATURAL PACE The American Walking Pony's paces are inherited, but they do require some training to show them to their full potential. The walking paces are remarkably light and smooth.

Assateague

ORIGIN United States
ENVIRONMENT
BLOOD
USES
HEIGHT 12.0 hh (1.22 m)
COLOURS All colours

Named after the island they inhabit off the west coast of North America, Assateagues are small and very hardy, owned and cared for by the United States Parks Authority. It is believed that they arrived on the island by accident, having swum ashore from a Spanish ship that had capsized off the coast in 1600.

| BLACK | BROWN | CHESTNUT | DUN | GREY | BAY | PALOMINO | COLOURED |

ORIGINS AND CHARACTERISTICS
Two groups of ponies evolved from the 17 Arab horses (*see* pp 184–87) that survived the wreck: the Maryland Herd, known as Assateague Ponies, and the Virginia Herd, known as Chincoteague Ponies. The ponies have adapted well to the harsh environment; they forage on sand-dune grasses, rosehips, and bayberry twigs. The herd is kept to approximately 160 ponies to ensure that they have enough to eat.

MANAGEMENT
The Assateague mares are administered a contraceptive vaccine to help reduce the number of pregnancies.

Asturcon

ORIGIN Spain
ENVIRONMENT
BLOOD
USES
HEIGHT 11.2–12.2 hh (1.17–1.27 m)
COLOURS Black, brown, or bay

Many centuries ago, it was recorded that a small horse breed had been developed in northwest Spain. The Romans referred to these horses as Asturcons. They became popular in the Middle Ages, and because of their unusual but natural ambling gait (the legs move in lateral pairs), they became a popular ladies' mount. The Asturcon is also known as the Asturian Pony.

| BLACK | BROWN | BAY |

ORIGINS AND CHARACTERISTICS
The pony is thought to descend from the Garrano (*see* p 326) and Sorraia (*see* p 357) but another influence must have produced the ambling gait.

The Asturcon has a small but sometimes rather heavy head, with a straight profile, small ears, and bright, alert eyes. The neck is long, with a flowing mane. The withers are high and the shoulders are sloping, while the back is straight and strong. The tail is low-set. The feet are tough and well shaped.

PROTECTED PONY
The breed has been close to extinction, partly due to living in a feral state under difficult conditions. Recently groups of activists have formed to protect the pony.

Australian Pony

ORIGIN Australia
ENVIRONMENT 🌿
BLOOD 💧
USES 🏇
HEIGHT 12.0–14.0 hh (1.22–1.42 m)
COLOURS All solid colours, including dun

The Australian Pony Stud Book Society, formed in 1929, officially made this a breed in its own right. Ponies were first imported to Australia in 1803, and the first distinctive type was established in 1920. The Welsh Section A Pony (*see* p 362) stallion 'Dyoll Grey Light' is considered the most important of the foundation sires.

BLACK   BROWN   CHESTNUT   DUN   GREY   BAY

WINNING PONY Although it is an excellent pony in conformation, action, temperament, and in the competitive show ring, the Australian Pony is little known about outside of its native country.

ORIGINS

Australia had no native ponies of its own, and it took 100 years to breed this distinctive pony. Influences include Arabs (*see* pp 184–87) and Exmoors (*see* p 322).

CHARACTERISTICS

The body is deep and well ribbed, with defined withers; the back is short and powerful; and he has well-shaped hindquarters. The action is free and smooth, allowing flexion of the joints without any exaggerations. The stride is straight and true. In general, the pony has good presence and show quality. It should stand square with its feet placed under.

ARAB INFLUENCE
The Australian Pony has a fine, Arab-like head, with large bright eyes. It has a good crested neck leading to a sloping shoulder that should show no sign of heaviness.

Avelignese

ORIGIN Italy
ENVIRONMENT 🔺
BLOOD 💧
USES 🐎 🐴🐴
HEIGHT 13.3–14.3 hh (1.40–1.42 m)
COLOURS Chestnut

The Avelignese gets its name from the Avelengo area of the Alto Adige, in Italy – the first official record dates from 1874. The Avelignese Pony is Italy's version of the Haflinger (*see* p 328), to which it bears a striking resemblance both in build and colour, although the Avelignese is stockier. Both breeds can be traced back to an Oriental stallion, 'El Bedavi'.

ORIGINS

The Avelignese is considered to be Italy's most prolific native breed, and is bred widely throughout Tuscany, Emilia, and central southern Italy.

Versatile as both a riding and harness pony, it is used to work the land in areas inaccessible to motor vehicles, as well as being a successful trekking pony. They are capable of carrying adults, which makes them an ideal family pony.

CHARACTERISTICS

Although they are stocky, like the Haflinger they are attractive with good confirmation. They are short and thick through the neck, with a slightly upright shoulder that makes the stride fairly short. They have broad chests and compact backs; the hindquarters are well muscled and round; the legs are short, with

hard, dense bone and good joints. The hooves are large and hard, allowing them to cope with their tough, mountainous environment.

DISTINCTIVE COLOURING Similar to the Haflinger, the Avelignese is always chestnut with a flaxen mane and tail. It can have white markings on the legs with light feathering on the fetlocks.

IN HARNESS The cold-blooded Avelignese has a calm temperament, making him an ideal harness horse. He is able to do farm work on the steep and rough mountain terrain as well be driven for pleasure.

Bardigiano

ORIGIN Italy
ENVIRONMENT ▲
BLOOD ◊
USES 🐎
HEIGHT 13.0 hh (1.32 m)
COLOURS Black, brown, or bay

BLACK   BROWN   BAY

Based on ancient stock in the northern Apennines in Italy, it is believed that the Bardigiano Pony is related to the Abellinum from which the Haflinger (*see* p 328) and the Avelignese (*see* p 300) evolved. It resembles some of the British natives, such as the Exmoor (*see* p 322). It is a tough, hardy pony breed having had to adapt to its harsh, mountainous habitat.

ORIGINS
Bred predominantly nowadays as a riding and light-draught pony, the Bardigiano was once raised for meat production. It came close to extinction due to many crossbreedings with lighter types, and it began to lose its typical traits.

However, in 1977, the official stud book was recognized and the breed was then protected.

CHARACTERISTICS
The Bardigiano has a noble pony head, which is broad between the eyes, with small, sharp ears. The neck is extremely thick and heavily muscled and the forehand, too, is exceptionally strong. The shoulders tend to be rather upright, giving a short stride, but allowing the pony to climb steep rocky slopes easily, which is a notable adaptation to the breed's mountainous habitat. The body is short and compact with a well-sprung ribcage. The legs are conformationally correct, with good hocks, and a well-muscled second thigh. The hindquarters are particularly well muscled and round.

HARDY AND AGILE The Bardigiano is a pony of considerable character. He is extremely hardy with a good temperament, but also very agile and quick.

Bashkir

ORIGIN Russia
ENVIRONMENT 🔺 🌾
BLOOD 🔥
USES 🏇 🐎
HEIGHT 13.0–14.0 hh (1.32–1.42 m)
COLOURS Chestnut, bay, or palomino

CHESTNUT   BAY   PALOMINO

The Bashkir is an ancient breed that has lived for thousands of years in the Ural Mountains, former USSR. They are probably related to the steppe horses of western Asia, and may contain other influences probably of Turkish origin. In 1845, government breeding centres were set up to improve the stock for agricultural purposes, including meat and milk.

ORIGINS

Two types of pony were developed: the mountain type, which is more suitable for riding; and the heavier steppe variety, often used for light draught and other farm work.

Bashkir endurance is legendary; it is claimed that a Bashkir troika (carriage/sleigh) can cover 120–140 km (75–85 miles) a day in the snow. The breed is hardy and the herds live out in deep snow and

BASHKIR CURLY
The Bashkir was originally sought after by Native Americans. Today they are gaining popularity in the United States with over 1,000 registered Bashkir Curlys in the country.

blizzard conditions at temperatures that fall between -10 and -40 degrees centigrade (between 14 and -40 degrees Fahrenheit).

The 'Bashkir Curly' is a United States breed. Some insist that it is related to the Russian Bashkir while others say that it is not. It remains a mystery how these ponies came to the United States, but they are gaining in popularity. It is understood that they were first sought after by Native Americans living in the northwestern states.

CHARACTERISTICS

The Bashkir Pony's legs are short and strong with very hard hooves that are capable of dealing with the rough terrain of Russia's Ural Mountains. The mane and tail of the Bashkir Pony tend to be curly and full. and its winter coat is similarly curly and very thick. The hair can be combed, spun, and then woven to produce cloth. Interestingly, people who suffer allergies to horses can wear the cloth made from this pony's coat.

HEAVY-HEADED PONY
The Bashkir has a heavy head, which is straight in profile with bright eyes. The long neck leads to a deep chest and sloping shoulders. The withers are low, and sometimes the back can be dipped and the tail low set.

Basuto

ORIGIN South Africa
ENVIRONMENT 🔺
BLOOD 🌢
USES 🐎 🐎 🐎 🐎 🐎
HEIGHT 14.2 hh (1.47 m)
COLOURS Brown, chestnut, grey, or bay

The Basuto is the indigenous pony of South Africa, achieving its popularity in the 19th century during the Boer War. The Basuto is a stocky pony with great stamina, and very surefooted – often being required to travel at speed over rough, rocky terrain. The breed became so popular that many were exported.

BROWN   CHESTNUT   GREY   BAY

ORIGINS

The four founder horses of the Basuto Pony breed were first introduced to the Cape area in 1653 by the Dutch East India Trading Company, although their precise breeding is unknown. It is likely that they would have been of Arabian (*see* pp 184–87) and Persian descent. These four horses are also the founders of the Boerperd Horse (*see* pp 194–95). Due to exportation and the Boer War, the Basuto faced extinction by 1940. There has been a programme to re-establish it

CHARACTERISTICS

The Basuto has a long neck, with prominent withers and a long, straight back. The head can be rather heavy. The shoulders are a little straight, but the quarters are well muscled and sloping. Basuto Ponies have good, sound, and tough legs. They have a natural affinity and affection for people. While they have inherited characteristics such as spirit, intelligence, and stamina from their Oriental ancestors, they remain, above all, sensible animals.

HORSE-LIKE BREED Although it is small, the Basuto has many horse-like qualities, and is considered by many to be a horse rather than a pony. It certainly has the long stride of a horse, which makes it comfortable to ride for many hours.

Batak Pony

ORIGIN Indonesia
ENVIRONMENT
BLOOD
USES
HEIGHT 13.0 hh (1.32 m)
COLOURS Black, brown, chestnut, dun, grey, bay, or palomino

| BLACK | BROWN | CHESTNUT | DUN | GREY | BAY | PALOMINO |

The Batak Pony was upgraded using Arab influences throughout the 20th century. It is now employed to upgrade the quality of horses and ponies on many Indonesian islands. These ponies' speed makes them popular for racing as well as being quiet enough for children to ride.

ORIGINS

Originating from central Sumatra, the Batak Pony is thought to have descended from the Mongolian Pony (*see* p 338) with some Arab (*see* pp 184–87) influence, and was once used as a sacrificial animal to appease the gods. This is a willing breed and quite hardy, able to survive on little forage, often of poor quality.

CHARACTERISTICS

The Batak is an elegant pony, whilst still being strong and sturdy. It mostly has a good, correct conformation; any faults are likely to be a result of the poor nutrition, as the ponies usually fend for themselves. It has a fine head with a slightly dished face, from the Arab influence. The neck is short and thin, and often weak. It tends to have a prominent wither and a long back. The tail is set and carried high on sloping quarters, which can be poorly muscled. The legs tend to lack muscle and have long and slender cannon bones.

ARAB INFLUENCE As with so many horses and ponies worldwide, the potent influence of the Arab can be seen in the Batak.

RELIABLE AND HARDY Although the Batak lacks somewhat in refinement, it is very well suited to the purposes of the Indonesians, making a good all-round working and pleasure animal.

Burmese

ORIGIN Burma
ENVIRONMENT 🔺
BLOOD 💧
USES 🐎 🐎 🐎
HEIGHT 13.0 hh (1.32 m)
COLOURS All solid colours

Also known as the Shan Pony, the Burmese originates from the Shan State of eastern Burma. The breed today is still used by locals as a work pony. It is not a particularly pretty pony, but it has become extremely surefooted, tough, and has great powers of endurance, able to cope with its mountainous environment.

BLACK   BROWN   CHESTNUT   GREY   BAY

ORIGINS

The Burmese resembles the Manipuri Pony (*see* p 336) of the Himalayan Mountains in India, suggesting the breeds have similar origins. The Burmese is slightly larger on account of the influence of more Arabian (*see* pp 184–87) blood.

CHARACTERISTICS

The Burmese has a rather straight, common head, with a muscular neck. The back can be long with sloping quarters, and it does not have a prominent wither. The upright shoulder gives it a short, choppy stride, which is a desirable trait in mountainous terrain, helping it to cope with steep and rocky hillsides. The chest is deep and wide, and like many ponies bred in mountainous areas, the legs are short and strong and have extremely small but hard hooves.

They have a quiet temperament and a willing nature, which makes them reliable and popular mounts for novices and children. They are neither fast nor athletic, but strong and hardy and able to cope with the harsh environment of the mountains.

MULTI-TASKING PONY Once used by British colonials for polo, Burmese Ponies are now used more for farm and pack work, as well as making very good trekking ponies thanks to their surefootedness over difficult terrain.

Camargue

ORIGIN France
ENVIRONMENT 🌿
BLOOD 💧
USES 🏇 🏇 🏇
HEIGHT 13.1–14.1 hh (1.35–1.45 m)
COLOURS Grey

The indigenous white horses of the Camargue, in the Rhône delta of southern France, are also called 'the horses of the sea'. The harshness of their environment and their isolation from outside influences have made them very distinctive. They are the traditional mounts of the Camargue herdsmen but are finding a new role as trekking ponies for tourists.

ORIGINS

The Camargue has only been officially recognized since 1968, but there is no doubt it is an ancient breed, possibly prehistoric. It is similar in size and proportions to the skeletons of the prehistoric horses found at Solutré. This area of France would have seen many armies come and go and each would have brought horses that could have bred with the native Camargue. A strong Barb (*see* pp 190–91) input may have occurred as a result of Moorish invasions in the 7th and 8th centuries, and prior to this there could have been Asian and Mongol influences.

WELL MADE The main failing is in the short, straight shoulder, but otherwise the Camargue is compact and muscular, with excellent limbs and feet.

CHARACTERISITICS

The herds of 'white' horses running freely through the saltwater marshes are a beautiful sight, although on closer inspection the Camargue is a little plain. His primitive origins show in the heavy, slightly coarse head, but he is an exceptionally strong, sound, and hardy little horse.

BULL PONY The Camargue is the traditional mount of the guardians of the herds of bulls, which also roam the Camargue region.

Caspian

ORIGIN Iran
ENVIRONMENT
BLOOD ◊
USES 🏇
HEIGHT 10.0–11.0 hh (1–1.2 m)
COLOURS All solid colours

The Caspian is classified as a pony because of its size, but it has all the refinement and proportions of a horse. In 1965, a small herd of 'miniature horses' were found at Amol in northern Iran, in a mountainous area close to the Caspian Sea. They are believed to be related to the small horses depicted on ancient artifacts.

| BLACK | BROWN | CHESTNUT | GREY | BAY |

ORIGINS AND CHARACTERISTICS

Since the Caspian's rediscovery, bones of its early antecedents, dating back to over 3,000 years ago, have also been unearthed in Iran.

It has long been accepted that just prior to domestication, four sub-species of horse had evolved. The Type 4 horse was the smallest yet most refined of this group with a distinctive concave profile and high-set tail. This is believed to be the ancestor of the Caspian. A breeding programme was set up to maintain and protect the breed, and it is now bred in many countries.

The Caspian's skeleton has several unique features: it has an extra molar on each side of the upper jaw and the bones of its head and scapula are different in form to those of other horses.

The Caspian has a gracefully arched neck, sloping shoulders, and defined withers. The body is slim and the tail is high set. The limbs are slender but strong, and the feet are hard and sound.

AGILE AND ATHLETIC Despite its small stature, the Caspian has the ground-covering stride of a horse and is also an exceptionally talented jumper. It has a kind and willing nature, and is also very intelligent.

HORSES OF THE SEA Herds of white Camargue ponies have run free on the salt marshes of the Rhône delta for centuries. They are a feature of the country's heritage and are a great tourist attraction.

Cayuse

ORIGIN United States
ENVIRONMENT
BLOOD
USES
HEIGHT 14.0 hh (14.2 m)
COLOURS All colours, but often roan

Little is known of the history of the Cayuse Pony, but it is believed the foundation stock is the Barb (*see* pp 190–91) and Spanish horses, which came to America with Spanish settlers, as well as escaped or stolen ponies from American settlers. They also have links to the Missouri Foxtrotter (*see* pp 250–51).

BLACK   BROWN   CHESTNUT   DUN   GREY   BAY   PALOMINO   ROAN

ORIGINS
The Cayuse is one of the little-known ponies from the 'Wild West' period of American history. The breed was recognized – and infamous – early in the 1800s as the ponies ridden and bred by the Native Americans.

The Cayuse got its name from the Cayuse Indians who were incredible horsemen and further developed the breed. Today, only a handful of these ponies exist and the Wild Horse Research Centre in California is trying to increase breed numbers to protect the Cayuse from extinction.

CHARACTERISTICS
The small, stocky Cayuse has typical pony conformation other than a couple of characteristics that set it apart. It has a high withers and relatively long cannon bones. The pasterns are also long and sloping. It is usually heavily muscled and is very powerful.

RARE BREED The Cayuse Pony is a small but powerful breed. It is now very rare, and in the 1990s disaster struck when over 100 of the ponies were killed by the accidental spraying of their pasture with toxic herbicide.

Chincoteague

ORIGIN United States
ENVIRONMENT
BLOOD 🜄
USES 🏇 🐎
HEIGHT 14.2 hh (1.47 m)
COLOURS Coloured or roan

COLOURED   ROAN

Named after the island they live on, Chincoteague Ponies are small and hardy. It is believed their ancestors swam to the island from a Spanish ship that had capsized off the coast in 1600. To survive, they had to live off coarse grasses and drink salt water. This foundation stock evolved into the breed known today.

ORIGINS AND CHARACTERISTICS
Two groups of ponies have descended from the original 17 Arab Horses (*see* pp 184–87) that survived the shipwreck: the Maryland herd, and the Virginia herd. The Virginia herd is larger and is managed by the Volunteer Fire Department. The Maryland herd is more feral, and is owned and cared for by the United States Parks Authority.

CHILD'S PONY The Chincoteague makes a good child's pony, excelling in American show classes, as well as jumping and driving, either under Western or English saddle.

LONG MANE The mane and tail are long and thick and they also grow a very thick winter coat to protect them from the harsh climate.

The Chincoteague Pony Association was established in 1994. All ponies sold by the Chincoteague Volunteer Fire Department are eligible for registration, as well as those bred by private breeders.

CHARACTERISTICS
The Chincoteague Pony is a very good doer, requiring little food even by the standards of most other ponies. It is well proportioned, strong, and muscular. The pony has a good, kind nature, and seems to love being around people.

Every year the ponies swim the seawater channel from the island to Virginia, where they are gathered and the offspring sold to keep the number of ponies on the island at a manageable level.

Coloured

ORIGIN United Kingdom
ENVIRONMENT 🌱
BLOOD 💧
USES 🐎 🐎
HEIGHT 14.0–15.0 hh (1.42–1.52 m)
COLOURS All colours, but most popularly coloured

Coloured Ponies are defined by their colour and are not, as such, a breed. However, there is a certain stamp of Coloured Pony, also known as the 'Vanner' or 'Gypsy Pony', that is recognizable. Light-draught animals, they are common in many parts of Europe, pulling the colourful caravans of Gypsy travellers.

BLACK   BROWN   CHESTNUT   DUN   GREY   BAY   PALOMINO   COLOURED

ORIGINS

The word 'vanner' has been used since the 18th century to describe the working horses used in towns and cities to pull the carts and vans of the travelling tradespeople. These horses and ponies had to be strong but quiet and patient. They can be developed from a mixture of any number of breeds, but are often produced from Friesian (*see* p 216), Clydesdale (*see* pp 138–39), Shire Horse (*see* pp 164–65), and Dales Pony (*see* pp 314–15) bloodlines. Originally, they would most likely have been solid coloured and clean limbed to look smarter about town.

HONOURED Gypsies have always valued their horses and ponies as they rely on them for their livelihood : 'Gypsy gold does not chink and glitter. It gleams in the sun and neighs in the dark.'

CHARACTERISTICS

Because the Gypsy Ponies have to thrive 'on the road', with no stabling and often sparse grazing, they have to be a tough, hardy stamp of animal. Hence the development of the heavier-boned and feathered-leg type seen today. There is a Gypsy Vanner Horse Registry that uses the traditional Gypsy descriptions to define the colours of the modern Coloured Ponies: black-and-white ponies are 'piebald'; brown-and-white or tri-coloured ponies are 'skewbald'; solid colours with splashes of white are 'blagdon'; and any other colour is simply 'odd coloured'.

POWERFUL PONY Immensely strong and hardy animals, Coloured Ponies are also renowned for their exceptionally quiet, gentle, and patient temperaments.

Connemara

ORIGIN Ireland

ENVIRONMENT

BLOOD ◊

USES

HEIGHT 13.0–14.2 hh (1.32–1.47 m)

COLOURS All colours, but predominantly grey

BLACK	BROWN	CHESTNUT	GREY	ROAN

The Connemara is named after a small area in the Connaught region of Western Ireland. The habitat is bleak, bordered on one side by Galway Bay, and on the other by the Atlantic Ocean. This is Ireland's only indigenous breed and it has had to be tough to survive. It is an exceptional performance pony.

ORIGINS

It is unclear how this breed developed; one theory is that it originated from imported Barb (*see* pp 190–91) and Spanish horses that bred with the native stock. Or it may have evolved from stock brought to Ireland by the Celts, including Icelandic (*see* p 331), Shetland (*see* pp 353-55), and Norwegian Fjord (*see* p 342) Ponies. Its quality would suggest that, either way, it has been influenced by Spanish or Arab (*see* pp 184–87) blood. The

Connemara Pony Breeders Society, founded in 1923, has helped to produce an outstanding quality pony.

CHARACTERISTICS

The Connemara is an athletic pony and is free, fluent, and true in its paces. It makes an ideal child's pony, but is also becoming very popular for small adults. It excels in all competitive disciplines from eventing to dressage and carriage driving.

ELEGANT PONY The Connemara has an elegant head with a long neck giving a good length of rein. The body is deep and compact with short legs.

GREY COLOUR The Connemara Pony is predominantly grey; dun and palomino were once common, but are now very rarely seen.

Dales

ORIGIN United Kingdom
ENVIRONMENT 🌾
BLOOD 💧
USES 🐎 🐎
HEIGHT 13.2–14.2 hh (1.37–1.47 m)
COLOURS Predominantly black, with some brown, grey, bay, or, rarely, roan

The Dales Pony originates from northern England on the hills of the Pennines, and it gets its name from the river valleys. The foundation stock is believed to be Scottish Galloway. The Dales shares a lot of its ancestry with its close neighbour the Fell Pony (*see* p 324). The Friesian (*see* p 216) influences both breeds.

BLACK	BROWN	GREY	BAY	ROAN

ORIGINS

The Dales Pony, like its ancestor the Friesian, is predominantly black in colour. Over the centuries, the breed has been crossed with, firstly, the Norfolk Roadster, and later, during the 19th century, horses of Welsh Cob (*see* p 365) and Clydesdale (*see* pp 138–39) bloodlines.

The Dales was originally used as a pack pony, particularly in the lead-mining industries, working both above and below ground, in and around the mines. As the mines became more mechanized and the ponies were no longer needed, the local farmers realized that their strength, intelligence, and agility over

STUD BOOKS The Dales Pony stud book was opened in 1916. However, World War II meant that selective breeding was limited and, by 1955, only four ponies remained registered.

LONG MANE The Dales pony has silky feathering on its legs, and an abundance of mane and tail hair.

rough country would be useful. Its ability to haul loads of over a ton, plough, and also take the farmer to market in style made the Dales a firm favourite. Later, the pace of the Dales made it popular as a light carriage horse, providing a speedy means of transport. Today, it is employed mainly for riding and carriage driving, competing successfully in many disciplines.

FALL AND RISE

During World War II, the breed declined drastically, but since 1963, with the formation of the Dales Pony Society, the breed has been much improved, and there has since been an increasing interest in this tough and adaptable pony.

CHARACTERISTICS

The attractive Dales Pony has a neat, intelligent head, with bright eyes that are set well apart. The ears curve slightly inwards. The neck of the Dales is long and strong, leading to muscular, sloping shoulders. The withers should not be too fine. The body is compact, deep through the chest, and has well-sprung ribs. The hindquarters are extremely powerful, with well-developed and muscular second thighs. The tail is well set with plenty of straight hair that should reach the ground. The strong legs show plenty of flexibility but should have no coarseness, with good bone on the cannon of about 20 cm (8 in), with defined tendons. The feathering on the legs of the Dales Pony is usually abundant and silky. The feet are large and open, with good open heels and a well-developed frog.

SMART MOVER The Dales Pony, with its distinguished looks and elegance, has a high knee movement and hock action. It has tremendous energy and stamina as well as being courageous, intelligent, and kind.

Dartmoor

ORIGIN United Kingdom

ENVIRONMENT

BLOOD

USES

HEIGHT 12.2 hh and under (1.27 m)

COLOURS Traditionally black, brown, or bay, but occasionally dun or grey

BLACK BROWN DUN GREY BAY

Ponies have been running free on the moorlands of Dartmoor in southwest England for centuries. The earliest reference to them was in the 11th century. Over time they served as pack ponies, being used for light farm and carriage work and, today, they are bred for the show ring and as general riding ponies for children.

ORIGINS

The exact origins of the breed are not known. They inhabit a wild and harsh environment, but not in a particularly isolated area as they lived on the path of an important trade route between Plymouth and Exeter. This would have led to the breed being easily influenced by other bloodlines. Some of the Arab (*see* pp 184–87) and Barb (*see* pp 190–91) horses brought back to England by the crusaders could have escaped onto the moors, and the 19th century saw the introduction of trotting, Thoroughbred (*see* pp 284–87), Welsh Pony (*see* pp 362–65), Cob (*see* p 206), and Exmoor (*see* p 322) blood.

Certainly, the bleak and rugged nature of the moorland shaped the stamp of pony most likely to survive on it. There is very little shelter to be found on the moors; the landscape is undulating, but open to the weather from all directions. Larger ponies are distinctly disadvantaged by the lack of shelter. The first stud book was opened in 1899 and allowed for ponies up to 14 hh (1.42 m) for 'political' rather than practical reasons. At the time, in 1898, the Polo Pony stud book was keen to make use of the native breeds as foundation stock for Polo Ponies. A larger pony would be needed for this purpose, which is why attempts were made to encourage the larger type. But, in 1899, when the ponies were gathered up and brought in for inspection and entry in the stud book, three quarters of them were 12.2 hh (1.27 m) or under! In 1924, the height limit was reset at 12.2 hh (1.27 m) in recognition of the forces of nature.

Dartmoor Ponies are often bred in the 'comfort' of private studs, and many of the ponies on

PART-BREDS There are many part-bred ponies on the moor today, leading to a range of shapes, sizes, and colours. The Dartmoor Pony Society carries a Part-Bred Dartmoor register open to ponies by a licensed stallion and which have at least 25 per cent Dartmoor blood. One parent or grandparent must be a registered Dartmoor.

the moor today are crossbreds. There is a risk that random crossbreeding and breeding 'off the moor' will lead to the loss of some of the pony's hardiness and characteristics. To encourage the continuation of purebred ponies on the moor, there is a scheme whereby approved mares are kept in fenced off areas of the moor called 'newtakes', where they run with a purebred Dartmoor stallion.

CHARACTERISTICS

The Dartmoor should have a small, relatively fine head, with large, kind eyes and small ears. As he is primarily a riding pony, the neck of the Dartmoor should be a good length. The shoulders must be well laid back and sloping. The body should be strong and deep, and of medium length.

Most of the ponies originally entered in the stud book were black, brown, or bay, with just a handful of greys and duns in existence. Today, there are many more colour variations. There was originally very little to be seen in the way of white markings. Some carried a white star, or white spot on the nose, with maybe the occasional white fetlock. White markings continue to be discouraged by the breed society today.

SOUND BREED
The rugged moorland terrain has led to the development of a tough, sound pony. The limbs have plenty of bone, with short, flat, hard cannon bones. The forearm and second thigh should be muscular, and the feet are well shaped and hard.

PUREBRED DARTMOOR PONIES To encourage purebred stock, a selection of mares is kept with a registered purebred Dartmoor stallion in enclosures called 'newtakes'. The offspring produced are inspected and, if approved, are entered in a supplementary stud book. Over time, as they are bred again to a purebred stallion, the offspring will be eligible for entry as registered purebred Dartmoors.

Dulmen

ORIGIN Germany
ENVIRONMENT
BLOOD ◊
USES
HEIGHT 12.0–13.0 hh (1.22–1.32 m)
COLOURS Usually dun, but also back, brown, or chestnut

BLACK	BROWN	CHESTNUT	DUN

Since the extinction of the Senner Pony, the Dulmen is the only native pony in Germany. It roams in the Meerfelder Bruch nature reserve on the Duke of Croy's estate. There is written evidence of the ponies in 1316, but numbers have decreased significantly. Crossed with an Arab (*see* pp 184–87), it makes a useful riding pony.

ORIGINS AND CHARACTERISTICS

Only the strongest of the Dulmen Pony herd survive as they are left to run truly wild. They must find their own food and shelter, and cope with illness and death without any human intervention.

As with many of the primitive breeds, the Dulmen is usually dun in colour. Nowadays, however, other colours do exist, which indicates some outside blood having been introduced, possibly by ponies from Britain and Poland. Their mixed ancestry means that they do not breed true to type.

PRIMITIVE MARKINGS The Dulmen are usually dun with black points – characteristic of their primitive breeding. They also have many conformational faults, including weak hindquarters.

Eriskay

ORIGIN United Kingdom
ENVIRONMENT ▲
BLOOD 💧
USES
HEIGHT 12.0–13.2 hh (1.22–1.37 m)
COLOURS Black, grey, or bay

BLACK   GREY   BAY

The Eriskay is listed as critical by the Rare Breeds Survival Trust, and the Eriskay Pony Society is working closely with the Trust to ensure its survival. Eriskays are descendants of the original native ponies that once roamed the Western Isles of Scotland. They have connections with ancient Celtic and Norse ponies.

ORIGINS AND CHARACTERISTICS

Until the middle of the 19th century, the Eriskay was found throughout the Scottish islands as the crofters' ponies, being used as pack ponies transporting peat and seaweed, pulling carts, and working the fields. Natural and human selection of the best ponies has played a large role in the development of the breed. As it was mainly women and children who had to handle the ponies, only the best temperaments could be accepted. Numbers declined with the introduction of mechanization and the increasing popularity of larger breeds. By 1970, only 20 purebred ponies were left on the island of Eriskay. The breed society was established, and the Eriskay numbers are now increasing with over 400 ponies registered.

The Eriskay has an excellent temperament, and enjoys being with people. They have fine legs with only a small amount of tufty feathering on the back of the fetlock. They generally have good conformation with good joints and feet.

MAINLY GREY The Eriskay is very distinctive in that it is often born black or bay and then, as it matures, turns grey. A few remain black or bay into adulthood, but no other colours occur – a similar trait to that of the Lipizzaner!

WATERPROOF The dense waterproof coat, and the abundance of mane and tail, enables the Eriskay to live out in the harshest conditions.

ERISKAY ISLAND The Eriskay Pony is usually born black or bay, and will turn the typical grey colour as it matures. They are subject to harsh conditions on the island, and survive on small amounts of forage.

Exmoor

ORIGIN United Kingdom
ENVIRONMENT 🌾
BLOOD 💧
USES 🏇 🛷 🐎
HEIGHT 12.2–13.3 hh (1.27–1.40 m)
COLOURS Bay, brown, or dun

BROWN   DUN   BAY

The Exmoor is the oldest of the United Kingdom's mountain and moorland breeds, having roamed on Exmoor since the Bronze Age, 4,000 years ago. The earliest breed records can be traced back to 1820, but the breed society was not formed until 1921. They are branded on the shoulder with a star and herd number; on the nearside hindquarters is the pony's unique number.

ORIGINS AND CHARACTERISTICS

Herds of ponies still run wild today on Exmoor, although numbers are not huge. The robust build and constitution of the Exmoor makes it an ideal riding and driving pony. Correctly handled, it also makes an excellent first pony for a child, as well as being a good all-round performance pony for the older child or small adult. When crossed with Thoroughbreds (*see* pp 284–87), they make very useful competition horses.

The Exmoor has a clean-cut face, with a broad forehead. He has a good length of neck with well-laid shoulders. He has a powerful body with a deep chest. The legs are short and clean with small, strong feet.

HOME-BRED PONY If bred away from Exmoor, the breed tends to lose type. The purity of the breed requires a return to breeding from ponies on the moor in order to retain its ancient characteristics.

HEAVY EYELIDS A noticeable characteristic of the Exmoor pony is its pale-coloured muzzle. It has large eyes that have heavy upper eyelids. Like the muzzle, the eyes are surrounded by lighter-coloured hair.

Falabella

ORIGIN Argentina
ENVIRONMENT 🌾
BLOOD 🜄
USES Novelty
HEIGHT 7.0 hh (70 cm)
COLOURS All colours

The Falabella is a miniature breed developed near Buenos Aires, in Argentina, by the Falabella family. They crossed the smallest Shetland (*see* pp 353-55) with a very small Thoroughbred (*see* pp 284–87), and continued to breed from the smallest offspring. Unfortunately, this process has caused conformational defects.

| BLACK | BROWN | CHESTNUT | DUN | GREY | BAY | PALOMINO | COLOURED |

ORIGINS AND CHARACTERISTICS

The International Falabella Miniature Horse Society maintains a breed registry to ensure that the breed remains pure. However, conformational defects are common, such as weak, straight hocks, crooked limbs and heavy heads, often with a ewe-neck. The breed has also lost the inherent toughness and vigour that is characteristic of the Shetland Pony.

A Falabella should have a head similar to a Shetland Pony and, ideally, the head should be in proportion to its body. Overall, a Falabella should have the proportions of a horse. Since it first developed, many different breeds have been used to produce the Falabella and, as a consequence, they come in many interesting colours including spotted patterns and skewbalds.

The foals are very small when born, just 40 cm (16 in), but they grow quickly in their first year. The gestation period of the Falabella is two months longer than that of any

MINI HORSES Falabellas have the appearance of scaled-down horses rather than ponies. Although rare, they continue to be bred in Argentina, and also in the United Kingdom.

other horse or pony; they also have two fewer vertebrae and ribs than a normal horse or pony.

The Falabella is friendly and intelligent, and thrives on attention. It requires regular grooming, care, and attention and usually needs to wear rugs during cold weather.

The Falabella tends to be kept as a pet as it is too small to be ridden, or for any other purpose, although they are occasionally seen in harness. They are delicate and need looking after like a Thoroughbred Horse.

MINIATURE PET Falabellas are often shown in hand at breed shows, where they will be judged on conformation, temperament, and movement. They are no bigger than an average-sized dog.

Fell Pony

ORIGIN United Kingdom
ENVIRONMENT 🌿
BLOOD 🜁
USES 🐎 🐎
HEIGHT 14.0 hh (1.42 m)
COLOURS Black, brown, grey, or bay

The Fell is related to the Dales Pony (*see* pp 314–15) and the Friesian (*see* p 216). Some trotting blood has been added, and the breed was used in harness in the 18th and 19th centuries. The Fell is lighter than the Dales, although the distinction was only recognized in 1916 when the two breed societies formed.

BLACK   BROWN   GREY   BAY

VERSATILE When crossed with a Thoroughbred, the Fell Pony makes an excellent versatile competition horse.

ORIGINS AND CHARACTERISTICS

The Friesian and the extinct Galloway were the main influences on the Fell. The Galloway was a swift, strong mount, used by raiding Celts, as well as Scottish drovers.

A fast active walk and trot makes the Fell an excellent carriage horse. It is able to carry up to 16 stone (100 kg), which makes its a popular choice among farmers as a hunter; it is also a reliable packhorse.

The head is small and well set on the neck, with a broad forehead, and bright and prominent eyes. It has a good, sloping shoulder that makes the paces comfortable, and has a strong, deep body with muscular loins. The hindquarters are strong with a well-set tail. It has strong limbs with good, flat bone below the knee.

The strong neck is longer than that of the Dales, giving a better length of reins, which is very desirable in a riding horse.

ROYAL PONIES Queen Elizabeth of the United Kingdom is a keen breeder of Fells and, for many years, HRH Prince Phillip has competed with a team in horse-driving trials, which involve dressage, a marathon with obstacles, and a course of cones.

French Saddle Pony

ORIGIN France
ENVIRONMENT
BLOOD ◊
USES
HEIGHT 12.2–14.2 hh (1.27–1.47 m)
COLOURS All colours

The French Saddle Pony, also known as the Poney Français de Selle, is a relatively new breed, with a breed organization founded in 1969 and the stud book in 1972. The French Saddle Pony has developed into a versatile breed that is an ideal family pony, capable of being ridden by both adult and child.

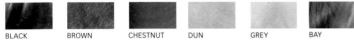

BLACK   BROWN   CHESTNUT   DUN   GREY   BAY

annual show to approve new mares and stallions. The largest numbers of this breed are found in the Mayenne, Normandy, and Brittany. However, it occurs throughout France and is gaining popularity across Europe.

CHARACTERISTICS

French Saddle Ponies are good tempered, but also quite lively to ride. The head is attractive with a long neck set on sloping shoulders. The back tends to be straight with developed withers, a sloping croup, and a well set tail. The French Saddle Pony excels in all competitive disciplines and will take his rider through most of the levels.

ALL-ROUND QUALITY The conformation of the French Saddle Pony is generally excellent. It excels in all competitive disciplines and jumps very well. It is also a fine leisure pony.

ORIGINS

Connemara (see p 313), New Forest (see p 339) and Welsh Pony (see pp 362–65) stallions were the foundation sires for this breed. The mares were native. The aim was to breed a pony with the looks and agility of a horse. The National Association of the French Saddle Pony and Sports Pony controls its breeding. Each year it organizes an

FINE HEAD The head is fine with a kind eye and alert ears. The neck is of good length and set on a deep, wide chest.

Galiceno

ORIGIN Mexico
ENVIRONMENT 🌵
BLOOD 💧
USES 🏇 🐎
HEIGHT 12.2–14.0 hh (1.27–1.42 m)
COLOURS Any solid colour, including black, brown, chestnut, dun, grey, or bay

BLACK	BROWN	CHESTNUT	DUN	GREY

The ancestors of Mexico's horses and ponies are Spanish and Portuguese, and the Galiceno is no exception. It is based on two ponies: the Garrano (*see* below), and the Sorraia (*see* p 357). It stands at 14 hh (1.42 m), which makes it a pony but, in its native country, it is always called a horse.

ORIGINS AND CHARACTERISTICS
The Galiceno Pony developed from mountain ponies brought to Mexico from Spain by Hernán Cortés in the early 16th century. These ponies had been captured in the Galicia region of Spain and showed the refined features as well as the gait, known as the Spanish gait (running walk), that is inherent in Andalucian (*see* p 180), Sorraia, and Garrano breeds. The Galiceno was officially recognized in 1958, and has slowly spread northwards into North America where it is seen as an ideal child's mount.

FINE BUILD The Galiceno is finely built and narrow, but retains strength, power, and stamina. It is hardy, quick and athletic.

Garrano

ORIGIN Portugal
ENVIRONMENT ⛰️
BLOOD 💧
USES 🏇 🐎
HEIGHT 10.0–12.0 hh (1.00–1.22 m)
COLOURS Brown, chestnut, or bay

BROWN	CHESTNUT	BAY

The Garrano, or Minho, is believed to come from similar ancient stock to the better-known Sorraia (*see* p 357), most likely from the Asian Wild Horse and the Tarpan (*see* p 12). It originates in northern Portugal, in the provinces of Garrano de Minho and Traz do Montes.

ORIGINS AND CHARACTERISTICS
The Garrano is a hardy, surefooted pony, with the ability to travel over difficult and steep ground. Recently, the Portuguese Ministry of Agriculture introduced some Arab blood (*see* pp 184–87) to upgrade the stock, losing some of the more primitive features in the process. The Arab influence shows in the fine head and dished profile. The neck is long, the shoulders straight, and the body short and compact.

PACK HORSE Once popular for use in trotting races, today he is more of a workman, used by locals and the army as a pack pony or to haul timber.

Gotland

ORIGIN Sweden
ENVIRONMENT ▲
BLOOD ◊
USES 🏇 🛞 🐎 🐎
HEIGHT 12.0–12.2 hh (1.22–1.27 m)
COLOURS Black, chestnut, bay, or palomino

The Swedish Gotland, or Skogruss, is probably the oldest of the Scandinavian breeds. Originating on the Swedish island of Gotland, it has been relatively free of other influences, although the Arab (*see* pp 184–87) has been added in the last 100 years. Breeding is now selective and governed by the Swedish Pony Association.

BLACK   CHESTNUT   BAY   PALOMINO

ORIGINS AND CHARACTERISTICS

This ancient pony is considered to be an excellent child's pony and has a good jump. It trots so fast that it was traditionally used in trotting races.

The Gotland is a light and elegant pony, with small, alert ears and large eyes. Although light in bone, it is very strong. The neck tends to be short, while the back is long with round, short hindquarters. The shoulder is long and sloping.

Once restricted to the island that gave it its name, nowadays the Gotland Pony is also bred on the Swedish mainland.

WILD PONY Today, the Gotland still runs wild in the forests on the island of Gotland, and some sport the primitive dorsal-stripe marking.

Hackney Pony

ORIGIN United Kingdom
ENVIRONMENT 🌱
BLOOD 🐎
USES 🛷🐴
HEIGHT 12.2–14 hh (1.27–1.42 m)
COLOURS Black, brown, or bay

BLACK   BROWN   BAY

The Hackney Pony is a small version of the Hackney Horse (*see* p 223), both based on the Norfolk and Yorkshire Roadsters. Christopher Wilson, who crossed his Roadster stallion with Fell mares (*see* p 324), started this pony version, which is exported and exhibited all over the world.

ORIGINS AND CHARACTERISTICS

The key feature of the Hackney Pony is the high knee action, which should be fluent with the foot flung forwards in a rounded movement. The hocks should come well underneath the body. The Hackney Pony has a small and intelligent head, a long neck, powerful shoulders, and a compact body. He is full of courage and has great stamina.

TEST Hackney Ponies compete in driving classes where they are judged on confirmation, action, and manners.

Haflinger

ORIGIN Austria
ENVIRONMENT 🔺
BLOOD 💧
USES 🐴 🛷🐴
HEIGHT 14.0 hh (1.42 m)
COLOURS Chestnut

The Haflinger Pony is sturdy and good natured, making it popular with the Austrian hill farmers. It has been used as a pack horse during times of peace and war. Just before World War II, the German government promoted the breed as a means of transportation in the mountains.

ORIGINS AND CHARACTERISTICS

The attractive and popular Haflinger Pony is named after the Austrian village of Hafling in the South Tyrol mountains. His exact breeding is uncertain, but the first written evidence was in 1868 when the stallion 'El Bedavi XXII' was used to improve local herds. Over the years, inbreeding has resulted in a distinctive pony, particularly remarked upon for its chestnut colour and flaxen mane and tail.

BRAND MARK Haflingers that are registered in the stud book are branded with an edelweiss flower with an 'H' in the centre.

Highland

ORIGIN United Kingdom
ENVIRONMENT 🔺
BLOOD 💧
USES 🏇 🐴
HEIGHT 13.0–14.2 hh (1.32–1.47 m)
COLOURS Commonly dun, but also black, brown, chestnut, grey, or bay

The Highland is one of the strongest and heaviest of the mountain and moorland breeds in the United Kingdom. It has had input from both Arab (*see* pp 184–87) and Clydesdale (*see* pp 138–41) blood. The Dukes of Atholl have been influential breeders, and they introduced Oriental blood as early as the 16th century.

BLACK   BROWN   CHESTNUT   DUN   GREY   BAY

IN DEMAND The Highland has a broad face, with kind eyes. The head is carried high on a strong, arched neck. He is in demand today, especially on the sporting estates in Scotland, where he is used to carry game panniers.

STRIKING The striking colouring features varying shades of dun, usually with a dorsal stripe – a sign of primitive breeding.

ORIGINS
In the early 16th century, some Percherons (*see* pp 156–59) were given to King James II of Scotland by Louis XII of France. These, along with Spanish horses, were used to upgrade the native stock of ponies. The resultant Highland Pony used to vary from area to area, with the smaller and faster Highland coming from the Western Isles and heavier ponies coming from the mainland. The Highland Pony Society, which was formed in 1923, no longer recognizes these distinctions, which have been largely lost with crossbreeding.

The Highland Pony is versatile, being used both as a pack and a riding horse, and he can be found competing in driving as well as dressage. Crossed with a Thoroughbred (*see* pp 284–87), the Highland makes an excellent hunter and event horse.

CHARACTERISTICS
The sturdy Highland has laid-back shoulders and a compact body. The hindquarters are powerful with well-developed thighs and second thighs. The cannon bones are short and strong. The Highland has light feathering but a long, flowing, silky mane and tail. Most show a dorsal stripe and some have 'primitive' zebra markings on the legs.

Hokkaido

ORIGIN Japan
ENVIRONMENT ▲
BLOOD 💧
USES 🐎 🐎🐎 🐎🐎 🐎
HEIGHT 13.0–13.2 hh (1.32–1.37 m)
COLOURS All solid colours, but commonly roan

The Hokkaido pony is an ancient, but now quite rare, breed. In Japan it is called Do-San-Ko. Hokkaido is the most northern island of Japan, and remains a wildlife refuge. It is mountainous terrain, and the Hokkaido has developed into a tough individual that has to be able to fend for himself in this harsh landscape.

| BLACK | BROWN | CHESTNUT | GREY | BAY | ROAN |

ORIGINS AND CHARACTERISTICS
The Hokkaido Pony is believed to have been brought to the island by fisherman between the 1600s and 1800s. The islands were uninhabited, and the fishermen brought the ponies to transport their catch. When the fishing season ended, they left the ponies on the island and didn't return until the following spring. The mountains of Hokkaido are covered in snow in the winter, and the only vegetation is bamboo grass, so only the hardiest survive.

MOUNTAIN TRANSPORT The hardy little Hokkaido Pony is still used for transportation in the mountainous regions, but it is also now popular for pleasure riding.

Hucul

ORIGIN Romania/Poland
ENVIRONMENT 🏔 ▲
BLOOD 💧
USES 🐎 🐎🐎 🐎🐎 🐎
HEIGHT 13.0–13.2 hh (1.32–1.37 m)
COLOURS All solid colours but usually bay

Also known as the Carpathian, the Hucul pony is a small draught breed that is still used to haul timber. The pony originated in the Carpathian Mountains, in Eastern Europe, an area that is now Romania. The borders in this area have changed many times, and both Romania and Poland claim the Hucul as their own.

| BLACK | BROWN | CHESTNUT | DUN | GREY | BAY |

ORIGINS AND CHARACTERISTICS
The Hucul probably originated in the 13th century by crossing the Tarpan with Mongolian ponies (see p 338). Many Huculs have a dorsal stripe, and zebra stripes on the legs. The harsh, mountainous terrain has fitted these ponies for a hardworking life in domestication. In 1856, a stud farm was established in Roaduti, Romania.

PONY TYPES Different types of Hucul have been developed, ranging from a light saddle type to a heavier draught animal, as seen here.

Icelandic

ORIGIN Iceland
ENVIRONMENT
BLOOD ○
USES
HEIGHT 12.3–13.2 hh (1.29–1.37 m)
COLOURS All colours

The isolation of the Icelandic makes him one of the purest breeds in the world. The small, sturdy horses that were his ancestors were taken to Iceland from Norway and Britain by settlers as early as the 9th century. A law passed in 930AD forbade the importation of more horses, so the breed has hardly changed since the Vikings.

| BLACK | BROWN | CHESTNUT | DUN | GREY | BAY | PALOMINO | COLOURED |

ORIGINS AND CHARACTERISTICS

Apart from its natural evolution in its harsh environment, the Icelandic Pony has been the subject of selective breeding since 1879. Selection trials were first held at Skagafjordur, Iceland's

BUILT TO WORK The diminutive Icelandic Pony has enormous strength and can carry a full-grown man for many hours without a problem.

main breeding area. Conformation is taken into account, but the main criterion is the quality of the horse's paces. The Icelandic Pony has five distinct paces: the fetgangur (walk), the brokk (trot), the stokk (gallop), the skeid (a rapid lateral pace), and the most famous of all, the tolt (a running walk that is used when covering rough terrain).

TOUGH LITTLE PONY The pony has a heavy head, which it carries well on a good neck. The deep body ends in muscular hindquarters.

Indian Country Bred

ORIGIN India
ENVIRONMENT ▲
BLOOD ◊
USES 🏇 🐎
HEIGHT Up to 12.0 hh (1.22 m)
COLOURS Most solid colours, but often grey or dun

The name Indian Country Bred is now used to cover most native Indian ponies. The individual breeds, such as the Spiti, Bhutia, and Tibetan Pony, have interbred for so many years that their distinguishing characteristics have been lost. Any conformational faults are usually the result of a lack of good nutrition.

| BLACK | BROWN | CHESTNUT | DUN | GREY | BAY |

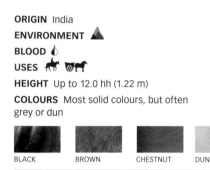

ORIGINS AND CHARACTERISTICS
The Indian Country Bred copes well with the mountainous environment of parts of India, but does not handle the heat and humidity as well as some breeds. Lack of nutrition limits their height, and overall they look slightly underdeveloped. They have a heavy head with a pronounced jaw; a short neck; short, upright shoulders; and sloping hindquarters. But they are tough little ponies, and are generally quiet and gentle to handle.

USES The ponies are used mainly for work, although they are perfectly suitable for leisure riding. They have great stamina and endurance and are often used as pack ponies.

Java Pony

ORIGIN Indonesia
ENVIRONMENT 🌵 ▲
BLOOD ◊
USES 🏇 🛞 🐎 🏇
HEIGHT 11.2–12.2 hh (1.17–1.27 m)
COLOURS All colours

Also known as the Kumingan Pony, this breed was developed on the Indonesian island of Java during the 17th century. The Dutch East India Company, which introduced horses to South Africa, also brought Oriental horses to many Indonesian islands from the 1600s onwards.

| BLACK | BROWN | CHESTNUT | DUN | GREY | BAY |

ORIGINS AND CHARACTERISTICS
The Java was bred by crossing native ponies to the imported Arabs (*see* pp 184–87) and Barbs (*see* pp 190–91). Today's Java Pony resembles the Arab in conformation and endurance. A tough, wiry pony, it pulls Indonesian taxis with relative ease. The Java has an attractive head with bright, alert eyes. The back can be long, leading to a sloping croup, with a high-set tail. The legs are poorly formed but strong.

WORK PONY
The Java Pony is very good tempered, and is a hard and willing worker, well suited both to pack and carriage work.

Kiso

ORIGIN Japan
ENVIRONMENT
BLOOD
USES
HEIGHT 13.0 hh (1.32 m)
COLOURS All colours

Indispensable for working on farms and for mounted infantry, the Kiso has inhabited Japan for over a thousand years. It is believed to be descended from either the Mongolian horses or the plateau horses of Central Asia. Some Kisos have a dorsal stripe, now considered an indication of their pureness.

BLACK   BROWN   CHESTNUT   DUN   GREY   BAY   PALOMINO   COLOURED

ORIGINS AND CHARACTERISTICS

During World War II, the Japanese government ruled that all purebred Kiso stallions should be castrated. Fortunately, one was missed, and in 1951, he was put to a Kiso mare, resulting in a foal called 'Dai-san Haruyama'. Kisos descend from this foal. Although not the most well-built ponies, they have a gentle nature.

WILLING CHARACTER The Kiso has a large head, flat withers, and upright shoulders. The body is short and compact. He is renowned for his kind and willing temperament.

Konik Pony

ORIGIN Poland
ENVIRONMENT 🌿
BLOOD 💧
USES 🐎 🏇 🛞 🐎 🐎
HEIGHT 13.0 hh (1.32 m)
COLOURS Dun

Although technically a pony, the Konik has many horse-like characteristics. The Konik's relationship with ancient breeds is revealed in the primitive dorsal stripe, and sometimes transverse zebra stripes on the legs.

ORIGINS AND CHARACTERISTICS

The Konik Pony's resemblance to the Tarpan clearly illustrates how closely related it is to that primitive horse. Although the Konik Pony has long been produced throughout Poland, breeding is now centred at the state studs in the Rzeszow province, and a uniform type of pony has existed for many years.

The head is large, with a short, strong neck. The shoulders are upright, giving a short stride. With low withers and a wide body, the legs are strong but tend to have 'cow' hocks.

TARPAN COPY
Konik mares are sometimes bred to Przewalski Horses, and the result is an animal even more similar than the Konik itself to its forefather, the Tarpan.

Landais Pony

ORIGIN France
ENVIRONMENT 🐎
BLOOD 💧
USES 🐎 🛞 🐎
HEIGHT 11.3–13.1 hh (1.19–1.35 m)
COLOURS Black, brown, chestnut, grey, or bay

| BLACK | BROWN | CHESTNUT | GREY | BAY |

Also known as the Landese, the Landais is an old breed that has had various improvements since the 8th century. Numbers decreased during World War II, and Welsh blood has since been used to keep the breed going.

ORIGINS AND CHARACTERISTICS

The Landais Pony descends from semi-wild ponies that lived in the forested region of Landes, south of Bordeaux, France. It is one of the foundation breeds of the more modern French Saddle Pony (*see* p 325).

An excellent child's mount, the pony has a small head and a heavy sloping shoulder. The chest can be narrow and under-developed, with pronounced withers. The back is short and wide.

ARAB INFLUENCE It is believed that Arabic blood had already been introduced by the time of the Battle of Poitiers in 732AD, an influence that has been repeated several times in the breed's development and is evident in its overall good quality.

Lundy

ORIGIN United Kingdom
ENVIRONMENT
BLOOD ⬥
USES 🏇 🐎
HEIGHT 13.2 hh (1.37 m)
COLOURS Chestnut, dun, bay, palomino, or roan

The Lundy is a fairly new breed, originating in 1928. It was developed on Lundy Island but, in 1980, the herd was moved to Cornwall. Each year the ponies return to the island to breed, returning to Cornwall for better grazing. The ponies swim behind a boat when making this move to and from the mainland.

| CHESTNUT | DUN | BAY | PALOMINO | ROAN |

ISLAND PONIES Since 1980, the semi-feral herd of Lundy Island Ponies has been moved to Cornwall, but each year ponies are moved back to the island to breed.

off the island, and the young stallions started to fight. They had to be culled so that the remainder could survive and continue to breed. The Lundy Pony Breed Society was formed in 1984.

CHARACTERISTICS
The modern Lundy Pony is attractive and versatile, with a kind nature. This makes them popular children's ponies. The head is broad, with fine cheekbones and a wide, strong jaw. Its eyes are large, alert, and gentle. The Lundy Pony has a compact body, with good hindquarters and a set-back shoulder. When viewed from the side, the body and legs should ideally make a square. The neck is strong and muscular, with a shaped crest. There should be a good depth through the chest, and no coarseness.

FOUNDATION PONY
'Pepper' was the first true Lundy stallion, who proved to be an excellent stud stallion. His creamy dun colouring and black mane and tail are common throughout the breed.

ORIGINS
The Lundy Pony was the result of a breeding experiment carried out by the owner of Lundy Island. New Forest (see p 339) mares were crossed with a Thoroughbred (see pp 284–87) stallion, but the result of this cross struggled to cope with the harsh conditions on the island. So Welsh Mountain (see p 362) blood was used to breed a tougher pony.

During World War II, it was impossible to move any young stock

Manipuri

ORIGIN India
ENVIRONMENT 🌵
BLOOD 💧
USES 🏇 🏇
HEIGHT 11.0–13.0 hh (1.12–1.32 m)
COLOURS Black, brown, chestnut, grey, or bay

The strong and hardy Manipuri is one of the purest and most prestigious Indian breeds and is claimed to be one of the oldest types of Polo Pony. Bred in the northeastern state of Manipur as a cavalry mount, it was also used by the British Army and taken to Burma in 1945, where it showed endurance and intelligence.

| BLACK | BROWN | CHESTNUT | GREY | BAY |

ORIGINS AND CHARACTERISTICS

The Manipuri is a cross between the Arab (*see* pp 184–87) and the Mongolian Wild Horse (*see* p 12). The sloping shoulder gives the Manipuri a fast, long stride, with little knee action. The neck is well muscled.

The pony has a compact body, strong knees and hocks, as well as muscular hindquarters.

The Arab influence shows in the concave face with alert eyes and small, pointed ears. The mane is usually coarse and stands upright.

MULTI-PURPOSE PONY Manipuri Ponies are still used for polo, racing, and in the military, where their speed, endurance, and intelligence are highly regarded.

Merens

ORIGIN France
ENVIRONMENT 🔺
BLOOD 🜄
USES 🐎 🐎
HEIGHT 13.0–14.1 hh (1.32–1.45 m)
COLOURS Black

The Merens Pony, also known as Merenguais, is claimed to have existed in the Ariège Pyrenees, in France, since prehistoric times. It takes its name from a small village high in the mountains close to Andorra. The Merens is very similar in appearance to the Fell Pony (*see* p 324) and the Friesian (*see* p 216), both of which are related.

ORIGINS AND CHARACTERISTICS

The breed is believed to have been influenced by Oriental bloodlines, as it has a much more refined head than other French native ponies. His isolated mountain environment has helped retain the breed's purity. A stud book and breed society (SHERPA) was formed in 1908. Although gentle and hardy, the Merens has a strong character. He is also supple and agile and able to work well on steep slopes.

ENDURING BREED The attractive Merens Pony is ideally suited to his mountain home and has been a good workhorse for farmers and soldiers.

TRUE BLOOD A 'true' Merens is one that has run free with the herd in the high Pyrenees, in the same way as his ancestors.

FINE FEATURES The Merens' head is fine with small ears and wide nostrils. The neck is strong with well-shaped withers.

Miniature

ORIGIN Worldwide
ENVIRONMENT 🌱 🐎 ⛰ 🌾 🌾
BLOOD 💧
USES Pets
HEIGHT Less than 39 in (1 m)
COLOURS All colours

The Miniature horse is bred all over the world, using many different small breeds, including the Shetland (*see* pp 353–55) and Dartmoor (*see* pp 316–17). The designation of a Miniature Horse for breed registration is dependent solely on its height, which is usually less than 1 m (39 in).

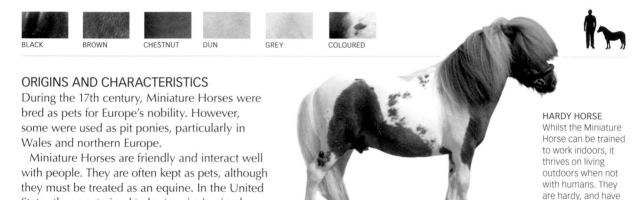

BLACK　BROWN　CHESTNUT　DUN　GREY　COLOURED

ORIGINS AND CHARACTERISTICS

During the 17th century, Miniature Horses were bred as pets for Europe's nobility. However, some were used as pit ponies, particularly in Wales and northern Europe.

Miniature Horses are friendly and interact well with people. They are often kept as pets, although they must be treated as an equine. In the United States they are trained to be 'service' animals, playing a similar role to that of guide dogs.

HARDY HORSE
Whilst the Miniature Horse can be trained to work indoors, it thrives on living outdoors when not with humans. They are hardy, and have a lifespan of 25–35 years.

Mongolian

ORIGIN Mongolia
ENVIRONMENT 🌱
BLOOD 💧
USES 🐎 🏇 🏇
HEIGHT 12.2–14.2 hh (1.27–1.47 m)
COLOURS Commonly dun, but also black and bay

The Mongolian Pony is an ancient type, with foundations in Przewalski's Horse, or the Asiatic Wild Horse (*see* p 12). They are bred by Mongol tribes, whose movement throughout Asia has led to the spread of this breed. Because of differences in ancestors, climate, and forage, the breed has no true type.

BLACK　DUN　BAY

ORIGINS AND CHARACTERISTICS

The Mongolian Pony has been used as important foundation stock for other breeds such as the Spiti and Manipuri (*see* p 336). The Mongolian saddle is very tall with a wooden frame, making the control of the paces limited. Unless essential to dictate otherwise, the rider generally leaves the pony to choose his own pace.

COARSE PONY The Mongolian Pony evolved from the Asiatic Wild Horse and this shows in his heavy head, somewhat coarse appearance, and commonly dun colour. The shoulders are also heavy, whilst the back is short, and the tail set high.

New Forest Pony

ORIGIN United Kingdom
ENVIRONMENT
BLOOD
USES
HEIGHT 13.2–14.2 hh (1.40–1.47 m)
COLOURS All solid colours

The New Forest Pony still runs free in the woodland and common land of the New Forest in Hampshire, England. The ponies are a great tourist attraction, and they are friendly and trainable by nature. An annual 'drift' (roundup) is used to sort out those to be sold and those to remain in the forest as breeding stock.

BLACK   BROWN   CHESTNUT   DUN   GREY   BAY

ORIGINS

Ponies have run wild in the New Forest since the passing of Canute's Forest Law in 1016. The New Forest Pony that we recognize today has certainly achieved a uniformity of type despite its very mixed ancestry. Welsh Ponies (*see* pp 362–65) were introduced in the 12th century, and

MADE FOR RIDING The New Forest Pony is popular throughout Europe as a children's riding and competition pony.

high-class stallions ran with the mares for a while, including the Thoroughbred (*see* pp 284–87) 'Marske', famed as the sire of the greatest racehorse of all time, 'Eclipse'!

HORSEY HEAD The head of the New Forest Pony is more like that of a horse, with a broad forehead, and narrow muzzle.

CHARACTERISTICS

The New Forest Pony is renowned as being a good child's riding pony, although he is sturdy enough to carry an adult also. The attractive head is more horse-like than that of most ponies, but it is the shoulders that are particularly noteworthy, being long and sloping, giving the pony a long, low, easy action. As with all native ponies, the New Forest is surefooted, tough, and sound.

Nooitgedachter

ORIGIN South Africa
ENVIRONMENT 🌾
BLOOD 🔥
USES 🏇 🏇 🏇
HEIGHT 13.2–15.0 hh (1.37–1.52 m)
COLOURS Mostly bays and greys, also brown, chestnut, or roan

| BROWN | CHESTNUT | GREY | BAY | ROAN |

The Nooitgedachter is a descendant of the Basuto Pony (*see* p 303) and is recognized as South Africa's first indigenous pony breed. It has a natural affinity towards people. It is named after the farm near Ermelo where it was first bred. There are now over 100 breeders dedicated to improving the breed.

ORIGINS

The breed only came into being when the South African Department of Agriculture decided to revive the old Cape Horse. They used Basuto Ponies that most resembled the Cape Horse, and began a breeding programme on Nooitgedacht farm. Similar to the larger Boerperd Horse (*see* pp 194–95), the Nooitgedachter was established as a breed in 1976.

CHARACTERISTICS

The modern Nooitgedachter is a compact horse capable of carrying 80–90 kg (13–14 st) for many miles. It has a fine, attractive head with large, intelligent eyes and alert, well-shaped ears. The hindquarters are well muscled, and its good, sloping shoulders give it a comfortable gait. The hooves are strong, and it is usually worked unshod.

ADAPTABLE PONY The Nooitgedachter is a good workhorse as well as a competition prospect. It is highly popular as a child's pony for competing.

Northlands

ORIGIN Norway
ENVIRONMENT ▲
BLOOD ◊
USES 🏇 🐴
HEIGHT 12.0–14.0 hh (1.22–1.42 m)
COLOURS All solid colours except dun or coloured

BLACK   BROWN   CHESTNUT   GREY   BAY   ROAN

The Northlands has much in common with the Icelandic Horse (*see* p 331), the Shetland Pony (*see* pp 353–55), and the Exmoor Pony (*see* p 322), and is considered to be descended from the Asiatic Wild Horse (*see* p 12). The breed has developed differently in different regions through crossing with various breeds.

ORIGINS

Prior to its near-extinction after World War II, there were two types of Northlands Pony: one from the Lyngen and the other from Norland (or Northlands). The Lyngen type was big and strong, and mainly chestnut in colour, while the Norland type was smaller with a thicker mane and tail and a variety of colours. The distinction is less evident today due to the crossbreeding that was required to revive the breed after World War II, and it was the more northern type that increased in numbers. The stud book was founded in 1969, but the breed is still endangered.

CHARACTERISTICS

The Northlands is energetic, good tempered, easy to train, robust, and healthy. Its overall confirmation is generally good.

MULTI-TALENTED He has a good-shaped head, straight in profile with small upright ears. The shoulders are well shaped leading to a good, strong back and a slightly sloping croup.

Norwegian Fjord

ORIGIN Norway
ENVIRONMENT ▲
BLOOD ○
USES 🏇 🐎
HEIGHT 13.0–14.0 hh (1.32–1.42 m)
COLOURS Dun

The Norwegian Fjord is an instantly recognizable pony with his distinctive dun colouring and striking bi-coloured mane and tail. He is believed to have inhabited his homeland since prehistoric times, and bears a strong resemblance to the Asiatic Wild Horse (*see* p 12). A black dorsal stripe runs from the forelock to the tip of the tail.

ORIGINS

The Fjord Pony is believed to be related to both the Asiatic Wild Horse and the Tarpan. The overall shape and colouring is very similar to the Asiatic Wild Horse, but he is more refined than that particular ancestor, indicating a link to the Tarpan also. The Fjord Pony is depicted in Viking carvings, and it was the Vikings who began the tradition of cutting the mane in a distinctive crescent shape, with the central dark hair standing out above the silver. Its harsh and arduous mountain landscape has helped to create a pony that is very strong, hardy, and surefooted. He has proved to be a great workhorse to the Norwegians, ploughing difficult terrain and easily negotiating steep, hazardous mountain tracks as a pack horse.

CHARACTERISTICS

The Fjord has a typical pony head, with small ears, wide-set eyes, and a narrow, light-coloured muzzle. The neck is thick and strong, and the body barrel-like with a broad chest. There is little definition through the shoulders and withers, but overall he is a perfect little powerhouse of strength. The limbs are exceptionally good, being short and strong, with

ACTIVE MOVER Popular for both riding and driving, the Fjord Pony has the good, active paces, particularly in trot, so often found in mountain breeds. The distinctive dun colouring seen here is always paired with the unique silver-and-black mane and tail.

good joints and plenty of bone. The feet are very hard and well shaped. Today, the pony is popular in other countries outside Norway, proving itself an excellent little riding and driving pony. He is popular as a riding pony not only because he is sound and surefooted, but also because he is a very attractive pony.

WILLING WORKER The Norwegian Fjord has a kind, and willing temperament although, like most tough pony breeds, he will sometimes have his own opinions about life.

Peneia

ORIGIN Greece
ENVIRONMENT ▲
BLOOD 🜄
USES 🐎 🐎🐎
HEIGHT 10.0–14.0 hh (1.00–1.42 m)
COLOURS Black, chestnut, grey, bay, or roan

The Peneia Pony, also known as the Pinia Geogalidiko or Georgaludiko, originates from the semi-mountainous northwest regions of the Peloponnese peninsula, in Greece. It is the least-known of the Greek ponies. 'Peneia' is a poetic name for the peninsula, often referred to in Greek Classical literature.

BLACK   BROWN   CHESTNUT   GREY   BAY   ROAN

ORIGINS

Peneia Ponies are found in the areas of Ilia and Achaia in Greece, but are very rare – there are thought to be no more than 300 of them. Greece is a difficult environment for horses: the sparse vegetation means that the indigenous breeds are generally small. The Greeks relied on importing larger, more refined stock such as Eastern types and Scythian horses. It is believed that the Peneia Pony is related to the Pindos (see p 346), which descended from the old Thessalonian Horse, noted for its beauty, courage, and endurance. During the early 20th century, the Peneia breed was influenced by using Anglo-Arab (see p 181), Anglo-Norman, and Nonius (see p 257) bloodlines. The herd book was only established in 1995, and is kept by the Greek Ministry of Agriculture.

PENEIA PONY WORKING Although rare, the Peneia Pony is still used as a riding and pack horse, more than capable of coping with the mountainous terrain of the Peloponnese.

CHARACTERISTICS

The Peneia is a very capable, useful pony. Its amenable temperament makes it a good riding and pack animal, as well as being used in agriculture. Stallions are crossed with donkeys to produce Hinnies (mules).

Although their conformation is not ideal, it is functional. They have great stamina and a strong constitution. Their legs are strong and sound, making them surefooted across rough terrain. The Peneia is quite heavily framed with a coarse head and a strong, muscular neck. They have a good back, but the hindquarters can be weak and underdeveloped.

The natural gait of the Peneia is rather stilted, so they are taught another gait called the 'Aravani', which, like the Icelandic 'tolt', makes the pace smoother and more comfortable for the rider.

NORWEGIAN FJORD PONIES These striking ponies are a truly ancient breed, popular with the Vikings for riding but also, less happily, for horse-fighting. Fortunately, their uses today are far less violent.

Pindos

ORIGIN Greece
ENVIRONMENT 🔺
BLOOD 💧
USES 🏇 🐎
HEIGHT 13.0 hh (1.32 m)
COLOURS Black, brown, grey, or bay

BLACK   BROWN   GREY   BAY

The Pindos Pony originates from the Pindus mountain ranges in Epirus and Thessaly, in Greece. It is probably a descendant of the Thessalonian, with influences from the ancient Peloponnese, Arcadian, and Epidaurian breeds. There is also evidence of Arab (*see* pp 184–87) blood.

ORIGINS AND CHARACTERISTICS

The Pindos is extremely surefooted and agile, and for centuries has been used for pack, farmwork, riding, and driving (as it still is today), but they do have a reputation for being difficult and stubborn. He is light framed, with a long and undermuscled neck. However, the back is strong and the shoulders sloping. The quarters can be weak and underdeveloped, but the Pindos is agile and able to carry loads over rough terrain.

ELEGANT The Pindos Pony is slightly larger and more elegant that the better-known Greek Skyros Pony. Pindos mares are often crossed with male donkeys to produce mules.

Pony of the Americas

ORIGIN United States
ENVIRONMENT 🌾
BLOOD 💧
USES 🏇 🐎
HEIGHT 11.0–14.0 hh (1.12–1.42 m)
COLOURS Coloured

The Pony of the Americas (or POA) was developed in 1954 by Leslie Boomhower. It was bred to provide a pony that had good looks, speed, and stamina for the teenage rider. The breed has attractive Appaloosa (*see* pp 182–83) colouring, which can vary from 'blanket' to 'leopard spots'.

ORIGINS AND CHARACTERISTICS

The POA has a refined head, showing Arab (*see* pp 184–87) influence in the dished face, with large eyes and fine pricked ears. Other influences include the Thoroughbred (*see* pp 284–87) and Quarter Horse (*see* pp 267–69). The shoulders are sloping with a wide, deep chest. The quarters are substantial and the legs have plenty of bone. They can also have sclera on the eye, mottled skin, and striped hooves, which is further evidence of the Appaloosa ancestry.

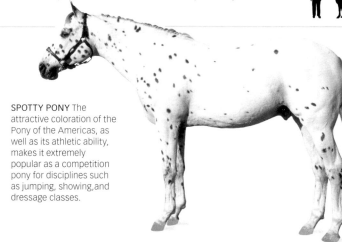

SPOTTY PONY The attractive coloration of the Pony of the Americas, as well as its athletic ability, makes it extremely popular as a competition pony for disciplines such as jumping, showing, and dressage classes.

Pottock

ORIGIN France
ENVIRONMENT
BLOOD 🌢
USES 🐎 🛒 🐎 🐎
HEIGHT 11.0–13.0 hh (1.12–1.32 m)
COLOURS Black, brown, grey, bay, or coloured

BLACK   BROWN   GREY   BAY   COLOURED

The Pottock, also known as the Basque Pony, is one of France's few indigenous semi-wild ponies. Once a year they are rounded up off the Pyrenees and Atlantic Cantons where they still roam. The breed's survival is aided by the fact that the ponies are early maturing – they reach maturity at 2–3 years of age.

ORIGINS AND CHARACTERISTICS

The Pottock descends from the Tarpan, and there has been some recent upgrading with the introduction of Arab (*see* pp 184–87) and Welsh (*see* pp 362–65) blood. He is a hardy pony, capable of living on sparse amounts of forage. The ponies are rounded up in January, and either sold or returned to the mountains. The Pottock copes well with being domesticated, and is a popular child's pony. It has some conformational defects, however, being weak in the hindquarters and long in the back. Although its legs are often lacking in bone and 'cow hocked', they do stand up to, and cope with, a good deal of hard work.

DEPRESSED Pottocks are often coloured. They have a small body and a large head, which has a small depression between the eyes.

MOUNTAIN ROOTS The Pottock's renowned toughness is testament to the challenging environment in which the breed developed.

Quantock

ORIGIN United Kingdom
ENVIRONMENT 🌿
BLOOD 💧
USES 🏇 🏇
HEIGHT 11.0–13.0 hh (1.12–1.32 m)
COLOURS Black, brown, grey, bay, or coloured

| BLACK | BROWN | GREY | BAY | COLOURED |

The Quantock is a 'type' rather than a breed. A herd of Exmoor ponies (*see* p 322) were introduced to the Quantock Hills in Somerset, England, for conservation grazing. Over the years, the commoners have used different stallions to develop and upgrade the offspring, which are sold at auction each year.

ORIGINS AND CHARACTERISTICS

Quantocks are very similar to the Exmoor and Dartmoor Ponies (*see* pp 316–17), but they tend to be slightly larger and finer, showing the influence of an Arab (*see* pp 184–87) stallion that was allowed to roam with the herd. Recently, a coloured Cob (*see* p 207) stallion was introduced. The ponies are rounded up every September. The stallion and the crossbred foals are taken off the moors for the winter as they do not cope well with the harsh conditions. The rest of the herd are returned to the moor.

ADDED COLOUR In recent years, a coloured Cob was introduced to the herd to increase the height and add colour, to help make the pony more popular and easier to sell.

Quarter Pony

ORIGIN United States
ENVIRONMENT 🌾
BLOOD 💧
USES 🏇 🐎 🐴
HEIGHT 13.0–14.2 hh (1.32–1.47 m)
COLOURS All colours

The Quarter Pony has been around for many years. It is derived from any Quarter Horse (*see* pp 267–69) that does not reach the Quarter Horse Association's minimum height of 14.3 hh (1.50 m), and it can be of any colour including mixed colours. The Quarter Pony must display the same characteristics as the Quarter Horse.

BLACK   BROWN   CHESTNUT   DUN   GREY   BAY   PALOMINO   COLOURED

CHARACTERISTICS

The Quarter Pony makes an ideal child's pony, with its quiet disposition and even temperament, but it is also capable of carrying an adult. He has a well-defined head, and is alert and intelligent looking. The face is broad with small ears. Another important characteristic of the Quarter Pony is that the head of the pony joins the neck at a 45-degree angle, with good distance between the neck muscle and the jaw bone, which is well developed. As with the Quarter Horse, the hindquarters are heavily muscled and full through the thigh, stifle, and gaskin down to the wide, deep, and straight hock. The hind legs are muscled both inside and out. The shoulders are sloping and the withers high, which helps to hold the saddle in position. The chest is broad and deep leading to a deep girth. The foreleg blends in to the shoulder, and the well-muscled forearm blends well in to the knee. The cannons are short.

GOOD BALANCE The Quarter Pony should be perfectly at ease when standing still, with the legs well underneath him. This gives the pony its ability to move quickly in any direction; he can stop and turn with ease and balance.

Riding Pony

ORIGIN United Kingdom
ENVIRONMENT 🌾
BLOOD 🌢
USES 🏇
HEIGHT 12.2–14.2 hh (1.27–1.47 m)
COLOURS All solid colours

The Riding Pony was developed over the last half of the 20th century to be a trainable and athletic pony for children. It may be registered with the National Pony Society stud book. The Riding Pony is now a very definite type; it is essentially the pony version of the Hack (*see* p 222).

BLACK   BROWN   CHESTNUT   GREY   BAY

ORIGINS
Breeders crossed Thoroughbreds (*see* pp 284–87) and Arabs (*see* pp 184–87) with the native pony breeds to produce this elegant pony. The success of this policy has led to many other countries following a similar breeding procedure. As the Riding Pony is a child's mount, it must be sensible and safe and give its young rider confidence.

CHARACTERISTICS
The Riding Pony's conformation must be correct and the paces true, straight, and free, with a long and low action similar to that of the Thoroughbred. The head is attractive, with a bold and intelligent eye. The shoulder is sloping, and the withers prominent. The neck is long, giving a good length of rein. The back is strong with sufficient depth through the loin, while the quarters are round with the tail well set and the hind leg well underneath. The second thigh and hocks are strong; the limbs have sufficient bone to withstand the work required of a child's pony.

The Riding Pony is popular in the show ring, where it is shown in classes according to its height. In addition, there are working pony classes. The Riding Ponies that tend to do well in these classes have more substance – a result of showing more of its pony characteristics than that of the Thoroughbred or Arab.

A lot of these ponies do not enter the show ring but are used for hacking and general riding.

SCALED-DOWN THOROUGHBRED The Riding Pony looks like a small Thoroughbred, but retains the characteristics of a pony. A good sloping shoulder and length of neck are needed to give the freedom of movement required.

Sable Island

ORIGIN Canada
ENVIRONMENT
BLOOD 💧
USES 🏇 🐎
HEIGHT Under 14.0 hh (1.42 m)
COLOURS Solid dark colours

It is thought that there have been horses roaming on Sable Island since the 16th century. A stallion called 'Jolly' was taken there in 1801, and bred with ponies already living on the island. It is likely that the original ponies were of Spanish descent, brought to America with the arrival of the *conquistadores* in the 1500s.

BLACK	BROWN	CHESTNUT	BAY

ORIGINS AND CHARACTERISTICS

The romantic belief is that the Sable Island Ponies are descended from equine survivors of various shipwrecks off the coast of Canada, but it is more likely that they descend from horses that were taken to the island. The ponies are tough and hardy, but do have conformational faults: the head can be overly large, and the hindquarters relatively weak.

WINDSWEPT Battered by the wind and the seas, the grazing on the island is sparse and the ponies are affected by the sand eroding their teeth and reducing their grazing ability.

Sandalwood

ORIGIN Indonesia
ENVIRONMENT 🌾
BLOOD 💧
USES 🏇 🐎 🏇 🐴 🐎
HEIGHT 12.0–13.0 hh (1.22–1.32 m)
COLOURS All colours

The Sandalwood Pony originated on the islands of Sumba and Sumbawa, off Indonesia. Named after the sandalwood trees that are exported from Indonesia, it is a quality pony greatly influenced by Arab (*see* pp 184–87) blood.

BLACK	BROWN	CHESTNUT	DUN	GREY	BAY

ORIGINS AND CHARACTERISTICS

The exact origins of the Sandalwood Pony are not known, but there was certainly a good injection of Arab blood at some stage, which shows in the pony's fineness of features, particularly in the head. He also has the Arab's speed, energy, and agility. The pony is considered the best of the local breeds and has been extensively exported. In Australia, they are popular as riding ponies; in Thailand, they are used for racing; and in Malaysia they have been bred to Thoroughbreds (*see* pp 284–87).

BAREBACK RACER Fast and agile, Sandalwood Ponies are used for flat racing and harness racing. They are also the mounts for the traditional bareback races held on the islands.

Sardinian Pony

ORIGIN Sardinia
ENVIRONMENT
BLOOD 🜄
USES 🐎 🐴 🐎
HEIGHT 12.0–13.0 hh (1.22–1.32 m)
COLOURS Dark solid colours

BLACK   BROWN   CHESTNUT   BAY

The Sardinian Pony is thought to be an ancient breed, but it is now quite rare. The first documented evidence of the breed was in 1845, but they probably existed several centuries earlier. More like a small horse than a pony, the Sardinian may well be another example of a breed stunted by the limitations of its environment.

ORIGINS AND CHARACTERISTICS

Also known as the Giara Pony, after their natural habitat the Giara plateau, the exact origins of the Sardinian Pony are not known. However, its native country was well positioned for trade with North Africa, which supports other evidence of Barb (*see* pp 90–91) influence. Arab (*see* pp 184–87) influence is also likely. The pony has a nicely arched neck; good, sloping shoulders; a short, strong back; and a deep, wide chest. The limbs look light but are strong and sound.

HORSE-LIKE The agile Sardinian has the proportions of a horse, shown in its good length of neck and body, and in the long limbs.

Shetland Pony

ORIGIN United Kingdom
ENVIRONMENT
BLOOD ◊
USES 🐎 🐴 🐎
HEIGHT Under 42 in (107 cm)
COLOURS All colours except spotted

The Shetland is the smallest of the United Kingdom's natives, but is probably one of the best known worldwide. There have been ponies on the Scottish Shetland Islands for centuries, although their exact origin is not known. Despite their stature, they have greater strength relative to their size than most other equines.

BLACK BROWN CHESTNUT DUN GREY BAY

SMALL WONDER The Shetland Pony has a small but broad head and an intelligent eye. Large nasal cavities allow air to be warmed before entering the lungs.

CHARACTER The strong character of the Shetland Pony is legendary. Though small, they are strong-minded and will not be dominated, as many a young rider has found out.

ORIGINS AND CHARACTERISTICS

The Shetland Pony probably descends from the primitive Tundra-type horse, descendants of which were probably brought to the Shetland Islands over 10,000 years ago. The isolation of the islands, as well as the bleak and harsh environment, would have shaped the evolution of these early animals. The Shetland Islands offer little shelter and sparse grazing; so the smaller the animal, the more chance he has of finding sufficient food and shelter.

GOOD ACTION The Shetland Pony has a double thickness coat (hence the cuddly, shaggy look), and a very thick, long mane and tail to protect him from the elements. The rocky terrain of the Shetlands has ensured he has strong feet.

Siberian Pony

ORIGIN Russia
ENVIRONMENT
BLOOD
USES
HEIGHT Up to 14.0 hh (1.42 m)
COLOURS Most colours, including spotted

Siberian Ponies are made up of a number of different types that evolved to suit the work required of them. They are most famous for their role in the ill-fated Antarctic expeditions of 1910–13. No ponies survived: those that might have made it to the end of the journey were shot to feed the men and sled dogs.

BLACK	BROWN	CHESTNUT	DUN	GREY	BAY

ORIGINS AND CHARACTERISTICS

Siberian Ponies evolved in the vast open stretch of land running from the Ural Mountains to the River Yenisei in northern and eastern Siberia. They evolved from the ancient Mongolian breeds and are used for riding, light draught, and pack work, as well as providing meat, milk, skin, and hair. They have been invaluable to the nomadic tribes of Siberia, and are renowned for their docile natures.

BREEDING The Siberian Pony has evolved to be extremely hardy. Attempts to improve them by crossing to Orlov Trotters and Thoroughbreds were unsuccessful as the progeny lost this vigour.

Skyros Pony

ORIGIN Greece
ENVIRONMENT
BLOOD
USES
HEIGHT 14.0 hh (1.42 m)
COLOURS Black, brown, or bay

The Skyros Pony, or Skyrian Small Horse, descended from the primitive Pony Type 1, which inhabited northwest Europe just prior to domestication. These animals resembled the present-day Exmoor Pony (*see* p 322), and this is evident in the small, stocky stature of the Skyros Pony.

BLACK	BROWN	BAY

ORIGINS AND CHARACTERISTICS

The ponies were brought to Skyros Island between the 5th and 8th centuries BC. During the winter, they live in the mountainous part of the island, the *Vouno,* where grazing and water are plentiful. In summer, they head north to find food and water. The Skyros Pony has a broad forehead with prominent eyes, short ears, and a wide mealy muzzle. They are deep bodied with wide loins and a low-set tail.

IN DECLINE The ponies' existence is threatened partly because they mate with the many wild donkeys! Fewer than 100 remained at the 20th century's end. Efforts are underway to promote them as children's ponies.

Sorraia

ORIGIN Portugal
ENVIRONMENT 🌾
BLOOD 💧
USES 🏇 🏇 🏇
HEIGHT 13.2–14.2 hh (1.37–1.47 m)
COLOURS Dun

The Sorraia Pony is an ancient breed, indigenous to southern Iberia, believed to have descended from both the Tarpan and the Asiatic Wild Horse (*see* p 12). The Sorraia is, in turn, an ancestor of both the Andalucian (*see* p 180) and Lusitano (*see* p 244) breeds. They have proved to be good riding horses, popular for herd work as they have natural agility and balance.

LONG-LEGGED Despite being called a pony, the Sorraia is very horse-like with horsey proportions and long slender legs. They are also surefooted and agile.

MARKINGS The Sorraia is always dun in colour and often has a dark face or muzzle, as well as black-tipped ears. The black mane and tail hair are often interspersed with paler hair.

ORIGINS AND CHARACTERISTICS

The name is derived from the area in which the breed was rediscovered in the 1920s – a region called Coruche in the lower Sor Raia. A land bridge existed between Spain and Africa up until the Ice Age, and this would explain the early influence of the Barb (*see* pp 190–91). More Barb blood would have been added when the area was invaded by the Moors. The Sorraia have horse-like proportions and are renowned for their ability to cope with climatic extremes.

South African Cob

ORIGIN South Africa
ENVIRONMENT 🌾
BLOOD 💧
USES 🏇 🏇 🐎 🏇
HEIGHT 13.2–15.2 hh (1.37–1.57 m)
COLOURS All solid colours

The South African Cob was developed from imported Welsh Cobs (*see* p 365) crossed with a variety of native and imported breeds. It is a type rather than a true breed and, although not yet as well known as other South African breeds, it is increasingly popular as a versatile, quiet-natured animal suited both to adults and children.

| BLACK | BROWN | CHESTNUT | DUN | GREY | BAY | PALOMINO | ROAN |

ORIGINS AND CHARACTERISTICS

The South African Cob does not have breed status, but it does have a stud book. A number of Welsh Cob mares and stallions were imported to start a breeding programme – most South African Cobs are pure Welsh Cobs that are registered in the South African stud book. There is also a South African Welsh Pony and Cob Society. The Cob is popular for trail riding, low-level dressage and showjumping, carriage work, and farm work.

The South African Cob should have a deep strong body, short limbs with plenty of bone, and an attractive but workmanlike head on a well-set neck. They have a good temperament and showy paces.

GOOD CHARACTER The quiet, good-natured South African Cob is generally easy to look after, adding to its popularity.

Sumba

ORIGIN Indonesia
ENVIRONMENT
BLOOD
USES
HEIGHT 13.0 hh (1.32 m)
COLOURS Any colour, but predominantly dun

BLACK	BROWN	CHESTNUT	DUN	GREY

Named after the island on which they are bred, the Sumba Pony is a descendant of Mongolian and ancient Chinese stock. Although small, they are incredibly strong and ridden by adults in traditional mounted games.

ORIGINS AND CHARACTERISTICS

The Sumba Pony is very similar to another of the Indonesian island ponies, the Sumbawa, which also takes its name from the island it inhabits. Both descend from the same stock. The Sumba is usually dun and displays the primitive markings of the dorsal stripe and black points, but they can also be any other colour. They are heavy in the head, with a short, muscular neck leading to flat withers. The back is usually long but strong. The legs are fine with tough hooves.

GAMES PONY The Sumba is quick and athletic. It also has great stamina, which, along with a willing temperament, makes it an excellent games pony both for adults and children.

Tibetan Pony

ORIGIN Tibet
ENVIRONMENT
BLOOD
USES
HEIGHT 12.2 hh (1.27 m)
COLOURS Any colour

BLACK	BROWN	CHESTNUT	DUN	GREY	BAY

Tibetan Ponies are highly regarded in Tibet and are kept both by rich and poor. The Dalai Lama has used them to travel through the mountains. They were given as gifts to Chinese Emperors, especially during the Ming and Tang Dynasties.

ORIGINS AND CHARACTERISTICS

Descending from ancient Chinese stock and the Mongolian Pony (*see* p 338), the Tibetan Pony has been pure bred for centuries. Valued for their great strength and endurance, they are surefooted and resilient to the harsh climate of the mountains, and are able to withstand freezing winter conditions. The head is straight in profile, and the neck is muscular. The straight shoulder, powerful hindquarters, short, strong legs, and hard hooves help them to cope with the steep mountain terrain.

VERSATILE Tibetan Ponies, seen here threshing corn, are used for agricultural, light draught, pack, and riding purposes.

Tokara

ORIGIN Japan
ENVIRONMENT
BLOOD 💧
USES 🐎 🐴
HEIGHT 12.0 hh (1.22 m)
COLOURS Black or chestnut

The Tokara, also referred to as the Kagoshima Pony, is native to Japan. The breed has always been low in density. Even at the height of their popularity, the number of ponies was never over 100, and after World War II, it came very close to extinction.

BLACK	CHESTNUT

ORIGINS AND CHARACTERISTICS

In 1950, Dr Shigeyuki Hayashisa discovered a small herd of horses on the south side of the Tokara Islands from which the ponies take their name. He declared the ponies a national treasure, and sent them to the mainland to escape the difficult living conditions. Today, the Kagoshima University, Iriki Ranch, Kaimon National Park, and Nakano Island are breeding and preservation centres for the Tokara Pony.

SMALL AND RARE The pony has increased slightly in height with the selective breeding that is now in place. The breed often shows primitive characteristics.

Welara

ORIGIN United Kingdom and United States
ENVIRONMENT
BLOOD
USES
HEIGHT 14.0 hh (1.42 m)
COLOURS All solid colours

This new breed was established during the 1980s by a group of ranchers from California, by crossing an Arab (*see* pp 184–87) with a Welsh Pony (*see* p 363).

| BLACK | BROWN | CHESTNUT | DUN | GREY | BAY |

ORIGINS AND CHARACTERISTICS

The first person known to have made this cross was Lady Wentworth at the famous Arabian Crabbet Stud in Sussex, England. But it only gained its recognition and stud registry in 1981. Crossing the Arab and the Welsh Pony gives a breed with exceptional refinement and beauty. They possess great intelligence and a fine temperament, making them ideal as a riding, competition, and harness pony. Since the registry was established, the breed has become very popular worldwide.

NOBLE PONY The beauty of the Welara is paramount as a characteristic of this breed. It has a naturally arched neck and a dished face, with a high head carriage.

Welsh Pony (Section A)

ORIGIN United Kingdom
ENVIRONMENT ▲ 🌾
BLOOD 💧
USES 🐎 🏇 🐎
HEIGHT 12.0 hh (1.22 m)
COLOURS All solid colours, including dun and palomino

The Welsh Section A, also known as the Welsh Mountain Pony, is probably the most well-known and numerous of the British mountain and moorland ponies. It is considered by many to be the most beautiful of all the pony breeds. It is the base from which the three other divisions of Welsh Pony and Cob evolve.

BLACK	BROWN	CHESTNUT	DUN	GREY	BAY	PALOMINO	ROAN

ORIGINS

The evolution of the breed is vague, but it goes back, at least, to Roman times. The Romans crossed the native Celtic ponies with horses of Eastern origin. More recently, in the 18th century, the breed was enhanced with the use of Thoroughbred (*see* pp 284–87), Arab (*see* pp 184–87), and Barb (*see* pp 190–91) blood.

MOUNTAIN PONIES The Welsh Mountain Pony still roams the moors and mountains of Wales. This ensures that the pony remains hardy and thrifty, and strong and nimble.

CHARACTERISTICS

The head is small and set well on a neck of good length, and carried well on gently sloping shoulders. The withers are clearly defined, and the limbs are set square. It moves quickly and freely, with good hocks, and knees that flex well. It is popular as a child's pony as it is a good jumper and excels in the show ring. It is also becoming increasingly popular as a carriage-driving pony, especially in the competitive world of driving trials, in which speed and agility play important roles.

PURE BEAUTY The eastern influence is still clearly visible in today's Welsh Mountain Pony with its elegant head and slightly dished face; large, alert eyes; and wide, flared nostrils.

Welsh Pony (Section B)

ORIGIN United Kingdom
ENVIRONMENT 🏔 🌾
BLOOD 🌢
USES 🏇 🐎 🐎
HEIGHT 13.2 hh (1.37 m)
COLOURS All solid colours, including dun and palomino

The Welsh Section B, or Welsh Pony, is a more modern and slightly larger version of the Welsh Section A. Originally bred by the Welsh hill farmers to provide a means of transport and for herding livestock, in more recent years it has developed into an ideal pony for children.

BLACK   BROWN   CHESTNUT   DUN   GREY   BAY   PALOMINO   ROAN

ORIGINS

The Welsh Section B pony is very similar to the Welsh Section A, but the fact that it is slightly larger makes it a more versatile riding pony. It was bred from the Welsh Mountain Pony, using Welsh Cob (*see* p 365), Thoroughbred (*see* pp 284–87), and Arab (*see* pp 184–87) blood, and is generally taller and lighter in build than the Welsh Mountain Pony.

CONFORMATION The conformation of the Section B Pony is similar to that of the slightly smaller Section A Pony, with a good length of neck and sloping shoulders.

BRED WITH CARE The Welsh Pony and Cob Society was founded in 1901 to oversee the development of the four divisions of Welsh ponies.

CHARACTERISTICS

Its agility, balance, and speed made it an ideal pony for the hill farmer to check and move livestock. The legs are set square and are strong with short cannons. These attributes, combined with its natural talent for jumping and its good nature, have also made it an ideal competition pony for the younger rider. It is also highly sought after for both pleasure and competitive carriage driving.

Welsh Pony (Section C)

ORIGIN United Kingdom
ENVIRONMENT ▲
BLOOD ⬦
USES 🏇 🐴
HEIGHT 13.2 hh (1.37 m)
COLOURS Black, brown, chestnut, dun, grey, bay, or palomino

The Welsh Section C is also referred to as the Welsh Pony of Cob Type. It is the smaller of the two Welsh Cobs, the other being the Section D. This stocky pony has also been called the 'farm pony', as they were used for all types of farm work on the Welsh hills, as well as being used in the slate mines of North Wales.

BLACK   BROWN   CHESTNUT   DUN   GREY   BAY   PALOMINO

ORIGINS AND CHARACTERISTICS

Originally, this pony was usually the offspring of a Section A Pony (*see* p 362) and a small Cob (*see* p 206). However, it is now produced by mating registered Section C Ponies.

The Welsh Pony Section C retains many of the attributes of the Welsh Section A, being tough, hardy, and sound in constitution. The neck is thick and strong, and carried high and arched. Although the withers tend to be low, the shoulders are long and the action is energetic and ground-covering. The legs are clean and strong, and there is light, silky feathering at the heels.

ELEGANT PONY Like the Welsh Sections A and B, the Welsh Section C has cadence and elegance. Its overall conformation is compact and stylish, making it popular with children and adults alike.

ACTION PONY The Welsh Section C is renowned for its ability to trot for long periods of time, covering the ground with ease and elegance. They are often shown in hand.

Welsh Pony (Section D)

ORIGIN United Kingdom
ENVIRONMENT ▲
BLOOD ◊
USES 🏇 🐎
HEIGHT 14.0–15.0 hh (1.42–1.52 m)
COLOURS Black, brown, chestnut, dun, grey, bay, or palomino

For centuries, the Welsh hill farmers have used the Welsh Section D, also known as the Welsh Cob, as an all-round utility horse. It is believed that the Section D is influenced by the Section A (see p 362) and Andalucians (see p 180), which were bred in the Welsh Borders during the 11th and 12th centuries.

BLACK   BROWN   CHESTNUT   DUN   GREY   BAY   PALOMINO

CHARACTERISTICS

The Cob retains a pony-like head, which is full of character and quality. The ears are neat. The neck is crested and arched, and runs smoothly into strong shoulders that are nicely sloping. The body is compact, with good depth through the girth, and well-sprung ribs. The legs are muscled with defined joints and a good deal of bone.

GREAT ACTION The Section D has a free action; the knee bends allowing the whole foreleg to extend straight from the shoulder and reach forwards as far as possible.

ORIGINS

During the 18th and 19th centuries, the Section D was upgraded using the Norfolk Roadster and Yorkshire Coach Horses. Much sought after as a gun horse and for mounted infantry, until 1960, the Cob was also used on milk, bread, and general delivery rounds throughout Wales.

VERSATILE The Section D is popular as a riding horse; although small it is able to easily carry an adult rider. It has a natural jumping ability and is often a good competition horse.

Yakut

ORIGIN Russia
ENVIRONMENT
BLOOD ◊
USES 🐎 🐎
HEIGHT 11.0–12.0 hh (1.12–1.22 m)
COLOURS Brown, grey, or bay

| BROWN | GREY | BAY |

The Yakut is a rare breed with similar characteristics to those of the Shetland Pony (*see* pp 353–55). It originated by natural selection in the harsh conditions of northern and central Siberia. It is thought to have desended from the Tundra Horse. The pony has evolved into three types: the Northern Original, the Smaller Southern, and the Larger Southern types.

ORIGINS

The Yakut is larger than the other breeds of similar type and Mongolian origin. The Northern Original is the most sought after, despite its coarse head and straight neck. The chest is wide and deep and it has short legs with very strong feet so that they can

ILL-FATED The Yakut is the hardiest of all the equine breeds. It was used to pull sledges on the ill-fated expedition to the South Pole led by Robert Scott; neither the ponies, nor Robert Scott survived the journey.

scrape away snow and ice while looking for food. The mane and tail are thick and long. In winter, the body hair can grow up to 8 cm (3 in) in length.

The Larger Southern type has descended from the local Suntar, Megezh, and Olekminsk varieties. In more recent times, it has been crossed with trotters and the hardier heavy draught horses in an attempt to improve the breed. It is widespread throughout the regions of central Yakutia. The Smaller

Southern type has not been crossed with any of the 'improving' breeds.

CHARACTERISTICS

The thick coat is usually bay, grey-brown, or grey. The purebreds have a dark dorsal stripe and a transverse stripe over the withers. Some have a dark, grid-like pattern on the point of the shoulder. They have thick skin, and can store reserves of fat during the summer, which then act as insulation from the cold and a source of energy to draw upon during the winter.

The Yakut is extremely hardy, requiring no shelter despite living in the coldest climate in the northern hemisphere. They are able to fend for themselves during the long and bitter winters, living off a wide variety of grasses and plants that manage to survive under the snow.

Yakut Ponies were famed for two exploratory journeys. In 1890, a Cossack officer, Dmitir Peshkov, rode his Yakut 'Seriy' across Siberia in the depths of winter – a journey of 8,850 km (5,500 miles). In 1910, the British explorer Robert Scott used Yakuts to carry equipment for his expedition to the South Pole.

HUNTER'S MOUNT Here, a hunter travels on his Yakut at Korban in the winter time. The thick coats help the ponies to withstand the terrible conditions, which can see temperatures as low as minus 50 degrees centigrade (– 60° F).

USEFUL BOOKS AND ADDRESSES

USEFUL BOOKS

Draper, Judith. *The Ultimate Encyclopedia of Horse Breeds and Horse Care*. Hermes House, 2002.

Hartley Edwards, Elwyn. *Eyewitness Handbooks Horses*. Dorling Kindersley, 1993.

Hartley Edwards, Elwyn. T*he Ultimate Horse Book*. Dorling Kindersley, 1991.

Hyland, Ann. *Foal to Five Years*. Ward Lock, 1980.

Kidd, Jane. *An International Encyclopedia of Horse Breeds and Breeding*. Salamander Books Ltd, 1989.

Muir, Sarah & Debby Sly. *The Complete Horse and Rider*. Hermes House, 2001.

Porter, Valerie. *Horse Tails*. Guinness Publishing Ltd, 2004.

Sly, Debby. *Fun with Ponies*. Studio Cactus, 2004.

Various. *The Illustrated Encyclopedia of World Equestrian Sports*. Marshall Cavendish, 1990.

USEFUL ADDRESSES

British Horse Society

Stoneleigh Deer Park

Kenilworth, Warwickshire

CV8 2XZ

United Kingdom

+44 (0) 8701 202244

http://www.bhs.org.uk

Canadian Sports Horse Association

Box 98, 40 Elizabeth Street

Okotoks, Alberta T1S 1A4

Canada

+11 (403) 938 0887

http://www.c-s-h-a.org

Equestrian Federation of Australia

PO Box 673

Sydney Markets

NSW, 2129

Australia

+61 (0) 2 8762 7777

http://www.efanational.com

Equestrian Sports New Zealand

Level 4, 3–9 Church Street,

PO Box 6146,

Wellington

New Zealand

+64 (0) 4 499 8994

http://www.nzequestrian.org.nz

FEI (International Equestrian Federation)

Avenue Mon Repos 24

1005 Lausanne

Switzerland

+41 (0) 21 310 47 47

http://www.fei.org

Indigenous Horse Society of India

Dundlod House,

Civil Lines, Jaipur 302019

Rajasthan

India

+ 91 (141) 2211276

http://www.horseindian.com

South African National Equestrian Federation

PO Box 30875

Kyalami 1684

South Africa

+27 (0) 11 468 3236/7

http://www.horsesport.org.za

The Jockey Club

40 East 52nd Street

New York, NY 10022

United States

+1 (212) 371 5970

http://www.jockeyclub.com

United States Eventing Association

USEA Inc

525 Old Waterford Road

NW Leesburg, VA 20176

United States

+1 (703) 779 0440

http://www.useventing.com

United States Equestrian Federation

4047 Iron Works Parkway

Lexington, KY 40511

United States

+1 (859) 258 2472

http://www.usef.org

USEFUL WEBSITES

http://www.ansi.okstate.edu – Alphabetical listings, histories, and breed specifications of many horse breeds from the Oklahoma State University Horse Project.

http://www.arabianhorses.org – AHA is an equine association that registers and maintains a database of more then one million Arabian, Half-Arabian and Anglo-Arabian horses.

http://www.equiworld.net – Online community and informational site on all things equestrian, billed as 'the Internet's most extensive equestrian resource'.

http://www.horseandhound.co.uk – A first-class equestrian site with everything for horse enthusiasts from equestrian news to equestrian disciplines such as showjumping, dressage, and eventing.

http://www.horsecare.stablemade.com – Information and experience-sharing about various breeds of horses, basic horse care, and the nature of horses.

http://www.kyhorsepark.com – Official site of the famous American theme park that includes the most comprehensive horse museum in the world.

http://www.lexiqueducheval.net – Trilingual (English, French, German) online dictionary of the equestrian vocabulary, including an extensive list of world breeds.

http://www.takh.org – A fascinating bilingual (English, French) site celebrating the world's last remaining truly wild horse: Przewalski's Horse.

http://www.tbheritage.com – Thoroughbred Heritage offers portraits, race charts, pedigrees, and other historical information related to the Thoroughbred.

http://www.thehorse.com – Horse news and veterinarian-approved health care information.

http://www.thejoyofhorses.com – Online 'magazine' full of in-depth articles and quality photographs that are held online indefinitely.

http://www.thoroughbredrehabilitationcentre.co.uk – A UK charity dedicated to the welfare of ex-racehorses and now regarded as the role model of racehorse rehabilitation.

BREED SOCIETIES

American Paint Horse Association
PO Box 961023
Fort Worth
Texas
United States
+1 (817) 834 2742
http://www.apha.com

American Saddlebred Horse Association
4083 Iron Works Parkway
Lexington, KY 40511
United States
+1 (859) 259 2742
http://www.asha.net

Arabian Horse Association
10805 E. Bethany Drive
Aurora, CO 80014
United States
+1 (303) 696 4500
http://www.arabianhorses.org

Canadian Warmblood Horse Breeders Association
Box 21100, 2105 8th Street East
Saskatoon
Saskatchewan, S7H 5N9
Canada
+1 (306) 373 6620
http://www.canadianwarmbloods.com

Cleveland Bay Horse Society
York Livestock Centre, Murton
York, YO19 5GF
United Kingdom
+44 (0) 1904 489731
http://www.clevelandbay.com

Clydesdale Horse Society
Kinclune, Kingoldrum, Kirriemir
Angus, DD8 5HX
Scotland
+44 (0) 1575 570900

http://www.clydesdalehorsesociety.com

Dutch Warmblood Society
KWPN, PO Box 382
3700 AJ Zeist
The Netherlands
+31 (0) 313 069 34600
http://www.kwpn.nl

International Miniature Horse & Pony Society
Howick Farm, The Haven
Billingshurst
West Sussex, RH14 9BQ
United Kingdom
+44 (0) 7802 592136
http://www.imhps.com

Kaimanawa Horse Breed Society
8/46 Wingfield Place
Clurton Park, Wellington
New Zealand
http://www.kaimanawa.com

Missouri Fox Trotting Horse Breed Association
PO Box 1027
Ava, Missouri 65608
United States
+1 (417) 683 2468
http://www.mfthba.com

Nooitgedacht Horse Breeders' Society of South Africa
PO Box 12262
Clubview 0014
South Africa
+27 (0) 12 654 1420
http://www.sa-breeders.co.za/org/nooitgedachter

Oldenburg Horse Breeding Society
Grafenhorststraße 5

49377 Vechta
Germany
+49 (0) 4441 9355 0
http://www.oldenburghorse.com

Palomino Horse Breeders of America
15253 East Skelly Drive
Tulsa, OK 74116-2637
+1 (918) 438 1234
http://www.palominohba.com

Russian Warmblood Association
Moscow office
tatiana@russianwarmblood.com
http://russianwarmblood.com

Selle Français Breeders Society (ANSF)
56 av. Henri Ginoux – 92120
Montrouge
France
+33 (0) 146 12 34 00
http://www.sellefrancais.fr

Shetland Pony Stud-Book Society
Shetland House, 22 York Place
Perth, PH2 8EH
Scotland
+44 (0) 1738 623471
http://www.shetlandponystudbooksociety.co.uk

Shire Horse Society
East of England Showground
Peterborough
Cambridgeshire, PE2 6XE
United Kingdom
+44 (0) 1733 234451
http://www.shire-horse.org.uk

South African Sport Horse Federation
No 79 Swaanswyk Road

Tokai 7945, Cape Town
South Africa
+27 (021) 7121931
http://www.studbook.co.za/society/
sporthorse

Thoroughbred Breeders' Association
Stanstead House, 8 The Avenue
Newmarket
Suffolk, CB8 9AA
United Kingdom
+44 (0) 1638 661321
http://www.thetba.co.uk

Trakehner Breeders' Fraternity
Lower Lidham Hill Farm
North Lane, Guestling
East Sussex, TN35 4LX
United Kingdom
+44 (0) 1424 813830
http://www.trakehnerbreeders.com

Waler Horse Society of Australia
20 Glengarrie Road, Bargo
NSW, 2574
Australia
+61 (02) 4684 1512
http://www.walerhorse.com

Welsh Pony and Cob Society
6 Chalybeate St, Aberystwyth
Caredigion, SY23 1HP
United Kingdom
+44 (0) 1970 625401
http://www.wpcs.uk.com

World Arabian Horse Organisation
North Farm, 2 Trenchard Road
Standton Fitzwarren, Swindon
Wiltshire, SN6 7RZ
United Kingdom
+44 (0) 1793 766877
http://www.waho.org

GLOSSARY

A

Action Describes the horse's gait with particular respect to the movement of his limbs and how these define his various paces.

Aids The signals given by the rider to the horse, through the use of the rider's hands, legs, seat, and voice, to direct and influence the horse's actions.

All-weather surface An artificial surface for riding on, which remains suitable for use whatever the weather or climatic conditions.

B

Back at the knee A conformational fault where the forelegs slope backwards from below the knee.

Backing (breaking) The process of teaching a horse that has never been ridden to accept a saddle and rider on his back.

Bars The gums of the lower jaw between the molar and incisor teeth.

Bone Refers to the substance and strength of the horse's limbs based on the measurement of the circumference of the cannon bone just below the knee.

Boxy feet Small, square-shaped, often upright hooves.

Breed Group of animals bred selectively to be consistent in type and characteristics so as to be identifiably different to another group or breed of, in this case, horse.

Brushing A faulty action whereby the hoof of one limb brushes against the opposite limb. Brushing boots can be worn to protect against this occurrence.

C

Cannon bone The main bone of the foreleg between the knee and the fetlock.

Cantle The raised back of the seat of the saddle.

Carriage horse Relatively light horse, usually with a good trot, used for drawing a carriage.

Cart horse Heavier stamp of horse used for pulling a cart or wagon, or for other draught work.

Chaps Protective long or short over-trousers that protect the rider's legs from rubbing against the saddle and stirrup leathers.

Chestnut A small horny growth on the inside of each leg. Also a reddish-brown coat colour.

Clean-legged A horse that carries no feathering on the lower leg.

Close-coupled (short-coupled) A horse with a short back, which gives the impression of strength and good connection between the horse's forehand and hindquarters.

Clipping Shaving off the horse's winter coat hair to prevent him becoming too hot and sweaty when he is in work.

Coach horse A strongly built but still elegant horse used for pulling a heavy coach – more heavily built than a carriage horse.

Coldblood Word used to describe the heavy-horse breeds of the world – relates to the origin as well as their calmness of temperament.

Colic Abdominal pain in horses, which can prove to be fatal.

Collection When the horse works in what looks like a short outline as a result of lowering his hock and hindquarters and elevating his forehand.

Colt A male horse (uncastrated) under four years of age.

Concentrates Manufactured feeds for horses that supply all the nutrients, vitamins, and minerals in one diet. Different types of concentrate feed are given depending on how hard the horse is working.

Conformation How the horse is shaped and put together in terms of his skeleton and musculature.

Cow hocks Conformational fault where the hocks point inwards towards each other. It is an acceptable characteristic of mountain breeds as it appears to helps them climb steep slopes.

Crossbreeding Crossing (mating) two different breeds or types of horse to produce offspring.

D

Dam A horse or pony's mother.

Depth A measurement of the horse's body taken from the withers to the elbow. When the measurement is adequate or better the horse is described as having a good depth of girth.

Desert horse Horses originating from a desert environment, such as Arabs and Akhal-Tekes, which are genetically capable of handling heat, low water intake, and hard ground conditions.

Diagonal Describes the movement, as a pair, of one hind leg and the opposite foreleg. For example, the trot involves the horse moving his legs in diagonal pairs.

Dipped back A conformational fault where the horse's back appears to sink, or dip, in the middle. Also known as sway back.

Dished face Concave profile of the front of the face. Usually indicates Arab blood in the horse's breeding.

Dock The bony part of the horse's tail.

Dorsal stripe A line of dark hair running from the withers to the tail – often found on dun-coloured horses and ponies.

Draught horse A heavy horse used for pulling either a vehicle or machinery (usually agricultural). A draught horse is generally a very powerfully built animal with a calm temperament.

E

Elevating (the forehand) When the horse lightens and lifts his head, neck, shoulders, and withers as a result of carrying more of his weight on his hindquarters. This is the aim of flatwork training.

Elevation When the horse's paces show good lift and height in his action. The stride is less ground covering but more elevated and extravagant.

Engagement When the horse uses his hocks and hindquarters correctly to carry his weight and power himself forwards whilst allowing the rider to contain and direct the energy and movement that this creates.

Entire An uncastrated male horse (stallion).

Ewe neck A conformational or training fault that shows as too much muscle on the underside of the neck, and muscle wastage (a concave profile) along the top of the neck.

Extension When the horse lengthens his outline and stride by powering himself forwards off his hind legs and stretching out his shoulders and forelegs to extend his stride to its maximum length.

F

Feather Long hairs on the lower limbs, either from below the knee or on the fetlock and heels.

Feral A once-domesticated horse that has escaped or been released and now runs wild.

Filly A female horse under four years old.

Flexion The yielding and bending of the jaw, poll, neck, and back, as well as of the joints of the limbs.

Foal A young horse or pony under one year old.

Forearm Upper half of the foreleg, i.e. between the knee and elbow.

Forehand Front half of the horse's body, i.e. head, neck, shoulders, and forelegs.

Forelock The section of mane that lies between the ears and falls over the forehead.

Frog V-shaped rubbery pad that forms part of the underside of the horse's foot. It acts as a shock absorber and anti-slip device.

G

Gaited horse A horse displaying paces other than the conventional walk, trot, canter, and gallop.

Gelding A castrated male horse.

Goose-rump (jumper's bump) High area of muscle over the horse's croup (top of the hindquarters).

Gridwork Gymnastic jumping exercises for horses involving lines of fences set at different distances apart.

Gymkhana Anglo-Indian word used to describe games on horseback (mounted games).

H

Hack An elegant, lightweight riding horse. To go for a hack (out hacking) means to go for a ride.

Half-bred Cross between a Thoroughbred and any other breed of horse or pony.

Hand Unit of measurement to define height of a horse or pony. Measurement is taken from the ground to top of the withers. One hand measures 4 inches (10 cm).

Handicapping The requirement for additional weight to be carried to disadvantage or 'handicap' the higher class (more successful) horses in a horse race.

Haute École (High School) The discipline of teaching and riding the classical art of advanced dressage movements.

Heavy horse A very powerfully built horse used for draught work. Heavy horses are described as cold blooded and are noted for their calm temperaments.

Hindquarters The back half of the horse, i.e. from behind the saddle and including the hind legs.

Hinny A cross between a male horse (stallion) and a female donkey (Jenny).

Hotblood Word used to describe the purest-bred horses of the world. It relates to their origins as well as their temperament and includes the Arab, Barb, and Thoroughbred.

I

Iberian Horse A term used to describe the horses of Spain and Portugal.

Inbreeding Mating horses that are closely related in order to accentuate and perpetuate certain characteristics, i.e. mating a mare back to her own sire, etc.

L

Light horse A horse that is suitable for riding and carriage driving and that isn't a heavy (draught) horse.

Livery Having a horse kept and cared for by someone else other than the owner, i.e. in a livery yard.

Loins The area of muscle directly behind the saddle and either side of the spine.

Lope A slow 'unengaged' canter pace used in Western riding.

Lunging Working the horse on a circle on the end of a long line, with the handler standing in the centre of the circle. The horse is usually not ridden and is controlled by the handler who holds the 'lunge line' and a long 'lunging' whip.

M

Mare Female horse over four years old.

Mule A cross between a male donkey (Jackass) and a female horse (mare).

N

Native ponies The collective name given to the mountain and moorland pony breeds of Great Britain.

Numnah A rectangular or 'saddle-shaped' pad worn under the saddle to protect the horse's back by acting as a cushion between horse and saddle.

O

Oriental horses A term to describe the horse breeds of Eastern origin such as the Arab and Barb.

Outcross Mating horses that are not related in any way – introduces 'outside' blood to a breed.

Over at the knee A conformational fault where the forelegs appear to slope forwards from below the knee.

P

Pacing Where the horse trots using lateral (as opposed to diagonal) pairs of legs, i.e. off hind and off fore move together, followed by near hind and near fore.

Pack horse/mule A horse or mule used to transport goods and equipment in packs on his back.

Pedigree Recorded ancestry of a horse's breeding, i.e. sire, dam, grand sire, grand dam, etc.

Poached Ground that has become rutted and rough.

Pommel The raised front arch of the saddle.

Poultice A hot or cold substance applied to a wound or injury – heat is used to draw out infection, cold is used to reduce bruising and inflammation.

Primitive Describes the early sub-species that were the ancestors of the modern horse, i.e. Tarpan, Forest Horse, Tundra Horse, and Asiatic Wild Horse.

Purebred A horse that has no mixed breeding in its pedigree, i.e. a Thoroughbred.

R

Roach back A rounded or convex curvature of the backbone.

Roadster A trotting horse that was ridden under saddle; the forefathers of today's trotters and pacers.

Roman nose A convex profile of the horse's nose, often seen in heavy horse.

S

Saddle horse A riding horse.

Scope The horse's range and potential in terms of movement, speed, and jump. A horse described as 'scopey' will have a big stride and jump.

Sickle hocks Conformational fault – weak, bent hocks as opposed to strong, straight hocks.

Sire The male parent of a horse.

Skipping out Describes the practice of removing the horse's droppings from the stable bedding.

Slab-sided A flat-sided horse as opposed to a horse with a well-rounded rib cage.

Spooky A horse that over-reacts to sights and sounds by jumping away, stopping, or trying to run away.

Stallion A male (uncastrated) horse over four years old.

Stud A breeding establishment for horses – a stud farm.

Stud book A book kept by a breed society to record the pedigree of horses eligible for registration in that particular stud book.

Substance The size and strength of the horse in terms of his skeleton and musculature.

T

Tack General description of horse's bridle, saddle, and accessories.

Top line The outline of the horse across the top of his neck, back, and hindquarters.

Tree The framework around which a saddle is built.

Type A horse or pony produced for a particular purpose, which is not necessarily defined as a breed, i.e. hunter, polo pony, hack.

V

Vetting Having a horse checked over by a vet to determine his general health, soundness, and suitability for purpose. Usually carried out prior to purchase.

W

Warmblood A horse or pony that has both hot (Thoroughbred or Arab) and cold (draught horse) blood in its breeding.

White line A band of soft horn in the hoof separating the hard horn from the sensitive laminae tissues.

Whorl Where the coat hair changes its direction of growth it forms a circle or short line in the coat hair.

Z

Zebra stripes Horizontal bands of dark hair on the limbs, often accompanied by other primitive traits, such as dun colouring or a dorsal stripe.

INDEX

ACKNOWLEDGEMENTS

The author would like to thank her sister Elizabeth Roberts for her help in researching many of the breeds included in this book. Thanks also to my other sister, Kathy Lunt, and also Adriana Pretorius, for the information they provided as our 'South African connection'. On the home front, thanks to my husband, Martin Ewing, and to Sophie Allen for shouldering much of the work in keeping our yard of horses going whilst I tackled this project.

I am also hugely grateful to the many breed societies and studs that provide a wealth of information on the different breeds of horses and ponies. Researching this book has been a revelation; it has been fascinating to look at so many different breeds and to be reminded that, whilst they can differ hugely, they have all served man faithfully in some form or other. For some breeds their hour of glory has been and gone – the farm horses and war horses in particular; others have found a new role in the ever-expanding areas of sport and leisure riding. The virtues of the horses and ponies that have a role in our modern world are well recorded, but it has been particularly gratifying to see so many dedicated people determined to champion the cause of the breeds of yesteryear; their vital role in our society may be over but our debt to them can never fully be repaid. The least we can do is preserve, protect, and appreciate them.

Studio Cactus would like to thank Laura Watson for design, Sharon Cluett for original styling, Jennifer Close and Jo Weeks for editorial, Sharon Rudd for additional design, Penelope Kent for indexing, Rob Walker for picture research, Peter Bull and Claire Moore for illustrations, Phil Carre for DTP assistance. Special thanks to Kit, Debby, and Kate from Kit Houghton Photography.

Special thanks to the following owners and their horses:

American Crème (p 178) – Sheridan's Valour; owner: Tracey Burchell.

Appaloosa (p 33 leopard) – Sonora's Daydream; owner: Tracey Burchell.

Appaloosa (p 33 snowflake) – Patchy's Little Rosa; owner: Lane Rhodes, Rhodes Appaloosas, Kentucky, United States.

Chincoteague (p 311) – c/o Kentucky Horse Park, United States.

Clydesdale – (pp 138–39 main) Westforth; owner: David Mouland.

Cob (p 206) – Benetton; owner: Bartholomy.

Coloured (p 312) – Indiana Jones; owner: Mr and Mrs Jones.

Connemara (p 313 bottom) – Carra Cashel; owner: Sandra Burton.

Connemara (p 313 top) – Drumoore Castle; owner: Mrs J McCallum, Producer: Kirstine Douglas.

Dales (p 314 top) – Stonygill Will-o'-the-wisp; owner: Miss Lisa Waite.

Dales (p 314 bottom) – Dart Dale Bobby; owner: Lorraine Ahmet.

Dartmoor (pp 316–17 main) – Drumphin Concerto; owner: Molly Tompsett.

Exmoor (p 322 top) – Porridge; owner: Natalie Greasley.

Fell (p 324 top) – Neath Rose Georgie Girl; owner: Anne Carslaw, Exhibitor: Anne-Clare Worsdale.

Fell (p 324 bottom) – Severn Veils Grey Bobby; owner: Mrs J Robinson.

Hunter (pp 34–35, pp 228–29 main) – Togher Princess; owner: Mrs Sarah Clark.

PICTURE CREDITS

The publishers would like to thank the following for permission to reproduce copyright material:

Abbreviations: a = above, b = bottom, c = centre, l = left, r = right, t = top

Jacqueline Abromeit 24; Terry Alexander 20 (t); Animal Photography 212; 218–219; 240; 344–345; Jeff Banke 179 (b); Stacey Bates 263 (b); Vera Bogaerts 232 (br); Emmanuelle Bonzami 112 (t); 353 (b); Robert Broadhead 21 (t); Winthrop Brookhouse 239 (br); Joy Brown 32 (craa); 114 (b); 139 (c); Marcus Brown 305; George Burba 15 (t); BVA 89 (l); catnap 14 (b); 268–69; Cathleen Clapper 59 (c); Stephanie Coffman 32 (crab); 32 (bra); Condor 36 33 (trb); 38 (b); 65; 109 (b); Paul Cowan 346 (t); Christa DeRidder 93 (b); EcoPrint 103 (t); Pontus Edenberg 33 (c); Holger Ehlers 10 (b); Diane N. Ennis 23 (t); Kondrashov Mikhail Evgenevich 36–37; 118 (b); 174 (t); 175; 259 (br); 283 (l); 288 (r); Wendy Farrington 68–69; Jean Frooms 32 (t); Michael Furey 86 (b); Daniel Gale 20–21; 316 (b); GeoM 32 (b); Jorge R. Gonzalez 83 (l); Andreas Gurskos 100 (b); J. Helgason 331 (t); Patrick Hermans 92 (t); Robert Adrian Hillman 96; Ron Hilton 8–9; 33 (tra); iofoto 121 (r); Fukuoka Irina 89 (t); Neil Roy Johnson 26–27; 102 (t); 117 (b); 285 (b); Laila Kazakevica 184; Falk Kienas 101; Alexia Krusheva 30 (t); 31 (t); 32 (ca); 32 (trb); 258; 289 (b); Abramova Kseniya 23 (b); 32 (tra); 43; 179 (b); Bob Langrish 33 (br); 128–29; 143 (r); 155; 162 (b); 163; 189; 202; 209 (t); 211 (r); 236; 237; 239 (l); 243; 248; 264 (b); 281 (l); 290 (b); 292; 297 (all); 298 (all); 304 (all); 323 (all); 326 (t); 327; 330 (all); 332 (B); 333; 341; 351 (all); 352; 356 (b); 360; 361 (all); Geir Olav Lyngfjell 100 (t); Petr Masek 274 (b); MAT 98–99; Craig McAteer 164 (b); Chris Mole 73 (t); Pedro Jorge Henriques Monteiro 73 (b); Byron W. Moore 124 (b); Sharon Morris 29 (t); 46 (l); NHPA 2–3; 4–5; 11 (t); 12 (bl); 12 (br); 13 (cr); 13 (bl); 13 (br); 14 (t); 15 (b); 16–17; 84–85; 94–95; 106–107; 131; 170; 293 (b); 294–95; 308–309; 366; 367; Lee O'Dell 183 (b); OSF/Digital Vision 86 (t); Yiannis Papadimitriou 87; Sergey Petrov 102 (t); Photos.com 13 (t); 13 (cl); 19; 22; 88; 92 (t); 93 (t); 182 (t); Marco Regalia 32 (cb); Lincoln Rogers 157 (b); Shutterstock 72; 90–91; 137 (b); Otmar Smit 30 (b); Eline Spek 31 (b); 32 (brb); 33 (t); 134; 135 (b); 185; 216 (b); 342 (all); Claudia Steininger 32 (crbb); 143 (l); Michaela Steininger 328 (b); Studio Cactus 10 (c); 11 (c); 12 (cl); 12 (cr); 32 (crba); 38 (t); 42; 43 (t); 44 (b all); 46 (b); 47; 48; 49 (all); 50 (all); 51 (all); 56 (all); 57 (all); 58 (all); 59 (t); 59 (b); 60; 61 (b all); 63 (all); 64; 70 (all); 71; 74 (b); 75 (all); 77 (all); 78 (all); 79 (c); 79 (b); 80 (tl); 81 (all); 82; 83 (r all); 125 (b); 138–39; 156–57; 164–65; 166 (all); 166–67; 178; 179 (l); 183 (t); 199 (b); 206; 228–29; 252 (t); 276–77 (all); 282 (t); 290 (t); 307; 311 (all); 312 (b); 313 (all); 314 (all); 316-17; 319 (bl); 320–21; 322 (all); 324 (all); 329 (all); 335 (b); 338 (t); 339 (all); 349 (l); 350; 353 (t); 362 (t); 363 (all); 364 (t); Graca Victoria 138 (b); Filipchuk Oleg Vladimirovich 172–73; Dana Ward 102 (b); 124 (t)

All other images © Kit Houghton/Houghton's Horses

COVER IMAGES: Front cover top from left to right: Abramova Kseniya (1); NHPA (2); Sharon Morris (3); Ron Hilton (4). Front cover bottom from left to right: Kit Houghton/Houghton's Horses (1, 2, 3); Studio Cactus (4). Back cover top from left to right: Kit Houghton/Houghton's Horses (1, 2, 3); Joy Brown (4). Back cover bottom from left to right: Kit Houghton/Houghton's Horses (1, 2, 3, 4)